*Function and context
in linguistic analysis*

Function and context in linguistic analysis

A FESTSCHRIFT FOR WILLIAM HAAS

EDITED BY
D. J. ALLERTON,
EDWARD CARNEY AND
DAVID HOLDCROFT

CAMBRIDGE UNIVERSITY PRESS
CAMBRIDGE
LONDON · NEW YORK · MELBOURNE

Published by the Syndics of the Cambridge University Press
The Pitt Building, Trumpington Street, Cambridge CB2 1RP
Bentley House, 200 Euston Road, London NW1 2DB
32 East 57th Street, New York, NY 10022, USA
296 Beaconsfield Parade, Middle Park, Melbourne 3206, Australia

© Cambridge University Press 1979

First published 1979

Phototypeset by
Western Printing Services Ltd, Bristol
Printed in Great Britain by
The Pitman Press, Bath

Library of Congress Cataloguing in Publication Data

Main entry under title:
Function and context in linguistic analysis.

Includes bibliographical references and index.
1. Functionalism (Linguistics) – Addresses, essays,
lectures.   2. Context (Linguistics) – Addresses, essays,
lectures.   3. Haas, William – Addresses, essays,
lectures.   I. Haas, William.   II. Allerton, D. J.
III. Carney, Edward.   IV. Holdcroft, David.
P147.F86   410   78–11603
ISBN 0 521 22429 2

Contents

Preface	*page* vii
The Contributors	viii
William Haas: a short biography	1
The work of William Haas: (i) an overview	4
(ii) select bibliography	27

CONTRIBUTIONS

Some cases of metanalysis	30
C. E. BAZELL	
The jingle theory of double *-ing*	41
DWIGHT BOLINGER	
Modes of meaning and modes of expression: types of grammatical structure, and their determination by different semantic functions	57
M. A. K. HALLIDAY	
On the logic of relations	80
STEPHAN KÖRNER	
Idealization of ordinary language for the purposes of logic	94
CZESŁAW LEJEWSKI	
Knowledge and truth: a localistic approach	111
JOHN LYONS	
Grammatical function	142
ANDRÉ MARTINET	
Deep structure	148
P. H. MATTHEWS	

vi   *Contents*

The English appearance of Aspect   159
T. F. MITCHELL

Non-assertion and modality   185
F. R. PALMER

Functional syntax in mediaeval Europe   196
R. H. ROBINS

Some remarks on the stylistics of written language   206
JOSEF VACHEK

List of references (excluding the work of W. Haas)   216
General Index   222

Preface

This collection of papers on the general theme of Function and Context in Linguistic Analysis is dedicated to William Haas on the occasion of his retirement as Professor in the Department of General Linguistics at the University of Manchester. Many more scholars would have wished to contribute than could be accommodated in a single volume, but the editors have unfortunately been obliged strictly to limit the scope of the work and thus make some very difficult decisions. They have, however, been fortified by the willingness and efficiency of their contributors and by the knowledge that this tribute to Professor Haas has such widespread and enthusiastic support.

The Contributors

C. E. BAZELL — *Emeritus Professor of General Linguistics, University of London*

DWIGHT BOLINGER — *Emeritus Professor of Romance Linguistics, Harvard University*

M. A. K. HALLIDAY — *Professor of Linguistics, University of Sidney*

STEPHAN KÖRNER — *Professor of Philosophy, University of Bristol*

CZESŁAW LEJEWSKI — *Professor of Philosophy, University of Manchester*

JOHN LYONS — *Professor of Linguistics, University of Sussex*

ANDRÉ MARTINET — *Professor of Linguistics, University of Paris*

P. H. MATTHEWS — *Professor of Linguistic Science, University of Reading*

T. F. MITCHELL — *Professor of Linguistics, University of Leeds*

F. R. PALMER — *Professor of Linguistic Science, University of Reading*

R. H. ROBINS — *Professor of General Linguistics, University of London*

JOSEF VACHEK — *Emeritus Professor of Linguistics, Czechoslovak Academy of Sciences*

The Editors

D. J. ALLERTON — *Senior Lecturer in General Linguistics, University of Manchester*

EDWARD CARNEY — *Senior Lecturer in Phonetics, University of Manchester*

DAVID HOLDCROFT — *Senior Lecturer in Philosophy, University of Warwick*

William Haas: A short biography

William Haas was born in May 1912 in the industrial town of
(Moravská-)Ostrava, which was then part of the dual monarchy of
Austro-Hungary but which at the end of the first world war became
part of the newly constituted state of Czechoslovakia. His father, a
successful barrister in Ostrava, became actively involved in the cause
of welfare legislation for miners and founded a miners' welfare institution which, amongst other things, created a Slovakian spa (Rajecké
Teplice) as a holiday and rehabilitation centre for miners. During the
second world war he was an adviser to the Beneš government-in-
exile, and returned with it to Czechoslovakia; but he and his wife came
back to Britain in 1947, to join Haas and his sister in Cardiff.

Haas himself attended a Gymnasium in Ostrava and went on to
study law at the Czech University of Prague. Before qualifying as a
Doctor of Law, however, he transferred to the Charles University of
Prague, where he studied philosophy, although he also attended lectures given by members of the Prague School. He found time for
various extracurricular literary and political activities, including the
writing of an historical drama about the French Revolution, which
was reviewed prominently in the Czech press. His time spent at the
Charles University, from 1937 to 1939, of course coincided with a
tragic period in the history of Czechoslovakia, that 'far away country
of which we know little and care less'. The Sudeten Lands, and with
them a defensible frontier against Germany, were lost by the Munich
Agreement of 1938. Increasing disruption of the University, together
with an uncertain and unhappy political situation, led Haas to leave
Prague in the spring of 1939, and escape by way of Poland to Britain.
He then went to University College Cardiff, but was obliged to
interrupt his studies after one year and went to do forestry work near

Cambridge. In the following April, however, thanks to an award from the Czechoslovak government-in-exile, he was able to resume his studies, and returned to Cardiff, where he managed to prepare himself for his second year examinations in a matter of weeks. In his third year he seems to have again been characteristically busy, taking a Diploma in Economics and Allied subjects (the reason for his scholarship) simultaneously with a BA with first class honours in both Philosophy and German. Former colleagues at Cardiff recall this as a unique achievement, one that is still talked about today.

After a period spent doing war work, Haas was appointed to a lectureship in German at Cardiff in 1945, thus beginning his academic career at the relatively late age of 33. Though he was responsible for the teaching of philology and Middle High German literature, he also did his full share of other departmental teaching in language and literature. At the same time he maintained his more general linguistic and philosophical interests, and at this time began a lifelong friendship with the Professor of Philosophy at Cardiff, J. W. Scott. His first published paper, entitled 'General categories of language', was presented at the VIth International Congress of Linguists in Paris and appeared in 1949. He went on to publish a number of other papers on linguistics and philosophy during this period, and it was a natural step for him to move, in 1954, to become a Senior Lecturer in General Linguistics at the University of Manchester – the first appointment in the subject at that University, and, indeed, one of the first in the country outside London. He inevitably played an important part in the development of linguistics in Britain, becoming a founder member of the Linguistics Association, and one of the original members of the editorial board of the *Journal of Linguistics*. In 1963 he was appointed to the newly established Mont Follick Professorship of Comparative Philology. Under his guidance the Department at Manchester has grown to its present strength of seven, but has remained a Department of General Linguistics. From the beginning, Haas interpreted general linguistics as including phonetics and semantics, and as embracing both analytic and comparative studies. Moreover he has been active in developing a departmental contribution in areas in which linguistics has important applications, most notably, the teaching of English as a foreign language, and speech therapy. One notable feature of Haas's outlook has been his encouragement of interdisciplinary contacts which, as many former and present colleagues will testify, have been frequent and mutually beneficial.

Since his appointment at the University of Manchester he has produced a steady stream of publications which shows no sign of abating. In them he has consistently addressed himself to fundamental questions in linguistics, and has developed a point of view which owes little to prevailing orthodoxies, and which is both distinctive and original. His work has earned the widespread respect of linguists – indeed, he could be described as a 'linguist's linguist' – and it is to that work that this volume pays tribute.

The work of William Haas: an overview

THE EDITORS[1]

The theory of interpretation is obviously a branch of biology . . . We shall do better to think of meaning as though it were a plant that has grown – not a can that has been filled. (I. A. Richards)

Although when a student at the Charles University he attended lectures given by members of the Prague School, William Haas was at that time primarily a student of German and philosophy. Although now established as a general linguist, he has maintained a strong interest in philosophy, and one of his first published papers was an address to the Aristotelian Society (1951). In this paper he discussed a number of issues in the philosophy of language, which obviously continue to interest him, and which he has returned to in recent publications (1973a, 1975c). It is, moreover, clear that his work in linguistics is informed by deeply thought out positions in the philosophy of language and on the methodology of linguistics itself.

There are three main philosophical questions which have interested Haas: (i) the nature and status of statements of the form 'X is meaningful', 'X means that ". . ." ', etc; (ii) the difference between formal and natural languages; and (iii) the status of sentences which are categorically anomalous, e.g. *Quadruplicity drinks procrastination*. These questions are connected in various ways, though the first is the most important, not merely because of its intrinsic interest, but because the answer given to it by a linguist can have, and is seen by Haas to have, profound implications for the methodology that he adopts.

The positions about meaning which Haas wishes to overthrow all involve some version or other of a 'dualist' theory of the sign. Common to these theories is the view that the meaning of a sign is some

---

[1] The editors are grateful to D. A. Cruse for his helpful comments and constructive criticism of this essay, but its inadequacies remain their sole responsibility.

thing, e.g. an idea, or particular referred to, which both exists independently of the language to which the sign belongs, and is in principle
identifiable by someone who is not a language user. Such ideas and
referents might be called 'pure ideas' and 'pure references' respectively. The essential thesis of the theories that Haas attacks is that a sign
acquires meaning by being put into correspondence either with a pure
idea, or with a pure reference. In opposition to this he argues that

the 'of' in 'meaning of' cannot be interpreted as a correlation between two
orders of fact . . . if there are pure meanings, or pure external facts, there is
certainly nothing we can say about them. (1968a: 90)

Taking the case against meanings first, Haas argues that if we
consider what happens when we translate, we find that an appeal to
meanings has nothing to do with the case. Why, for instance, would
we count *knowest thou* . . . as a poor translation of *kennst du* in *Kennst du
das Land, wo die Zitronen blühn*? The reason is that

Kennst du . . . is a straightforward bit of colloquial language, as one might say
'Do you know the shop where the sale is on?' (*Kennst du den Laden/* . . . *Herrn
Schmidt/* . . . *meinen Bruder*, etc.), whereas 'knowest thou' would be unusual in
corresponding contexts. (1968a: 87)

A translation is a good one if the contexts in which the expression
being translated is habitually used are the same as those in which the
expression used to translate it is used, and the contextual relations of
the latter are the same as those of the former. We show that two people
are dancing the same dance by showing that certain correspondences
hold between their actual performances, not by discovering that each
is doing something which corresponds in the same way to a dancerless
dance. Similarly, we show that two expressions have the same meaning by showing that there are certain correspondences between
habitual ways of using them, rather than by showing that each is
related in the same way to a meaning. Just as reference to a dancerless
dance has no explanatory value, so neither does reference to a meaning, independent of language.

Undoubtedly, there is a widespread feeling that the ontological
status of meanings is obscure, and that their explanatory value is
slight. On the other hand, the status of the individual things which we
can use singular terms to refer to seems much less open to attack. A
theory of meaning that was rooted in the theory of reference would,
therefore, seem to escape the charge that it was committed to dubious
reifications. Nevertheless, Haas thinks that the theory of meaning

cannot be so rooted. This is not, of course, because he denies that we do refer to things, or even that, given that we already have a language, a new expression may be introduced by saying what it refers to (1968a: 93). What is at issue is not the existence of the things which we can use language to refer to, but the existence of what we earlier called pure references; i.e. the existence of things which both exist independently of any language and which are identifiable by someone who is not a language user. If there were such things, then it is possible that expressions acquire meaning by being put into correspondence with them. But, Haas argues, there are no such things.

There are various reasons why he thinks expressions cannot acquire meaning by being put into correspondence with pure references, but perhaps the most important is that the theory is committed to a fiction, which he calls the fiction of 'isolated reference'. What this involves is the possibility of referring to a particular in isolation from all other particulars, and by so doing giving an expression meaning in isolation from all other expressions. Perhaps the only sustained attempt to work out a view of this kind has been made by Russell who, as Haas notes, wrote that a word in the object language has meaning in isolation, and that it can be learnt 'without its being necessary to have previously learnt other words' (Russell 1940: 65).

Certainly, as Haas points out, the fact that we who have a language are familiar with the experience of being aware of something for which we have no name goes no way to establishing that there could be pure references:

Those things we seek a name for are not extra-lingual in the required sense. We can always say a great deal about them; . . . The fact that we may want another word for a thing, besides the many which are already involved with it, is nothing to establish a reference-theory of meaning. (1968a: 94)

Nor does the fact that children ask 'What is it called?' show that they can merely refer by use of the pronoun; for they can tell us a lot about 'it'. It is true, of course, that it is possible by use of pointing gestures to define something ostensively. But pointing is itself a sign, not a mere gesture; and its role when used in ostension is that of an auxiliary language which supplements the language to which the expression defined belongs. 'The ostensive definition explains the use – the meaning – of the word when the overall role of the word in the language is clear' (Wittgenstein 1953: §30). Thus ostensive definition does not establish the meaning of an expression which is neutral between languages. It is just another way of explaining the meaning of an expression which belongs to a language.

But if none of this shows that pure reference is possible, what shows it to be impossible? There seem, in Haas's view, to be two main reasons why it is. Firstly, we have to ask

whether an expression, by itself, could possibly be deemed to be significant; and it seems clear that such an expression, even if repeated and applied a hundred times, could never be said to have acquired *meaning*. It could not be viewed as 'having meaning' until, on some occasion we found it *inappropriate*, and said so: 'This and this and this is a cat. But *that* is not a *cat*. It's a *dog*'. A language, one might say, requires at least two words. Language and meaning take their origin from difference of meaning. (1968a: 99)

This is indeed plausible. Theories of abstraction which attempt to show how, for example, one could acquire the idea of yellow on its own by being presented with a representative sample of yellow things, fail because the sample itself does not tell one where to draw the line between yellow and orange on the one hand, and yellow and green on the other. Yet to have the idea of yellow is, amongst other things, to know where to draw that line.

Secondly, a related question concerns the identity of the expression used in the ostension. What entitles us to say that repetitions of it are repetitions of the same expression? The lesson of phonology is that linguistic signs have what de Saussure called a purely relational identity, i.e. that a sign is to be identified solely in terms of the relations in which it stands to other signs.

We cannot say, for any particular language, what counts as repetition, as occurrence of a 'similar expression', unless we know what counts as occurrence of a different one. The recurrent shape of 'cat' is determined by contrasts such as '*c*at/*p*at/*m*at; *c*at/*c*ot; *c*at/*c*ap/*c*an'. For a Japanese, *wrong* is a repetition of *long*, *right* of *light*, and *grammar* of *glamour*. This is simply because, in his language, though he does make use of both *l* and *r*, he has no need of their difference for distinguishing meanings. (1968a: 100)

This attack on the idea that words can acquire meaning by being put into correspondence with pure references is impressive. One conclusion to be drawn would be that a linguistic sign is meaningful only in a system of signs, a *langue*, a conclusion forcibly argued for by de Saussure. The attack also leads to the rejection of views, such as Hjelmslev's, that a text should be analysed into an 'expression line' and a 'content line'. For such views interpret the undeniable distinction between an expression and its meaning as a relation between two distinct orders of things, one of which, as Haas points out (1956b: 98), remains curiously inaccessible.[2] A third conclusion which Haas draws is that meaning has to be understood in terms of use. However, an important difference between the use of a sentence and that of a word has to be noted. The use of a word is its function in sentences, whilst that of a sentence is its function in social contexts. Hence, there is no reason why the use of at least some sentences should not be identifiable independently of the uses of the words they contain. This then opens up the possibility of explaining without circularity the meanings of those words in terms of the contributions they make to the meanings of sentences.

This conclusion has important methodological implications, for it entails that whilst it is perfectly in order for a linguist to count as data facts about the meaningfulness of sentences, with the aim of explaining facts about lower level linguistic units in terms of their functional role in sentences, the reverse process is not an acceptable alternative. If we begin with the smallest units, distinctive features, prosodic features, phonemes, etc., and try to construct higher level units out of these, we find that we constantly have to presuppose the results of our constructions in order to carry them out. This is a moral which Haas himself repeatedly draws. Commenting on the kind of hierarchical analysis proposed by Hill (1958) he argues that

At every level, as we try to make the proposed ascent through the 'hierarchy of language', contrastive substitution is one step ahead; it implies that we are already acquainted with units of the *higher* levels. (1960b: 259)

He goes on to point out that at every level it is necessary that some larger structure be available, and that

This is assured, if we *begin* with sentences. The decision that, for the purpose of a strictly linguistic analysis, we do not go *beyond* the sentence, but *begin* with it, immediately commits us to a minimum of primitive semantic intuitions – . . . (1960b: 259–60)

One question which has continued to interest Haas is the difference between formal and natural language. His position is that no formal language could be an adequate model of either the syntax or semantics

---

[2] Note also Haas's comment on Chomsky's *Syntactic structures*: 'The notion that the studies of Syntax and Semantics could be pursued along independent lines, only having their results "correlated" after they have run their separate courses (103, 108) is surely an illusion. It seems to derive from that plausible but notoriously stultifying theory for which the meaning of the expression is divorced from that expression – is something on another, a "parallel", plane'. (1958a)

of a natural language. The semantics of formal languages, he argues, misrepresent those of natural languages in various ways. Consider, for example, statements containing empty singular terms, e.g. *Pegasus flies*. Haas maintains, plausibly, that we do not ordinarily, assign the same truth value to all such statements simply because they contain an empty singular term. We might count *Pegasus is a philosopher* as false, but would we not count *Pegasus is a horse* as true? When we turn to formal languages, however, we find that the situation is quite different. Either they do not contain such statements at all, or else all such statements are treated in the same way, for example, all are counted as false, or lacking a truth value. This does seem unsatisfactory, even if it is only the occurrence of empty singular terms in extensional contexts that is in question.

However, is it clear that a formal language has to treat all statements involving extensional occurrences of empty singular terms uniformly? A system described by Smiley (1959), for instance, would not ascribe the same truth value to each of the following: *Pegasus flies, It is not true that Pegasus flies, Pegasus exists, It is not true that Pegasus exists*. Assuming that *Pegasus* is an empty name, these would be counted, respectively, as neither true nor false, true, false, and true. Admittedly, this might not agree with everyone's intuitions; but one might be sceptical whether there is anything like universal agreement among native speakers about the ascription of truth values in such a range of cases. Hence, sometimes at least, when it plumps for one possibility rather than another a formal theory cannot be accused of ignoring a deeply entrenched tendency of native speakers, for there is none.

It can, of course, be plausibly argued that there are many sentences of natural languages which cannot be satisfactorily translated into any existing formal language. Haas maintains, for instance, that a formal language employing only the syntactical categories of the kind of categorial grammar envisaged by Lejewski (1975) is intrinsically incapable of assigning distinct categories to important classes of items which should be so assigned. These are evaluative adjectives, e.g. *good, gifted, dubious, real*; adjectives of degree, e.g. *big–small, fast–slow*; and adverbs. It is difficult, however, to see that the last present an unsurmountable difficulty. Adverbs such as *hurriedly, awkwardly, carefully*, for example, plainly belong to the category :(:sn)(:sn). The problem of attributive adjectives is admittedly much knottier. However, even if no grammar of a formal language can give a satisfactory account of them, it is not clear that any other grammar can do much better. And if a categorial grammar did fail to provide an adequate model of the syntax of a natural language for this sort of reason, it would be unclear what *general* moral followed. The failure of a particular attempt does not entail the failure of all attempts of a similar kind. Certainly, many recent attempts to extend to natural languages techniques developed in the first place for formal languages have tried hard to grapple with the problems posed for syntax and semantics by adjectives, adverbs, referential opacity, etc. (Davidson 1967, 1969; Lewis 1972, 1975; Kamp 1975). Undoubtedly, there are many reasons why such attempts may fail; and arguments that theories of this sort cannot in principle constitute fully fledged theories of meaning command respect (Dummett 1975). It might be argued, for instance that provided we already know what it is for a name to stand for an individual, a formal theory can say what the 'meaning' of a name is by specifying the individual (or individuals in different possible worlds) which the name stands for. But the theory can neither explain what it is for a name to stand for an individual, nor what a person's knowledge that it does so stand consists in. It is, of course, clear that Haas would endorse an argument of this sort. What, however, is difficult to prove is that the attempt to develop a formal model of natural language must fail because of an inability to provide a rich enough syntax.

The problems posed by categorially anomalous sentences raise fundamental questions about the nature of grammatical rules. Should a grammar class such sentences as ungrammatical, or, as Haas argues, should some other account of their anomalous character be given?

If such a sentence as *Quadruplicity drinks procrastination* is ungrammatical, then there is some grammatical rule which it violates. But is there any such rule, and, anyway, how is *this* question to be settled? For Haas, the question of rule status depends on acceptability judgments:

The rule is valid if conforming utterances are acceptable, and non-conforming utterances are not; or at any rate, if any conforming utterance is more acceptable than any non-conforming one. 'Acceptable' is a primitive notion defined in terms of native speakers' responses to an utterance . . . (1973a: 141)

However, matters are complicated by the fact that there are two radically different types of deviant sentence. The first is such that there is no context whatsoever in which it can be uttered without oddity. The second, whilst odd in many contexts, and perhaps not acceptable in any normal context, nevertheless admits of contexts in which it can be uttered without or with a greatly reduced degree of oddity. Thus, to Haas, *Quadruplicity drinks procrastination* was a perfectly intelligible comment on the pointless deliberations of the occupying powers in Vienna after the war. He maintains that only sentences belonging to the first category should be classed as ungrammatical, and that attempts to bring grammatical considerations to bear on the second category by trying to identify degrees of grammaticality fail. For instance, the suggestion that there is a rule that certain verbs require animate nouns, and that any otherwise normal sentence which violates this rule is less grammatical than one which does not, would class *Rust is eating up the car* as more deviant than *The chimpanzee is eating up the car*. No doubt the rule could be made more sensitive, but only at the cost of producing what would amount to a description of the whole universe – an impossible task (1973a: 146).

But if sentences belonging to the second category do not violate grammatical rules, they are nevertheless deviant; and the question of the nature of that deviancy remains. As we shall see below, Haas makes a distinction between rules which are strict, in the sense of being exceptionless, and habits and tendencies, which admit of exceptions. Whilst syntax is concerned with rules that are strict, semantics is concerned only with what is for the most part so, i.e. with habits and tendencies. Thus, a semantic regularity is a norm which admits of deviations. The oddity of sentences such as *Quadruplicity drinks procrastination* is to be explained by the fact that they involve deviations from a semantic norm, rather than violations of a grammatical rule. And because they do no more than deviate from a tendency, they admit of an interpretation, given an appropriate contextualization.

Haas's theory at this point is both distinctive and original, contrasting as it does the 'rigidity' of syntax with the relative 'looseness' of semantics. For Haas, a language developing and growing, as it does, as a result of the creative choices of its users, is more akin to an organism than to a mechanical generative device. As a result, what was categorially deviant may cease to be so, for tendencies can change, and, indeed, rules can become tendencies and tendencies rules. At one time perhaps to speak of a chair leg was deviant, since there was a tendency to speak of legs only in relation to animate objects. But if there was such a tendency, it has long since lapsed. Clearly, one merit of Haas's position is that it admits of an intelligible account of linguistic change which need involve no abrupt discontinuities. Connectedly, it permits an explanation why, from an instrumental point of view, language is such a flexible instrument. It is precisely because any given syntactic form, far from being specially designed for each of its uses, is indifferent to all of them:

It is, for example, neither vagueness nor ambiguity but semantic neutrality that allows the syntactic category of 'noun' to apply to *lion* equally in *The lion pounced on its prey*, and in *The lion is a species*, and to apply to *prey* as well as to *species*. The ordinary-language category 'noun' is indifferently receptive of a wide range of semantic differences. (1975c: 164)

As Haas points out, if a language is to be an instrument of communication there must be

a certain structural rigidity: it must be rule-governed. But in order to admit of continual adaptation and change, the uses of this peculiarly organic instrument must not be subject to anything more stringent than directions and inclinations of habit . . . (1973a: 149)

One is always free to go against the tendencies inherent in usage by using an expression in a novel context. Indeed, not only is one free to do this, but language is powerless to stop one doing so. For – and it is this which dooms attempts to deal with categorially anomalous sentences by selection restrictions – there is no possible way of foreseeing and specifying all possible contexts. And because this is so, if a language is to be used in an appropriate way in any context, its rules must be somewhat insensitive to contextual considerations. Thus, speaking a language is a truly creative business, not simply a matter of blindly following rules, but of deciding which tendencies inherent in usage to extend, restrict, or even reject. As Haas himself puts it in a fine passage:

The truly creative work that is required of us, whether in managing our social affairs or in speaking a language, is not to be found in the observance of rules. It consists, as it does in the case of moral decisions, in a sifting and blending of inherited habits and tendencies, in choosing either to reinforce or to defy them, and, by doing so, in continually altering them. Genuine creativeness of this kind cannot be represented as the productivity of a generative device. It works, and has to prove its worth, in the uncharted and unchartable uses we make of that device. (1973a: 155)

It is probably fair to describe Haas as a general linguist who makes incursions into philosophy, rather than the converse. How then does his view of meaning affect his account of language? This is an important question, because, for him, meaning enters into all aspects of language study. His approach to meaning, as we have seen, is a functional one; he sees meaning as value in context. 'The fundamental task of Semantics, then,' he writes, 'appears to be to provide criteria of semantic value' (1964a: 1066).

Haas grades his semantic statements from the most basic 'Is X meaningful?' through the intermediate 'Does X mean the same as Y?' and 'How does X differ in meaning from Y?' to the most ambitious 'What does X mean?' In starting with the most basic question, Haas does not mean to imply that we do not recognize from the outset what constitutes a linguistic sign, but he wishes to go beyond specific intuitions about particular cases, to find a generally applicable method of description.

The basic requirement for meaningfulness is recurrent semantic value.

We should then say that a constituent form is significant, if substitution of some other form for it entails the *same* semantic contrast in different sentential functions. (1964a: 1067)

This approach obviously presupposes a knowledge of the meanings of sentences, but, as Haas frequently points out, some things must always be presupposed in any analysis. These presuppositions will, however, in their turn, form a topic of investigation for some other discipline or subdiscipline. Relying on native speakers' judgments about the meanings of sentences, we are therefore entitled to observe that replacing *jewel* with *hat* will effect the same change of meaning in *She bought a new jewel* as in *Her father is a jeweller*, while replacing *jewel* with *badge* will have a different effect in the two cases.

A consequence of this strict test of his for a minimum meaningful unit (which he is happy to refer to as a 'morpheme') is that words like *author*, *butcher*, which are frequently described in terms of 'unique morphemes' (Hockett 1958: 126–7) must be analysed as monomorphemic, and so classed together with items like *clown*, *priest*. Haas recognizes the unsatisfactory nature of this analysis in his later work by making use of the notion of 'marker' (see below, 16–17), which can be applied not only to items like the *-er* of *butcher*, but also to such elements as adverbial *-ly*, verbal *-ing*, etc. The latter type of markers fail the test for meaningfulness but are regular markers of a grammatical structure, and can therefore be assigned morpheme status.

Haas is equally strict in his treatment of morphological 'zero'. In a widely appreciated theoretical paper (1957c) he takes other linguists to task for their profligate use of this often useful but never indispensable descriptive device. Haas proposes that two requirements should be met before the use of a linguistic zero is entertained: the proposed zero morph should have at least one overt allomorph (ruling out, for instance, a zero noun singular suffix in English); and it should contrast with some overt morpheme (ruling out, for instance, a zero noun plural suffix for *sheep*, *(air)craft*, etc.). These principles place a severe restriction on our use of zero; they would allow it, for example, in the past verb form of *he/she cut*, but not of *I cut*. Haas stresses, however, that he only wishes to limit the use of zero morphs and morphemes. He is quite prepared to allow what he calls 'class-index zero' (1957c: 49–53), by which he seems to mean a mark of the neutralization of a grammatical distinction such as singular–plural or noun–verb.

Having established his morphemes, Haas is in a position to say something about their meanings, and for this purpose he asks his native speakers to make a different kind of judgment about sentences: they must assess the comparative normality of one sentence versus another, being willing to say, for instance, that *My cat had puppies* is less normal than *My cat had kittens* (to quote one of his own examples). Each sign or morpheme is then said to have a 'focal distribution' (1964a: 1069) of its occurrences in its more normal sentential environments, and this will distinguish it from all other signs (cf. Lyons's essay, 115).

A sign carries with it its typical distribution wherever it goes, and if this potential distribution is lacking, we do not have a true instance of the sign: so that *outlaw*, for example, turns out to contain neither the morpheme *out* nor the morpheme *law*; and this conclusion is confirmed by the lack of meaningful contrasts for either item. We can only applaud the consistency and empirical nature of these procedures, but we are left wondering if it is right to give *outlaw* the same monomorphemic status as *bandit*.

Haas criticizes Lyons's (1968) account of structural semantics for being based on truth-value relations, and therefore limited to cognitive meanings. Such an approach could in his view only claim to cover 'focal' meanings, and thus 'will have no room for metaphors, jokes, idioms, slang, poetic language or illuminating paradox' (1973b: 99). Such factors, as well as semantic change, would in Lyons's approach be 'allowed for' but not 'accounted for'.

In as yet unpublished work, Haas develops his own methods of semantic analysis to account for such phenomena as homonymy, polysemy, idioms, metaphors and semantic change. A homonymous item, for example, is said to have two or more separate focal distributions. Idioms emerge as unanalysable signs, while constituent parts of metaphors retain at least something of their original morphemic status.

Insisting on a strict semantic interpretation of the morpheme is for Haas simply a consequence of his functional view of language. 'The meaning of an element', he writes (1954a: 81) 'is the functions of its form.' Examining the functions of an element provides a synthetic definition and description, whereas examining its internal composition yields an analytic definition. While intermediate grammatical units such as phrases can be defined either synthetically or analytically, the maximum unit, the sentence, must in Haas's view be described analytically,[3] but the minimum unit, the morpheme, must be described synthetically. A functional or synthetic view of the morpheme is essential, if the merely distributionalist approach of Harris and other Bloomfieldians is to be avoided. In practice, he points out, no one would consider the items *rambling, sapling, cling,* and *not linger* to be natural instances of the English phonological contrast /bl/ versus /pl/ versus /kl/ versus /tl/, because linguists only consider contrasts within clearly defined functions and not in 'mere stretches of speech'. Functional analysis involves examining relevant distributions.

Despite agreeing with Firth (1957: 19–27) about the central importance of meaning at all linguistic levels, Haas is unwilling to attribute meaning to phonological elements. In fact he distinguishes three levels at which meaning may operate: (i) what he then called '*mere* semantic value', the distinctive value of phonemic features and phonemes (cf., in Martinet's essay, 'relevancy', 143); (ii) 'meaning proper', the relatively constant distinctive value of morphemes, words and constructions; and (iii) 'sentential meaning' or 'sense', the extralingual and relatively constant distinctive value of sentences.

What is applicable to elements at all linguistic levels is the notion of function:

The most important fact about the vast majority of linguistic elements is their instrumental value – their capacity of being chosen from determinate ranges and for determinate functions. (1960b: 263)

Any linguistic element is widely recognized as having syntagmatic relations (to its neighbouring fellow items in the text) and paradigma-

---

[3] This view undervalues the importance of discourse in defining and describing the sentence. Indeed, Allerton (1969) suggests that the only feasible definition of the sentence is synthetic. Even Haas himself later (1975b: 533n) refers to a 'rough functional distinction of "types of sentence" '.

tic relations (to competing items that might have occurred in its place); but these relations, Haas insists, presuppose a third kind of relationship, functional relations, which subsist between an item and the larger item of which it is a component part and within which it plays its functional role (for a slightly different view cf. Halliday's essay, 58–9). The verb *be*, for instance, has a syntagmatic relation to elements like the Adjective Phrase (*very*) *happy* or the Noun Phrase *a university teacher* that might follow it; it has a paradigmatic relation to elements like *become, remain* that are its 'rivals'; but it has a functional relation to whole Verb Phrases like *be very happy, be a university teacher.*

Using the term 'function' in its logical – mathematical sense, we are able to say with Haas that the constituent item gives a value to the higher level function. A function like *be very happy* is thus made up of two parts, the constant (—) *very happy* and the variable element (*be*). Since, as Haas points out,

. . . one and the same utterance may be viewed as value of a number of different functions (1964b: 126–7)

any one part may be viewed as either constant or variable; and corresponding to these two functional roles are two 'basic types of linguistic relevance', namely, diacritical power and determinant power. For an element, or better the difference between two elements, to have diacritical power, replacement of the one element by another must correlate with some (no matter what) difference of meaning or structure between the resultant function values. Diacritical power is a necessary and sufficient condition for phonological distinctiveness, but only a necessary one for (lexical–grammatical) meaningfulness.

Determinant power, on the other hand, is a matter of syntagmatic relevance. It is the power an element has, as a result of the syntagmatic restrictions on its occurrence, to determine what its neighbours shall be and what the higher unit shall be of which it is part. The notion applies not only in phonology, where Trubetzkoy's (1939/58: 242) 'Grenzsignale' and Firth's (1957: 123f) 'prosodies' are well known, but also particularly to grammar. Consider, for instance, the value of infinitival *to* or adverbial *-ly* in English: they have virtually no diacritical power (since they are irreplaceable when they occur), but they have an important role to play in identifying the grammatical structure of the sentence. Fries's (1952: 69–71, 106–9) 'structural signals' are fundamentally words and morphemes with determinant value. It is

Haas's merit here to have appreciated the general principles underlying these disparate phenomena: they are all 'markers'. He also makes it perfectly clear that it is quite normal for one and the same item, e.g. English /h/, or the English determiners *the, a, my*, etc. to have both diacritical and determinant power:

The distinction we shall have to make, then, is *not* between two kinds of *element*, but between two kinds of value. (1966: 129–30)

How are the values of a linguistic element to be established? Haas follows Firth in seeking techniques for justifying a description of linguistic data rather than discovery procedures, especially mechanical ones, which are an unrealistic goal. He describes his two basic operations as segmentation and substitution, and considers all others as variants of these. While it is easy to see how operations like expansion, reduction, insertion and omission (deletion) are variants of substitution, it is difficult to avoid viewing permutation (reordering) as something different in nature from its mechanical equivalent insertion-plus-omission.

Operational techniques were criticized on more fundamental grounds by Chomsky (1965: 19–27), who claimed that they were unreliable and inconclusive. The real test of a grammar, he asserted, was the extent to which it coincided with 'the speaker-hearer's linguistic intuition', although he conceded that the native speaker may not be 'immediately aware' of his own intuitions and may have to have them drawn out of him 'in fairly subtle ways'. The dangers of this view are clear (cf. Allerton 1970); but anyone who insists on empirical validation of analyses is condemned by Chomsky as being overconcerned with verification.

Unworried by the charge of 'verificationism', Haas sees an empirical justification of any proposed analysis as an essential check on its validity. Indeed he sees some operational tests just like the measurements of the physicist, as entering into the theory. He fully supports what he sees as Lyons's demand for 'rational principles of syntactic analysis' (1973b: 105), and rejects the proposition that the linguist's role is simply to evaluate given grammars. This he sees as a task of metalinguistics. Neatly turning the tables, Haas suggests that the techniques of generative grammar are most useful

. . . as precisely, a way of finding out whether, and in what respect, some independently proposed grammatical description may need to be amended or 'deepened' . . . (1973b: 72)

In other words, generative grammar turns out to be most helpful as a discovery procedure!

In any analysis of linguistic data it is essential, in Haas's view, to make a clear distinction between grammatical and semantic phenomena. The two are obviously closely related, since meaning plays a part in both, and they both need to be described in functional terms; but they are each associated with a different kind of unacceptability. Amongst unacceptable sentences, he distinguishes between syntactically deviant sentences like *They permitted to attend* which simply require correction, and semantically deviant ones like **John drank fish* that can be 'cured' by finding an appropriate context for their use (1973b: 82). He therefore criticizes Lyons for classing as 'ungrammatical' sentences like **The butterfly eats the cow*, which are clearly contextualizable. Syntactic phenomena can be described in terms of grammatical rules, whereas semantic phenomena need to be described in terms of interacting, and sometimes competing, tendencies, a state of affairs that has been obscured by 'a craving for uniform "models" of linguistic structure' (1973b: 84). While generative semanticists have attempted to subject everything to rules, some linguists such as Hockett (1968) and even Bolinger (1969) have detected tendencies everywhere. (For a further discussion, see Matthews's essay, 157 and Halliday's essay, 59–63, 70.)

Attractive though Haas's simple dichotomy between syntactic rules and semantic tendencies is, it is not always easy to apply in practice. In judging a particular sequence to be ungrammatical but corrigible with reference to a specific syntactic rule (or rules), we must, of course, assume that we know what meaning the utterer intends. In **They permitted to attend* we know that an overt subject for the *attend* needs to be inserted between *permitted* and *to*, but we have no way of knowing whether that subject should be *me*, *him*, *people* or whatever, unless we are aware of the intended meaning. Turning to semantically deviant sentences, we find that Haas asks us to find a possible context, which in effect means working out a possible intended meaning; so that *John drank fish* could be intended as meaning, for instance, 'John drank fish-juice or a fish-based drink' (cf. also Mitchell's example *John began to arrive* (165)). If, however, that is what the speaker means,[4] shouldn't

---

[4] It is of course possible that a speaker might use the semantically deviant sentence with a meaning not precisely equivalent to any other sentence, but with a new imaginatively devised meaning, involving a joke, a metaphor, or some other extension beyond the 'normal' use of language.

he say so, and shouldn't we, equally correct him? Haas would obviously point out that such a correction could not be based on any general syntactic rule. But this only takes us as far as the Sweet – Jespersen view (Sweet 1913: 31; Jespersen 1924: 32) that grammar deals with the general and lexicology with the particular, both prescribing rules, norms or tendencies for expressing particular meanings. It is now apparent, however, (Cruse 1973; Allerton 1978) that the meanings associated with such central grammatical categories as subject, object and indirect object are extremely subtle and complex.

For Haas, as a believer in an autonomous syntax, it is clear that syntax and semantics are separable. The question is: how are they related? Haas readily concedes that syntactic classes and constructions may be associated with particular meanings, but prefers to speak of 'semantic burdens'.

The semantic burden of a grammatical category or construction, like the 'meaning' of any lexical item, is explicable in terms of tendencies of co-occurrence. (1973b: 87)

Grammatical meanings must therefore be described in terms of tendencies: for instance, nouns only tend to be countable, and verbs only tend to allow the progressive. These semantic tendencies of grammatical items must not be mistaken for rules; indeed, unlike rules, they may compete and conflict with each other. This is why a semantically-based deep structure syntax runs into trouble, when it attempts to build these tendencies into a single, hierarchically organized description. Haas is quite willing to entertain rival deep structure proposals for sentences like:

They fly planes to Paris
Planes fly to Paris

because no single deep structure can express all the different strands of their meanings, such as that *planes* has in one sense a similar function in the two sentences (being like *aircraft, helicopters,* etc. the machine through which flying is achieved), but that at the same time *planes* is in the first sentence the thing flown (like *food, mail,* etc.) and in the second sentence the thing that does the flying (like *birds, bees*). Haas adduces numerous other verbs such as *move, grow, develop, love, (be) sad,* etc. which, like *fly* allow subtle shifts in the semantic role of their associated subjects, objects, etc. according to the lexical and situational context.

Semantic tendencies are realized WITHIN the framework of grammatical rules, but they are not part of that framework. (1973c: 292)

As a consequence he also rejects any attempt to set up a universal semantically-based deep structure, whether on a logical or on an anthropological base.

If we allow Haas his independent syntax, what does he make of it? Certainly not just 'surface structure', which he claims to find highly problematical, pointing out the paradox of its generally being considered inadequate but uncontroversial. What is generally assumed for the surface structure of a sentence is a labelled bracketing where all the constituents are continuous. If such surface structures inevitably need supplementation (in the form of deep and semantic structures), Haas argues, is it not preferable to abandon them and start afresh? Although some linguists would certainly defend surface structures (cf. Lyons's essay), no one would wish to exempt them from empirical scrutiny; and even Chomsky (1976: 83) now speaks of 'a suitably enriched notion of surface structure' (cf. further Matthews's essay).

In his syntactic investigations Haas looks for what he calls 'syntactic cohesion'. The cohesion[5] of two syntactic elements is established by examining the 'syntagmatic dependence' between them and/or the 'paradigmatic reducibility' of their cooccurrence (1973b: 107–11, 1975b: 533–6; cf. also Taylor 1976). He envisages three kinds of dependency relationship: (i) dependence for occurrence; (ii) dependence for position; and (iii) dependence for value. Dependence for occurrence (which is always assessed within a particular functional frame) refers to the requirement for an element only to occur in the presence of some other element (the dependence may be unilateral, when it corresponds to a strict syntactic notion of endocentricity, or it may be bilateral). In *the boy*, for instance, we find two elements that are bilaterally dependent, and in *the poor boy* a further element *poor*, which is unilaterally dependent on the discontinuous *the . . . boy*. Dependence for position relates to the (lack of) permutation potential of elements in sequence: in *a beautiful contemporary material*, for instance, the adjectives are fixed in position relative to each other, something that is not true of *a coarse contemporary material*. Dependence for value is a matter of status relative to (minimal) linguistic signs: a morpheme like adverbial *-ly* or verbal *-ing*, for instance, is a mere grammatical

---

[5] This term is intended, obviously, in a sense entirely different from that used by Halliday & Hasan (1976).

marker by itself and requires a preceding lexical morpheme (as in *quickly*, *flying*) before it can (jointly) assume the status of a linguistic sign.

Working from first principles on individual sentences, using his concepts of dependence and reducibility, Haas sees himself as establishing an empirically justified alternative to surface structure, one that is semantically neutral but in no way superficial. As he himself puts it:

We should try, once more, to subject 'labelling' and 'bracketing' to an explicit discipline of empirical inquiry. Computational formalization of intrinsically obscure formulae is not enough. (1975b: 532)

In phonology, Haas set himself the task of scrutinizing the criteria and methods of phonological analysis with a philosopher's theoretical rigour. Although the various theories of the phoneme have shown a certain practical similarity in the descriptions they have produced, their methods and assumptions differ widely, as do their relations to other branches of linguistic analysis. Since the practical results of phonological description have not differed seriously from school to school there has been a general reluctance to compare assumptions and look for consensus. Haas wryly remarks:

. . . the interest in method is rather frowned upon by some linguists. Where there is so much to do, they would rather get on with it. (1958b: 1)

His own theory of phonology was largely developed from the work of the prewar Prague School, but a second major influence was the work of J. R. Firth and his colleagues. Though Haas was unwilling to surrender the practical advantages of independent segments for the complexity of prosodic notation, he incorporated the insights of Firthian prosodic analysis into his treatment of elements with determinant value.

The contributions Haas makes to phonological theory are contained in a number of important articles spanning his whole career. His second paper to the Philological Society (1957a) examines basic concepts. In phonology his two basic types of operation, segmentation and substitution, serve to identify segments and features. These elements may have the two types of value discussed above: diacritical (here equivalent to distinctive) and determinant. In addition the process of phonological analysis establishes the same types of relation found at other levels. Within the syntagma there are relations of sequence; within each paradigm there are relations of substitutability. Such relations operate not in arbitrary chunks of speech but only within linguistic frame-units or functions. As we have seen, Haas views these functional relationships of the segment or feature to the unit within which it contrasts as a third kind of relation.

Among the practical difficulties of phonemic analysis has always been phonemic overlap – the same sound occurring in different contexts as a realization of different phonemes. Haas recast this as a problem of defining the limits of feature variation. He proposed flexible 'relative' features, whose value is read from different scales in different contexts. An ideal example would be features of tone such as 'high' – 'mid' – 'low'. Compared with them, the grades of place and manner of consonants (labial, dental, etc.) seem invariable. Yet Haas suggests that these too can be interpreted on a relative basis. The nasals of Hungarian could be analysed as /m n ŋ/ 'front', 'mid' and 'back' with the values read on two scales: [m ɲ ŋ] before /k g/, where all the values do contrast, and [m n ɲ] elsewhere. This neatly avoids a traditional analysis into /m n ɲ/ with [ŋ] as an allophone of /n/, which made it very difficult to specify the distinctive features of the /n/ and /ɲ/. Haas is confident that 'in operating with relative features we are not guilty of any hocus-pocus' (1958d: 484), but it is difficult to share his confidence, in the absence of any criterion of economy or naturalness with which to limit relativity.

In a generative approach to the Hungarian nasals, freed from the constraints which caused the problem, one would naturally generate [ŋ] as a conditioned variant of underlying /n/. On the other hand, a rule to shift the value [ɲ] to [n] and [ŋ] to [ɲ] or vice versa would be very cumbersome in any of the current feature systems. This might be taken as evidence of the unnaturalness of Haas's proposal for this particular case. Once we admit relativity along the category of place, we can easily lose control. Consider two suggestions for matching the four places of English fricatives with four places of stops, which clearly take relative features far beyond what Haas intended:

(i)	Hill	p	t	tʃ	k		(ii)	Jones	p	t	tʃ	k
	(1958)	b	d	dʒ	g			(1968)	b	d	dʒ	g
		f	θ	s	ʃ				f	s	ʃ	θ
		v	ð	z	ʒ				v	z	ʒ	ð

Here the relativity of place allows us to pack phonetically disparate elements into four grades, but the work done by the speaker-listener in processing the contextual conditions would be considerable. It would be more realistic to employ one or two extra grades at the expense of symmetry. To safeguard relative features from hocus-pocus, it is necessary to have a constraint of naturalness – a point with which Haas is in full sympathy.

Relative features also serve (1957a) as a basis for extending the Prague concept of neutralization to multidimensional oppositions, a suggestion which has been widely followed. A typical example is the absence of initial clusters */tl/, */dl/ in both English and German as against /pl/, /bl/, /kl/, /gl/. However, such problems inevitably hinge on the actual features used. Even in articulatory terms, if we admit a hierarchy of features (first, labial~lingual; then, apical~dorsal), we can still reduce this neutralization to binary and possibly privative terms. At the same time Haas also reacts strongly to the extreme relativity of Jakobson's binary acoustic-based features (Jakobson *et al.* 1952), then very much in vogue, and advocates a return to an articulatory basis.

Haas's view of the relations between phonology and grammar is consistent over a span of thirty years, in which a number of radically different approaches have been proposed. Like the pioneers of phonology – Sapir, Bloomfield, Trubetzkoy and Firth – he presupposes a knowledge of the boundaries of grammatical units in phonological analysis, since contrastive substitution and statements of distribution are only relevant within the frame of some grammatical unit. He was in profound disagreement with the attempts of the American structuralists of the 1950s, notably Bloch and Trager, to keep phonology free of grammatical prerequisites and of appeals to meaning, by relying exclusively on distributional criteria (1958b, 1967) and so progressing to grammatical description from an independently worked-out phonology. More recently he has been highly critical of extreme forms of generative phonology. He finds the approaches of Bloch and Chomsky to be the converse of each other:

The first will admit *no* grammatical information at the earlier phonological stage; while the second will insist on admitting *all* grammatical information into the later phonology. (1967: 228)

Haas draws an important distinction here between DESCRIPTIVE and EXPLANATORY morphophonemics. It is possible to make purely descriptive statements about allomorphic variation, but they are inevitably of a very restricted nature. The English noun-plural morpheme, for instance, is regularly marked by sibilance; this relation is observable within single utterances. Explanatory morphophonemics of the type which links the allomorphs of the stem in *president, presidency* and *presidential* to a single abstract underlying form requires a complete phonological and grammatical analysis of the language for the explanatory relationship to become apparent. It operates on descriptions of language, not directly on language itself. However valuable such explanatory statements may be, Haas maintains that they can only serve as a complement to, and never as a replacement for, the phonological analysis which restricts its grammatical prerequisites to a knowledge of unit boundaries.

Though his main concern in phonology has been to refine theory, Haas has always been interested in its practical applications in various fields. He has, for instance, taken a great interest in speech therapy (1962c, 1963, 1968b). His first paper in this field was a pioneering attempt to extract, from a small sample of the speech of a dyslalic patient, an independent sketch of the defective phonological system. By comparing this system with the target system he was able to suggest a treatment strategy which would gradually and most profitably extend the child's network of contrasts. Such an exercise is clearly educative for a student therapist, but in day-to-day practice it seems inevitable, as Haas realized, that assessment will largely be made by direct reference to the target. Even so, such a comparison will always be more rewarding if it takes account of contrasts, distinctive features and functional load than if it merely records segments correct, incorrect and omitted. Haas also drew attention to the importance of determinant value, particularly in lip-reading (1968b: 25). An utterance-initial /w/ is liable to have determinant value for a whole clause or sentence, and not to perceive it would be particularly serious, as experienced teachers realize.

Closely related to his work in phonology is Haas's interest in orthography. Here again, it involves not merely the refinement of theory, but the practical applications of such a deeper theoretical insight to the teaching of reading and writing and to spelling reform (1969, 1970a, 1970b, 1976b). In *Phonographic translation* (1970b) Haas examines the relationship between writing and speech. This is usually thought of as 'reference', and graphemes are considered to be 'signs' of phonemes. Yet in an orthography like that of English, almost every graphemic sign has multiple reference, and almost every phoneme corresponds to a range of 'synonymous' signs. Moreover there is only a tenuous link between this kind of 'reference' and that involved in meaning proper. Haas suggests instead that the relationship between phonemes and graphemes is really one of translation, and he explores the consequences of such a model for methods of teaching reading and writing, and for spelling reform. Even though phonographic translation, between the two mediums of speech and writing, is 'fast and curtailed by habit' (1970b: 42), Haas considers it to be a process of matching similar to that used in translating texts from one language to another. He compares the two translation processes to show various types of disjunctive correspondence and to show how choice is controlled by rules and tendencies. Contextual rules and transformational rules are both shown to be an essential part of the regularity of English spelling and he finds that they are not always given adequate consideration in reading schemes and proposals for spelling reform.

With this translation model, Haas has undoubtedly laid stronger theoretical foundations for teaching reading and for spelling reform. Those who follow him may need to develop the model further, however. It does not, for instance, incorporate the process of acquiring reading and writing (cf. Chomsky & Halle 1968: 331). As Haas presents it, the model describes a fully competent reader/writer.

For instance, he caters for vowel reduction by a set of 'transformation rules':

We learn to become sensitive to the advantage of marking these 'paradigmatic' relations, and therefore *not* to write what we hear. The rule . . . requires us to collect the 'full' vowels from any member of such a set [author – authority, etc.] and to write them in every case. (1970b: 69)

However, the child learning to write may very well not have these sets and so be unable to 'collect' the appropriate full vowel from his own linguistic experience. How the child is taught to cope with the full-vowel graphemes of English in the transition from reading to writing is in fact a critical test of any literacy scheme.

In one of his most recent works (1976b), Haas establishes a comprehensive taxonomy of writing systems – not by cataloguing and labelling existing scripts, but by exploring all theoretical options in the technology of writing. He suggests three binary classificatory features based on the relations contracted by graphemes: DERIVED – ORIGINAL ('interlingually' based on speech, or not); INFORMED –EMPTY ('intralingually' making a semantic contribution to the message, or not); MOTIVATED –ARBITRARY ('extralingually' related by pictorial representation to things referred to in the message). In using a completely new terminology for his theory, Haas wished to escape from the confusions inherent in terms such as pictographic, ideographic, or conventional.

Only three possible types of script prove to be feasible: (i) original, informed and motivated; (ii) derived, informed and arbitrary; (iii) derived and empty. Different types may mix to some extent, and this mixing together with the 'extension,' of motivated graphemes is a prime factor in the historical development of scripts. The question of which type is optimal is found by Haas to depend on the purpose for which it is used. To take a minor point, derived characters are not superior to original characters in road signs, chemical formulae and a whole range of metaphorical diagrams.

Although Haas's major contributions have been in theory of meaning and in linguistic analysis, he has never forgotten his earlier trade of Germanist. His article 'Of living things' (1957d), a contribution to the History of Ideas, brings together Goethe's (and Darwin's) views on biology, Schlegel's work on comparative philology and Herder's approach to literary criticism: they all seek to explain how living things can evolve and become differentiated, and yet remain the same. The explanation lies in describing and comparing part–whole relationships rather than individual parts on their own, in other words in adopting a functionalist approach. Haas's account of the development of the German standard language (1976a) also brings together his literary and linguistic interests. He has, moreover, always insisted that historical and comparative studies have a secure place in linguistics, and that linguistics has a part to play in the study of literature.

It is clear, therefore, that Haas wishes to see language studied not only in its own right, but also in a broader philosophical, literary and historical context. As a distinctively human phenomenon, language has the power to cope with complex and abstract thought alongside its apparently trivial, though vital, everyday functions. As a human institution, language also has enough flexibility to allow for imaginative and experimental use by poets and, inevitably, to undergo change as time passes.

In taking this broad view of language, William Haas shows himself to be the complete antithesis of a narrow linguistician. At the same time, as a general linguist first and foremost, he consistently points to the functional viewpoint as a guiding principle.

William Haas: Select Bibliography

1949 'General categories of language', *Proceedings of the VIth International Congress of Linguists* (1948). Paris: Klincksieck, 150–160

1951 'On speaking a language', *Proceedings of the Aristotelian Society 1950–1*, 129–66

1952 'Sense and commonsense', BBC talk, *The Listener* (6 March), 386–7

1953 'Value judgements', *Mind* 62, 512–17

1954a 'On defining linguistic units', *Transactions of the Philological Society*, 54–84

1954b 'The contemporary philosophy of language: I. Sounds and meanings; II. New methods in linguistic studies; III. Theories of language', Three talks given on the BBC Third Programme, 26 September, 2 and 14 October, unpublished

1956a Contributions to the discussions, *Proceedings of the VIIth International Congress of Linguists* (1952). Oslo: Oslo University Press, 12–13, 25–6, 39–40, 50–1, 86–7, 190–2, 241–3

1956b 'Concerning glossematics', *Archivum Linguisticum* 8, 93–110

1957a 'The identification and description of phonetic elements', *Transactions of the Philological Society*, 118–59

1957b 'On speaking with an accent', *Journal of the Lancashire Dialect Society* 7, 2–9

1957c 'Zero in linguistic description', in *Studies in Linguistic Analysis* (Special publication of the Philological Society), 33–53

1957d 'Of living things', *German Life and Letters* 10, 89–96, 251–7

1958a Review of N. Chomsky, *Syntactic structures* (1st ed. 1957), *Archivum Linguisticum* 10, 50–4

1958b 'Relevance in phonetic analysis', *Word* 15, 1–18

1958c Review of J. R. Firth, *Papers in linguistics 1934–51*, in *Bulletin of the SOAS* 21, 668–71

1958d Contributions to the discussions, *Proceedings of the VIIIth International Congress of Linguists*. Oslo: Oslo University Press, 483–4, 805

1960a 'General Linguistics in university studies', *Universities Quarterly* (April) 14, 118–43

1960b 'Linguistic structures', Review of A. A. Hill, *Introduction to linguistic structures*, *Word* 16, 251–76

1961 'Translation', *Proceedings of the Aristotelian Society, Supplementary Volume 35*, 217–23

1962a 'Two types of phonological value', *Proceedings of the IVth International Congress of Phonetic Sciences* (Helsinki, 1961). The Hague: Mouton, 625–9

1962b 'The theory of translation', *Philosophy* 37, 208–28. (Reprinted as 1968a)

1962c 'Signs and signals', in S. Mason (ed.) *Signs, signals and symbols*. London: Methuen

1963 'Phonological analysis of a case of dyslalia', *Journal of Speech and Hearing Disorders* 28, 239–46

1964a 'Semantic value', *Proceedings of the IXth International Congress of Linguists* (Cambridge, Mass. 1962). The Hague: Mouton, 1066–72; also contributions to the discussions, 365, 697, 994–5

1964b 'Why linguistics is not a physical science', paper read to the International Congress of Logic, Methodology and Philosophy of Science (Jerusalem, 1964), unpublished

1966 'Linguistic relevance', in C. E. Bazell *et al.* (eds.) *In memory of J. R. Firth*. London: Longman, 116–47

1967 'Grammatical prerequisites of phonological analysis', in J. Hamm (ed.) *Phonologie der Gegenwart*. Graz and Vienna: H. Bohlaus, 227–41

1968a 'The theory of translation', in G. H. R. Parkinson (ed.) *The theory of meaning*. Oxford: Oxford University Press, 86–108. (Reprinted from 1962b)

1968b 'Functional phonetics and speech therapy', *The British Journal of Disorders in Communication* 3, 20–7

1969 'From "look and say" to ITA', *Times Educational Supplement* (28 November)

1970a 'On spelling and spelling reform', in W. Haas (ed.) *Alphabets for English*. Manchester: Manchester University Press, 1–13

1970b *Phonographic translation*. Manchester: Manchester University Press

1972 'The science of language', Review of C. F. Hockett (ed.) 'A Leonard Bloomfield anthology', (1970) *Times Literary Supplement* (10 March)

1973a 'Meanings and rules', *Proceedings of the Aristotelian Society 1972–1973*, 135–55

1973b Review Article on J. Lyons, *Introduction to theoretical linguistics*, *Journal of Linguistics* 9, 71–113

1973c 'Rivalry amongst deep structures', *Language* 49, 282–93

1974 Review of P. Tartaglia, *Problems in the construction of a theory of natural language, Journal of Linguistics* 10, 194–7

1975a 'Phonology and General Linguistics (on the notion of linguistic function)', in W. U. Dressler & F. V. Mareš (eds.) *Phonologica 1972: Akten der zweiten internationalen Phonologie-Tagung*, (Vienna, 5–8 September 1972). Munich and Salzburg: Wilhelm Fink Verlag, 25–33

1975b 'What is surface structure?', *Proceedings of the XIth International Congress of Linguists*. Bologna: il Mulino, 529–38

1975c 'Syntax and semantics of ordinary language II', *Proceedings of the Aristotelian Society, Supplementary Volume 49*, 147–69

1976a 'The making of the German national language', in D. Daiches & A. Thorlby, *Literature and western civilization: the modern world I: Hopes*. London: Aldus Books, chapter 13, 327–49

1976b 'Writing: the basic options', in W. Haas (ed.) *Writing without letters*. Manchester: Manchester University Press, 131–208

1978 'Linguistics 1930–80', *Journal of Linguistics* 14, 293–308

Some cases of metanalysis

C. E. BAZELL

Though metanalysis is a familiar factor in linguistic change, it has not been exploited to the full. I shall begin with a well-known problem of early Germanic which receives a rather simple solution as soon as this factor is taken into consideration, and continue with a cluster of problems in the later history of English where the factor intervenes at several stages.

1. The Germanic problem has most recently been discussed by Seebold (1974). In several Old English dialects there are nominal forms which appear, at least superficially, to be dative plurals, but whose semantic interpretation as plurals is, to say the least, dubious. Hence the suggestion was long ago made that these forms are old instrumental singulars whose form collapsed by regular phonological change with the dative plural. The instrumental singular does not survive as an independent case except in the adjective in Old English, or at all in Gothic and Old Norse. Where it does survive in the noun, as in Old High German, the form is not that with which we are concerned.

A typical instance is the Old English form *meolcum* (Campbell 1959: 227). This looks like the dative plural of the word for 'milk', but one would not expect a plural in the text. An instrumental singular, on the other hand, would perfectly well fit the contexts. However, since there is no instrumental as such in the Old English noun, it would be an archaism, and one moreover to which there is only one possible parallel in Old English.

It is therefore only to be expected that some scholars should have tried to explain such forms as being precisely what they appear to be – just normal dative plurals. The classical account along these lines still remains that of Osthoff (1906). In the particular instance of *meolcum*, he refers to the fact that words for liquids often take a plural form: modern English *beestings* would be an example.

But Osthoff showed merely that each separate instance might be given some sort of explanation of this sort, and rather a different kind of explanation in each case. One might be prepared to put up with any one of these explanations individually if no better explanation were forthcoming, but surely not with their totality. Each of them has a difficulty of its own, yet the problem demands an overall solution.

The difficulty in the sample case we have chosen to start with is that *meolcum*, if at all a plural, is to be found only in the dative. We do not find a corresponding nominative or genitive plural. The comparison therefore with languages in which some nouns for liquids take normally a plural form, is quite irrelevant as a substantive contribution to the question of the Old English form; though I will argue later that the fact that nominals referring to liquids do, in some languages, have a regular and invariant plural form (*pluralia tantum*), is by no means irrelevant to the general question.

Seebold concentrates on the Gothic examples. He allows that *dagam jah nahtam* 'day and night' (as in 'they prayed day and night') could conceivably be a plural, although the Greek original shows singulars in accordance with a surely universal idiom across languages. He even allows that *in fragiftim* 'engaged with prospect of marriage', while most likely containing the singular *fragifts* 'engagement', could at a pinch be treated as containing the plural of this noun. Since Seebold is in general arguing in favour of a singular–instrumental interpretation, this is surely overgenerous, even though he finally concludes that there is one certain instance in favour of his view, namely *in gasinþjam* '(travelling) in company'.

Finally, that is, so far as the main body of the paper is concerned. But in a postscript he indicates that even here it is possible to conceive of a plural interpretation. He is the first to think of this possibility, and his conclusion from it, that his arguments after all fall short of anything like a proof, is needlessly modest.

The appearance of failure to prove anything derives from the fact that Seebold set out to decide between two opposite views: (i) that there are at least some survivals of pure instrumental singulars; (ii) that all putative instances of such a survival are merely dative plurals. But there is an intermediate view (iii) that old instrumental singulars survive only when they could be reinterpreted as plurals.

On this third assumption everything falls into place. We do not have to regret that there are no quite unambiguous instances of instrumental singular, for it is in the nature of the assumption that there cannot be; a metanalysis as dative plural is the price that the old singular forms pay for survival. But at the same time we now understand the extreme artificiality of most, if not all, of the attempts to treat the forms as spontaneous uses of the dative plural. In synchronic morphology they are rightly regarded as plurals, but semantically they are deviant – though not deviant beyond the point at which serious linguists could regard them as explicable without recourse to historical explanation.

There remains an example for which even defendants of a purely non-singular origin of semantic nature for the rest of the examples would not claim such an origin here. This is the example of Old High German *houbitum* which survives in the modern German *zu Häupten* 'at the head of' (the modern normal dative plural is *Häuptern*). Plainly, the plural is semantically unmotivated here, but it can be explained without recourse to the old Germanic instrumental singular, on the analogy of the natural plural 'at the feet of' which in non-literal contexts is the exact opposite. And this is presumably part of the explanation in fact.

But as a total explanation it fails dismally. For why is it that it is precisely in Germanic, which had other instances of putative old instrumental singulars, that this particular analogy took place? Osthoff cites parallels from such languages as Lithuanian, but they are not genuine parallels, but rather biblical imitations of Luther's Bible.

Seebold has noted this, as indeed he has noted all other weak points in Osthoff's treatment, so far as each individual instance is concerned. But he does not seem to be struck by the general weakness of Osthoff's paper. Osthoff treats each instance quite independently of the others, and does not appear to be in the least surprised that one and the same language group should present so many problems in this domain, each (according to him) with its own private solution. Seebold points out implausibilities in each separate solution, but he seems to see no grave difficulty in the fact that so many quite different solutions should be needed.

My conclusion is that Seebold's case for an instrumental singular origin for all these forms is far stronger than he himself believes. In a sense, all these forms have different explanations, but in another sense they are all to be explained in the same way. The motivation for the retention of the old forms is always just this: they could be interpreted as dative plurals. The mode of interpretation varied from instance to instance: it could be semantic, syntactic or morphological. But in each case there was a possibility of metanalysis whereby the old forms could be retained under a new system, albeit not so fully integrated into this system as not to betray their origin in an earlier system. Where the possibility of metanalysis was absent, the old forms were lost.

2. The following three problems of English have not to my knowledge ever been seen as in any way connected:

(a) So-called 'people-deletion'; cf. Pullum (1975)
(b) The underlying form of the common plural morph; cf. recently Miner (1974)
(c) Singular–plural homophony in such nouns as *Swiss* and *Japanese*; cf. *OED* under the relevant headings.

Let us begin with seventeenth-century English. This is similar in the relevant details to the modern language, except that (i) *Swisses* and *Japaneses* were the norm both as generic plurals and count-plurals; (ii) the generic ('people-deleted') *the Spanish* was unknown as against the still normal *Spaniards*.

For seventeenth-century English we can then state the general rule: People-deletion takes place if and only if the adjective has fewer syllables than the count-plural.

Hence *the English, the French*, etc. (not *the Englishmen* etc., which as generics are not grammatical). Hence also *the Poles, Arabs, Finns, Turks*, etc., not *the Polish, the Arabic*, etc., and hence also when the number of syllables is equal: *the Icelanders* not *the Icelandic*.

However this is true only under the assumptions (i) that it was the underlying number of syllables (vocalic segments), not the phonetic number, that was relevant, and (ii) that the underlying form of the plural morph was -*z* rather than -*iz*. Only so can we account for *Swisses* and *Chineses* as having no more underlying syllables than the corresponding adjectives, the extra syllable being inserted under merely phonological rules. Since the decision about the underlying form of the plural (and similar forms) is rather finely balanced, and since none of the arguments so far presented depends on a consideration of historical developments, the latter should now be allowed their place.

On these assumptions, the replacement of generic *the Japaneses*

(*Portugueses, Swisses*) at the turn of the century by the now normal *the Japanese*, etc., is to be accounted for by the replacement of the underlying syllabic form by the surface syllabic form as decisive factor. (There was no change in the underlying form of the plural itself; plainly it would make nonsense of the whole distribution if one supposed that *-iz* had become the underlying form, for then *Poles* and *Polish* would start off with the same number of syllables.)

However, while this accounts for the peculiar treatment of the generics ending in a sibilant (the only nouns in which underlying and surface syllabicity differed), it does not at all account for the replacement of *Japaneses* as a count-plural by *Japanese*. Surely we have to deal here with a case of 'overspill': while the generic ('people-deleted') form underwent this change, *pari passu* the count-plural followed suit.

Overspill is quite familiar in its most uninteresting manifestation of hypercorrection. Hypercorrection does not normally involve any loss of generality. But if we are right about what happened around the turn of the seventeenth–eighteenth century a generality was lost in this instance.

Instances of this sort are not very rare, but they are commonly overlooked by historical linguists. I cite one instance from Middle English which, as is usual in such cases, has been obtusely misinterpreted, just because this sort of thing had not been looked for.

I refer to a development in the West Midland dialect of the thirteenth century; probably the development was more widespread than this, but it matters very little. In this dialect the old dative plural was replaced (as elsewhere) by the nominative plural in the most common declension: thus the old dative plural *englen* was replaced by *engles*. This looks very commonplace indeed.

But at this stage there was a remarkable development. The replacement of the old dative plural *englen* by nominative *engles* was as such just a 'global' substitution of the nominative for the dative in the most common declension; it would be mistaken to describe it as a substitution of *-es* for *-en*. Yet this was its secondary interpretation, as shown by well-attested forms in the West Midland dialect; *-es* was in fact to replace *-en* in such forms as *footes* (where the dative had no corresponding nominative) which thus remained distinct from the expected *feet*, and even more paradoxically in such forms as dative plural *limes*, distinguished from nominative *limen*, though historically *limen* would be expected in both cases. In other words the initially syncretistic tendency was frustrated by overspill.

My data are taken from an excellent study of a West Midland text by d'Ardenne (1936: 210). It is only fair to add that her own explanation of the facts is quite different. Among other things she assumes that the normal development of dative plural in the dialect would be *-e* rather than *-en*. It is surely most implausible to assume that OE *-um* could yield *-e* in this dialect while OE *-an* (in the nominative) yielded *-en*. However, there is no direct textual evidence against this assumption and its acceptance would entail only a minor modification of the view taken above.

I return now to the question of the replacement of the count-plural *Japaneses* by *Japanese*. This is a plain case of overspill: there is no structural (or functional) reason for the replacement. Quite simply, when the generic plural (people-deleted) adjective replaced the nominal plural the count-plural followed suit. Like most instances of overspill the results defeat the initial motivation.

In this modern instance of overspill we have independent evidence that something odd had happened. Many speakers are reluctant to use *Japanese* as a count-noun at all, though the only explicit reference I have found for this fact is in the well-known grammar of the American scholar Curme, who remarks that, while *three Chinese* would be avoided, *a million Chinese* is more acceptable. My own usage conforms with his observation.

Let us now turn to the other difference between seventeenth-century and later English, the growing popularity of *the Spanish*. The *OED* records it as 'rare' even for the later centuries, but at least it is cited. It is now fairly common, though still found less acceptable than *the Spaniards*.

Now almost alone among adjectives ending in *-ish* in the relevant domain, *Spanish* has the same number of syllables as the count-noun. In other words, with this type of adjective, when there is a larger number of syllables in the count-noun the latter cannot be used as a generic, when there is a smaller number it must be, hence *Poles, Turks, Finns* etc., and when there is an EQUAL number of syllables BOTH are permissible.

Spanish/Spaniards is not in fact the sole example of equisyllabicity, we also have *British/Britons*. So far as modern English is concerned, this simply confirms our rule.

But at this point a very reasonable objection may be raised against my argument, namely that *the British* is far earlier than the eighteenth century and that today it is preferred over *Britons* (except in patriotic contexts). Nothing similar can be said about *the Spanish*.

However it could equally be objected that I have singled out the suffix *-ish* for special consideration. Why? Because it is the suffix in the word *English*, which is the paradigm of the class. *British* is strongly parasitic on *English*; no wonder that as a generic it is earlier than *the Spanish*.

The appearance of generic *the British* before the eighteenth century is just the first instance of the upgrading of people-words in *-ish* which in modern English gives them a special status: only to them does the rule apply that when count-noun and adjective have the *same* number of syllables either may be chosen, *the Spanish* beside *the Spaniards*.

I have hitherto spoken as though the latter example is the only one of its kind, but there is at least one other: *the Flemish* beside *the Flemings*. It does not seem to have been mentioned in the grammatical 'literature' (because Flanders is not a political entity?) but is entirely parallel to the case of *Spanish* and *Spaniards*.

It is beyond the bounds of coincidence that the class of nouns having a number of syllables in the count-plural identical with the number of syllables in the adjective, is the same as the class of nouns allowing the alternatives of a normal count-plural and a 'people-deleted' adjective. The three members of both classes are identical.

The language to which this rule generally applies is my own rather normal form of English, which (matters of frequency apart) agrees with literary usage as recorded in the *OED*.

However there is one marginal exception to which R. M. Hogg has called my attention. My rules predict *Scots* alone, whereas both *the Scottish* and *the Scotch* are attested. Interestingly this is a point and perhaps the only one on which my usage departs from the *OED*. The *OED* records *the Scottish* (albeit as rare), whereas I could deviate from my own rule only by saying (hardly writing) *the Scotch*.

Hogg suggests that the avoidance of *the Scots* may be due to the avoidance of *Scots* as an adjective: if so this is a plain instance of overspill. But an additional factor was surely the upgrading of the suffix *-ish* which led to the early occurrence of *British* as a generic. This same factor accounts for the relative acceptability of *Scottish* two centuries later.

It is natural that *the British* should have been the first to profit from this upgrading, since it had the double advantage of equisyllabicity with count-noun and a special semantic relation to *English*. If syllabicity was the main factor, it is also natural that *Spanish* and *Flemish* were the next items to follow suit. Finally, if semantics played an essential but subordinate role, *Scottish* and *Scotch* would be next on the list, as hyponyms of British. All other hyponyms such as *Welsh* and *Cornish* could not be affected, since they were already fairly and squarely in the bag.

Although the close fit of rule to data leaves no room for talk of coincidence, it is of course natural to ask how such a strange rule came about. Obviously it must have something to do with markedness. In names for 'peoples' the generics are unmarked vis-à-vis count-nouns and so may be expected, all else equal, to have shorter or at least not longer phonological forms. Or as in many languages there may be no count-noun at all corresponding to the generic: OE *Dene* 'Danes' has no morphological count-noun equivalent.

Have I any parallel to offer for the admittedly unusual English development? Perhaps not a parallel, but at least an analogue. Just as the phonological markedness of a semantically unmarked term led to a reduction in 'bulk' via 'people-deletion' of the English generics, so in other languages did the phonological unmarkedness of a semantically marked term lead to an increase in 'bulk' via other devices.

The most remarkable known to me of such developments is that of the Serbian genitive plural. By a sound-law common to Slavonic languages, this generally terminated in zero. Some Slavonic languages have roughly maintained the zero–forms, while others have replaced them by readily explicable analogies. But Serbian has a new genitive plural which at first sight seems to have arisen out of thin air. This is absurd, but the only real explanation offered, though technically feasible, is so fantastic as to make my explanation of some facts of English look very commonplace indeed.

The explanation was this. There were (and are) some nouns in Serbian with a genitive singular in short *-i* and a genitive plural in long *-i:*, while the commonest type of masculine nouns had a genitive singular in (short)-*a*. By analogy there arose a genitive plural in long *-a:* and this spread into almost all other declensions.

Though this may not offend against the minimal requirements for a proportional analogy, it is otherwise as fantastic as any explanation could be. First, the starting point is in a minority declension (the old *i*-stems) which survives in most Slavonic dialects but never elsewhere plays any productive role. Secondly, its presumed role is to afford a model for the commonest masculine declension; but the *i*-stems were exclusively feminine, and morphological influences across gender are hard to find in the history of Slavonic languages. (It is striking that the main analogical contribution to the common masculine declension is from the original *u*–stems in most Slavonic languages, though as a class they nowhere survive. These were from the beginning mainly masculine nouns, and some Indo-European dialects which retain the *u*–declension (notably Old Norse) include no nouns of other gender.)

I cannot believe there is much to an explanation of this sort; I mention it only to show the problems which arise when a marked morpheme does not answer to a marked (non-zero) morph.

In the case under discussion, we have rather to do with the failure of morphemic unmarkedness to answer morphic unmarkedness: *men* in *Englishmen* might have been called an 'empty morph' in the days when this term was popular. However I cannot see any way in which the older structuralists could have described (let alone explained) the position.

For a transformational–generative grammarian, it would of course be quite easy to formulate the rules I suggested. However, he would object that they are not natural rules, since they involve transderivational complexities and a dubious use of the concept of markedness. But this is surely to miss the point. It is in the very nature of metanalyses that they give rise to rules that are not readily motivated synchronically. To revert to the Gothic example, it is sheer phonetic coincidence that an old instrumental singular became homophonous with the dative plural, and again a coincidence that some of these forms could be reinterpreted. It is therefore not surprising that rules that evolved in the process of metanalysis are not 'natural' rules in the way that rules arising from normal analogy are natural.

Moreover where the metanalysis involves overspill, as in the identification of count and non-count plurals *Chinese*, it is merely to be expected that the result should be in some way unnatural; indeed it might be said that this is part of the meaning of 'overspill'. And we have seen that here the unnaturalness of the rule is reflected in the behaviour of speakers, who, while accepting the rule in the sense that they do not infringe it, do not positively apply the rule, but rather avoid the forms which would result from its application.

3. Hudson (1972) has raised the question of the non-parallel distribution of probability adjectives in English. Thus we find with subject raising

He is likely to come
He is sure to come

but not

*He is probable to come
*He is inevitable to come

Hudson asks why there is not even a tendency to extend the construction to adjectives which do not normally allow it.

I do not claim to be able to answer this question, but can point to one fact that should surely be taken into consideration here. All these instances of subject raising are the result of metanalysis. For instance *sure to come* in its earlier uses in English invariably meant what is now expressed as 'sure of coming', i.e. *sure* was a genuine predicate of the nominal subject. The person, not the event, was sure. The same holds of *certain*, which in earliest examples occurs in contexts which preclude any other interpretation, e.g. in the imperative *be certain that* . . . which of course is still possible in modern usage, though now less usual than constructions in which *certain* must be taken as a predicate of S rather than of NP.

But this new construction is almost peculiar to English so far as adjectives of probability (including certainty as a limiting case) are concerned; there is no exact parallel in French or German. When Virgil describes Dido as 'certa mori' in the fourth book of the *Aeneid* (564), it can mean only 'determined to die' with *Dido* as the subject, not 'certain to die' with a phrase as the subject, and this not merely because the context demands it, but because a sentence subject of the sort demanded by English *Dido is certain to die* is in Latin a syntactic impossibility.

But in French there has recently arisen an almost parallel case, the difference being merely that we have to do with a verb rather than an adjective.

According to the standard usage as recorded in good French dictionaries, *Il risque de perdre* can have only the meaning 'He is in danger of losing' – and no doubt this is still the most normal interpretation. Here the verb *risquer* is predicated on the subject, as in English *He risks losing*. But there is now another interpretation 'he will probably lose'. Hence one may also say *Il risque de gagner* 'He will probably win', where the sense of 'risk' would be contextually most implausible. *Risquer* has become, by metanalysis, a phrasal predicate.

Are all the English examples the result of metanalysis? Some that I have not so far mentioned can only be so interpreted, e.g. *He is bound* (dialectally *tied*) *to come*. Here the phrasal interpretation is far later than

the interpretation as predicate on NP, as brought out by the fact that
it is bound that he will come has never existed.

The case of *likely* may be rather more problematic. *Likely* at the
relevant period (round the turn of the fourteenth century) meant
'able', 'suitable', etc. Now obviously 'able to be a king' could readily
be reinterpreted as 'likely to be a king'; the semantic change would be
small, and thus conceal the syntactic change whereby an NP-predicate
had become an S-predicate. Syntactic changes are apt to take place
under the cover of a semantic change.

It is easy to foresee an objection here: there is no evidence that *likely*
in its predicative use of an adjective on an NP is any earlier that its use
as a phrase-predicate. But this reflects the point I made before, that
reinterpretations do not necessarily follow in any temporal succession
some foregoing interpretation. It may be a shade paradoxical to say
that they take place at the same time, but I have dealt with this apparent
paradox above in connection with a morphological problem.

The earliest meaning of *likely* was 'similar, alike' and its semantic
development to 'probable' is not as such at issue here. Of interest is
rather the fact that as soon as *likely* became a synonym of *probable* it
was a synonym with different syntactic range, *likely* allowing
subject-raising while *probable* has to this day never acquired this
option. (It is curious however that in modern usage the relation is one
of syntactic overlapping, since *likely* is excluded from some positions
in which *probable* is allowed, e.g. in the adverbial *He will probably come*.
But while *He will likely come* is deviant, *He will very likely come* is
acceptable. This is an interesting oddity not without theoretical
import, but hardly relevant in the present context.)

It seems rather obvious to suggest that when *likely* took the new
meaning of 'probable', it retained at the same time its old role as a
predicate of NP, no longer of course in deep structure but merely in
surface syntax. Whereas *probable*, which at no stage had ever been a
predicate on NP, had no older role to preserve. Its distribution is very
similar to that of probability-adjectives in other European languages.

I cannot pretend to have solved Hudson's problem about the distribution of *likely* and *probable*. But I claim to have sketched in a bit the
background against which such problems must be seen. An essential
part of this background is the role of metanalysis.

The jingle theory of double -ing

DWIGHT BOLINGER

In his 'Grammatical prerequisites of phonological analysis' (1967), William Haas pleads for a middle ground between a phonology that ignores grammar, and a grammar that absorbs phonology (233). While phonology has emerged from its recent eclipse, we still find it taking second place to 'higher' levels. The controversy over when an -ing can be reiterated has focussed on the grammatical side, but should be looking at phonology and style. So we must take Haas's lead and redress the balance again.

Replying to J. R. Ross's 'Doubl-ing' (1972), Gary Milsark (1972) argues that successive -ings, as in *He was enjoying singing songs* and **He was keeping singing songs*, are normal when the -ing is a gerund but not when it is a participle. The formulation is neater than Ross's and contains a grain of truth, but offers no motive for the restriction. It makes no attempt even to explain what the acceptable constructions have in common – what there is, for example, about both *He was enjoying singing songs* and *He was keeping on singing songs* that makes them better than **He was keeping singing songs*. Nothing is said about how the expressions SOUND.

The primary condition of every signalling system is contrast. In language it manifests itself most strikingly in phonology, but it exists there only to guarantee its presence at higher levels. *Black* must not sound the same as *white*. The death of a homonym is only an extreme case of avoiding repetition, of making sure that different meanings are carried by different forms. And also of not diverting attention to the form when the intent is to focus on the message; as Wimsatt (1950: 10) points out, what is a virtue in poetry is a fault in prose; alliteration or rhyme can be distracting.

The result is one of those cases of what Talmy Givón calls 'overkill'.

To be on the safe side, speakers develop an AVERSION to repeated sounds when the repetition is close by and does not correspond to a clear parallel in sense. The practical becomes stylistic and is often mistakenly considered merely stylistic (Harris 1952: 10; Maclay & Osgood 1959: 43). A speaker is on the point of saying 'has dealt properly with *to hear* but has assigned too little structure to *to see*', and corrects it by inserting *the verb* before *to see*. An *if if* is changed to an *if supposing*, a *when when* to a *that when*, and a *had had* to a *had've had*. Alliterations like *mighty mild* and *quite quiet* haul one up short, and no one will be caught asking *Can eggs be coddled addled?* if the monstrosity can be foreseen in time.

The suffix *-ing* has a gift for calling attention to itself because of its consonant, the only one in English that virtually has to be morpheme-final. The velar nasal is widely exploited in sound symbolism and tends to be comical: *whang, bong, clang, ding-dong, sing-song, whingding, dingaling, King Kong, Gerald McBoing-Boing*. A repetition of *-ing* at close quarters is apt to attract attention, especially if prosodic and other factors set it off. Though double *-ing*s are not among the offensive repetitions that Fowler (1954, 1965) lists under 'jingles' ('I awAITED a belATED train'), they match his examples and his definition. For Wimsatt they would be 'the unhappy jingles of obliquely related like syllables' (1950: 8, 9).

This salience is the obvious reason why **He was keeping singing* is avoided. But it does not explain why *He was enjoying singing songs* is better, or why, in general, it is easier to repeat with gerunds than with participles.

I pause here to dispel the idea that asterisks can be evenly bestowed on participles and withheld from gerunds. Acceptability is graded, as has to be expected if the purpose is to avoid a clang. In the following, the gerund is worse than the participle:

> The bad thing about a strict diet is that you end up disliking eating
> (GERUND)
> I'm going fishing (PARTICIPLE)

Because of this indeterminacy, I put the remaining acceptability labels in parentheses. Most of the asterisked, and probably all of the queried instances, might well be found in a suitable context.

The acceptability of double *-ing*s is affected by two kinds of factors: grammatical–semantic, and phonological. An example of the first is gerund versus participle. To this must be added the class of participial adjectives, as in:

> You're looking ravishing
> Just being willing to help is the main thing

Also the very small class of participial prepositions:

> She is able to face anything, including dying
> Barring getting a divorce, I can't see any way out
> Even not counting making fudge this afternoon, I've spent more
>   time than I usually do in the kitchen
> Regarding helping your aunt, I have just this to say

Also lexical nouns in *-ing*:

> They were busy hanging bunting for the victory celebration
> Fixing ceiling prices safeguards the public
> I found the missing bearing

The gerund/participle split calls for a closer look. Shoemaker (1952: 109) points out the close kinship in a pair such as:

> I got the machine running
> I got the machine to running

Similarly:

> What can we accomplish just standing here?
> What can we accomplish by just standing here?

Historically, of course, the progressive embodied a gerund, with a preposition that is still manifest in *A-hunting we shall go*, and certain auxiliaries other than *be* still have divided usage (the last two examples are from Damon Runyon 1942: 32, 135):

> He was busy (at) doing his homework
> She got (to) thinking he didn't care for her any more
> The doll gets talking to him
> We happen to get to talking of wrong gees

While there are clear cases of gerunds, as in the example *including dying*, the really critical gerund/participle cases are all but impossible to tell apart. By Milsark's analysis, both of the following involve participles and hence are ungrammatical; the first example (with its asterisk) is his:

> (*)The police are stopping drinking (publicly) on campus
> California shows no signs of stopping growing (*Harper's
> Magazine* (June 1965), 82)

One can stop one's own drinking (*I stopped drinking*) or drinking in
general (*I stopped drinking*, i.e. prohibited it); this is a possible semantic
distinction between participle and gerund. On the other hand, one can
quit only one's own habit, in spite of which we find:

> Begin by quitting smoking (*Radio KGO, San Francisco, 10 p.m. 20
> August 1974*)

But this is no assurance that *smoking* is a participle, in view of the *it*
nominalization, and the lack of it, in:

> Quit it! – Quit what? – Quit smoking in here! I can't breathe!
> *Keep it! – Keep what? – Keep pushing! (OK: at it, at what)

Milsark's tests are inconclusive. His asterisked transformation, below,
is worse than my invented example only because he chose a bad
context in which to refer to a habit:

> (*)Drinking (publicly) on campus was hard for the police to stop
> Smoking heavily is hard for a person to stop, once he gets
> hooked

The intervening preposition in *I got the machine to running, She
got to thinking*, etc. points to one of the three most important factors:
SEPARATION. This is recognized by both Ross and Milsark, and
answers to the general principle of conflict: the closer the echo, the
worse it sounds. Two *-ings* with a preposition are better than two
without:

> To get talking you need a push
> (*)For getting talking you need a push
> (?)For getting to talking you need a push

The relative unimportance of the 'gerund' status shows in the awk-
wardness, still, of the last example. A 'participle' may even be better, if
the auxiliary is a phrasal verb with a particle between:

> (*)Just stopping complaining will be enough
> Just leaving off complaining will be enough
> Just giving up complaining will be enough
> To delay complaining would be fatal

(*)Delaying complaining would be fatal
Holding off complaining would be fatal[1]

Other intervening elements similarly:

(?)What can we accomplish just standing gabbing?
What can we accomplish just standing here gabbing?

Separation is also achieved prosodically. Though they seem unaware of it, most of Ross's and Milsark's unacceptable examples have a close juncture between the second of the two -*ing* forms and what immediately follows, creating a relatively more open juncture just preceding it. In the following I hyphenate the closer juncture. The first example is Ross's:

His avoiding contacting-Harriet is understandable
(*)What is not understandable is his avoiding talking

A phrase that increases the speed helps even more. The first example is again Ross's; in the second example the 'empty' (and hence de-accented) word *stuff* is flanked by reduced syllables:

(?)Red's attempting breathing-without a snorkel was ill-considered
Red's attempting eating-the-stuff-unseasoned was ill-considered
(*)It was ill-considered, Red's attempting running

It is impossible to say whether these are gerunds or participles. But when the first -*ing* is a verb of position or motion, the second is clearly a participle. The same junctural conditions obtain:

(*)He was lying gasping
He was lying gasping-for-breath
(*)Try sailing standing
Try sailing standing-up
(*)Try walking pushing
Try walking pushing-against-the-wind

Likewise with clear cases of gerunds:

(*)I'm missing playing
I'm missing playing-with-the-children

[1] The quasi-auxiliary status of *give up* and *hold off* can be seen in the behaviour of the particle. The following are progressively better: *He held complaining off*; (??)*He held his complaining off*; (?)*He held his complaints off*.

It is difficult to separate the effect of juncture from the second phonological factor, that of prominence, since adding something after the second *-ing* automatically removes it from the prominent end position. In the preceding asterisked examples, the second *-ing* receives the main sentence accent. Reducing its prominence has the effect of taking the heat off the second *-ing*, as can be illustrated with auxiliary *having*, unaccented:

> (?)Regretting being what she was caused her great anguish
> (?)More and more she was regretting being so gullible
> (*)Stupid and gullible was what I was most regretting being
> More and more she was regretting having been so gullible

The factor of prominence can be seen in its own right where relative juncture has been disposed of, as in the pair:

> But I don't think that continuing expanding is the answer to our economic woes
> (?)But I don't think that the answer to our economic woes is continuing expanding (is that of continuing expanding)

(I include the parenthesis to show that it is not the suggestion of a progressive in *is continuing* that causes the trouble.) End position can be bad even without accentual prominence:

> I don't líke being fired and I don't accépt being
> (*)I don't líke being fired and I'm not accépting being
> I don't líke being fired and I'm not accépting being fired

Separation is the clue to the greater acceptability of gerunds. Whatever one's views about how a verb phrase should be expanded, it seems clear that unless there were some especially close relationship between verbs – closer than between a verb and a complement noun – the notion of 'auxiliary' would never have been conceived. A participle is tied to its preceding verb more closely than a gerund usually is. Pauses and interpolations are easier in general with the latter:

> (*)Keep, if you can, running
> Continue, if you can, running
> (*)They will be, I suppose, competing
> They will resent, I suppose, competing

For would-be psychologizers, the structural separation between V and NP may be the thing; perhaps we only 'think' a separation. But

whether grammatical or prosodic, separation helps keep successive
-*ings* out of each other's way.

The third important phonological factor is rhythm. One rhythmic
factor already noted is toning down of the accent:

> (*)Denying being there was a mistake
> Denying having been there was a mistake

Even a rhyme can be mitigated:

> (*)That's what I was regretting getting
> (?)Regretting getting hurt won't heal the wound

But the rhythmic structure of the -*ings* also calls attention to itself
when the same beat is repeated. In the following, broken rhythms are
contrasted with more regular ones:

> (?)She was sitting waiting
> She was sitting embroidering
> (*)No congressman is venturing junketing after that scandal!
> I'm not venturing doing thát, not after the scandal!
> (*)You can please us by stopping pampering yourself
> You can please us by stopping overindulging yourself

Perhaps because of the availability and close synonymy of *Keep on*,
which could be used and would avoid a double -*ing*, a combination
with simple *keeping* is especially sensitive. The second example is
Ross's (79) with his asterisk; the third has the greatest rhythmic
contrast:

> (*)Her keeping fussing was a damned nuisance
> (*)Her keeping resisting him didn't help much, though
> Her keeping interfering all the time is what bothers me

It is notable how conscious one becomes of any additional repetition
of sounds once attention is attracted to this feature of the utterance. In
the second of the following there is a repetition of consonants as well
as rhythm, and the third adds rhyme:

> You end up hating entertaining
> (?)You end up hating eating (hunting)
> (*)You end up hating skating

One immediately senses an intentional reduplication, as in *helter-
skelter, hurry-scurry, pitter-patter*.

The tendency in English to regard trochaic (and dactylic) metre as more unusual than iambic may be an attention-getting factor in itself. We probably notice *Would Dakin waken?* more than *The accused refused*, or *It had gotten rotten* more than *We want the deceased released*. So something like *I dislike his shirking working* immediately flags us down.

The difficulties with prosody extend to combinations of attributive adjective in *-ing* plus nominal *-ing*. The familiarity of the adjective is a factor (see below), so that *the coming* ('future') *meeting* is less obnoxious than *the seeming* ('apparent') *failing*. But with degree of familiarity on a par, the effect of the prosody is evident:

> A telling discovery
> (?)A telling finding
> An interesting finding
> His exasperating acting
> (?)His exasperating operating
> (?)A burning longing
> (*)A burning yearning

Returning to grammatical–semantic factors, the second one is FAMILIARITY. The more commonplace a word or expression is, the less work speaker and hearer must perform to process it, and the less attention it attracts to itself. So double *-ing*s that occur in frequent colligations or that consist of elements that are individually familiar are less apt to be noticed than those that require closer attention.

This is why predicative adjectives trouble us less than either gerunds or participles. They are independently coded lexical items; the hearer does not have to compute them by referring them to a verb. Even one in accent position is not too bad:

> Most suspicious of all was his being missing
> The results were finally looking interesting

A less firmly established lexicalized *-ing* may cause trouble. *Grating* and *biting* are less easily recognized as adjectives than *loving* and *grasping*:

> (?)Sounding grating is bad where music is concerned
> (?)Being biting is not diplomatic when you make remarks about strangers
> Being loving is the surest road to a happy marriage
> Being grasping is no way to make friends

The same goes for gerunds as they approach the lexical status that accompanies institutionalized actions. In the following, the more familiar the operation (as it affects both the transitive verb and its object) the better the combination:

> He spends most of his time teaching writing (boxing, driving, dancing)
>
> These new forms are for testing reading
>
> Stay in your classrooms; interrupting learning can be traumatic for children
>
> (?) The hardest part of a job like that is overlooking grumbling (OK: is putting up with grumbling)
>
> (?) A linguist spends many hours observing talking (OK: studying writing)

It appears that what we have most occasion to say is what most effectively overrides the attention-catching *-ing*s. For a schoolteacher there is nothing outlandish about *She is taking beginning writing*.

Where familiarity has its most telling effect, is with the highly colloquial quasi-auxiliaries *get* and *go*. *Get* occurs in a specific type of inceptive, with certain verbs of motion, in the sense of 'getting under way', 'getting with it'. The two most common verbs are *move* and *go*:

> The poor guy's problem is just getting moving (getting going) – it takes him two hours to perk up in the morning

Other verbs are used with other forms of *get*, but are less likely with *getting*:

> Get hopping (cracking, humping)! We haven't got all day!
>
> Get walking (flying, spinning)! Move those feet!
>
> (?) It isn't easy getting walking (hopping, etc.) when you're not feeling well

Get is less likely with other verbs in a less specific inceptive sense, and double *-ing*s are very difficult:

> I got (to) talking to him, and found he was from Missouri too
>
> (*) Getting (to) talking to him, I found he was from Missouri too
>
> (*) For getting working you need a warm-up

Start is a less happy-go-lucky inceptive, and is bad with double *-ing*s:

> (?) Just starting moving is my problem

The difficulty with a low-frequency inceptive can be seen in combinations with *fall to*. Even with the intervening preposition the result is bad:

> He fell to wondering what might happen to him if he failed
> (*)Falling to wondering what might happen to him if he failed, he concluded that the danger was more imagined than real

Just as familiar as *get* is *go* (and to a lesser extent *come*) in an 'expeditionary' sense. The commonest verbs here refer to sports. (See Silva (1975) for a characterization of this construction.) Prosodically bad -*ings* readily get by:

> I'm góing rówing this afternoon
> Going shopping is fun
> The bastard is going wenching again
> Are you coming dancing (swimming, hunting) with me?

The construction is not used in a non-expeditionary sense:

> *This afternoon I'm going painting (studying, digging; OK: digging for clams).

Go and *come* are frequent in a non-expeditionary sense closer to their literal locomotive meaning. They form a group, an auxiliary-like set, along with the common verbs of position, *sit*, *lie*, and *stand*, and a few other verbs of motion. Their quasi-auxiliary status can be seen in the infrequency with which they are used independently. A sentence like *He sat* without a complementary *there*, *reading*, *down*, etc., or a simple *He strode*, rather than *He strode in*, is unusual, and *He was lying* would most likely be misunderstood. With complementary -*ing*, the finite forms are the usual ones:

> She lay dying
> He sat staring
> I stood gazing out to sea
> They strode laughing into the room
> She knelt praying
> I saw you come stumbling in

These verbs do fairly well with double -*ing*s:

> (?)I saw him going scurrying
> I saw him going scurrying-along (traipsing-along)
> I saw her coming gallivanting-by

(?)She was lying gasping
She was lying gasping-for-breath
(*)She was sitting staring
(?)She was sitting staring-at-us
She was sitting staring-at-us-and-making-funny-noises
(*)He was striding laughing into the room
(*)The ambulance was tearing screaming past my door

In the last pair the two *-ings* are forced together by the fact that the prepositional phrase modifies the combination. In an example like:

She was running clawing-at-her-face-and-body, trying to extin-
    guish the flames

the prepositional phrase pulls the second *-ing* away from the first. Furthermore, *run* is a relatively independent verb (*She ran* is normal), and we have now moved out to paired *-ings* in which the two verbs are relatively independent of each other and can ofter be punctuated with a comma between:

They were marching(,) singing away
I was riding(,) staring ahead

A step farther out are combinations using verbs other than those of motion and position, with actions more or less independent of each other brought together in some temporal or logical relationship:

(?)I was sleeping dreaming
I was sleeping(,) dreaming-of-marble-halls
(*)What she is suffering coughing!
What she is suffering(,) coughing-like-that!
How much are you losing(,) gambling?
How much are you earning(,) working?
They were eating(,) looking-out-the-train-window
How are you feeling(,) living in Detroit?
How is she doing(,) working for Macy's?

If the comma is inappropriate, the result is bad:

(*)Eating working is not a good idea
(*)It can be dangerous, reading walking

Relative familiarity is again evident in these examples: *losing gambling* and *earning working* are familiar associations; *suffering coughing* is not.

There are also high-frequency idioms that have developed from expressions of conjoined action. Two related ones are *What are you (is she, etc.) doing . . . -ing . . . ?* and *What are you (is she, etc.) thinking . . . -ing . . . ?* Both demand to know by what right something is happening:

> What are you doing eavesdropping? Get away from there!
> What's he thinking(,) telling me to do a thing like that?

The *doing* idiom is resistant to factors that work against double -*ing*. There would be no problem with *What are you doing cycling?* addressed to someone who is not supposed to be on a bicycle.

A final[2] set of high-frequency verbs that tend toward auxiliary status is made up of *intend* and its synonyms:

> When do you intend telling him?
> How do you figure doing it?
> That's not something I plan doing

These all yield possible double -*ing*s, though the infinitive would usually be preferred and is virtually required with a marginal member such as *aim* or *mean*:

> Do you mean getting rid of it?
> (*)Are you meaning getting rid of it?
> Are you meaning to get rid of it?

Think has the potential separation with *of*:

> What were you thinking of doing next (thinking to do next)?
> (*)What were you thinking doing next?

The sensitivity to double -*ing*s is such that if a construction already has one or two strikes against it, making it a double -*ing* is more difficult than ever. Take the case of *being*. There is no problem when *being* is the more usual copula and takes as its predicate a familiar adjective in -*ing*:

> She was being grasping when she was supposed to be generous
> Being amusing is rather essential for a comedian

But participles are foreclosed:

> Why didn't you take the call? – Being at work ((*)being working) I
>   couldn't. It was a personal call

---

[2] The final one for this paper. There must be many other semantically motivated verb clusters.

To be playing when you're supposed to be working is not a good
   idea
Playing when you're supposed to be working is not a good idea
(*)Being playing when you're supposed to be working is not a
   good idea

As the third example suggests, the auxiliary *being* is more or less
superfluous anyway, and while the infinitive in the second example
creates no conflict, the *-ing* in the last example is very bad. In fact, the
infinitive is a rather obvious dodge in the following, from a personal
letter, since *to mind* normally governs *-ing* (the auxiliary here is essential to the meaning):

I wouldn't mind to be breathing some of your Colorado air

The handicaps with *being* can be compared with other progressive
auxiliaries, which add some semantic content and provide a buffer
between the *-ing*s:

Your having been resisting so long has angered them
Your going around resisting now would only anger them
(*)Your being resisting now would only anger them

Despite the difficulties, the progressive with *being* is not to be ruled out
absolutely. In the following there is both prosodic and semantic
support; the closer juncture in *spinning-around* yields a relatively wider
juncture after *being*, and the temporal modifier *all that time* gives a
certain justification for not omitting the auxiliary. The sentence can be
paraphrased *being (spending) all that time spinning around . . . :*

Spinning made me dizzy
(*)Being spinning made me dizzy
Being spinning-around all that time made me dizzy

   The other copular verbs *seem, appear, look* lack the ability of *be* to
form both stative and non-stative constructions (*The light is blue, Don't
be impertinent*). They are normally stative, and even in their finite forms
are better with adjectives than with participles:

Mary seems impatient
(*)Mary seems talking

But progressives are occasionally found:

Schools seem moving toward such interdisciplinary offerings
   (*PMLA* (1968) vol. 83, no. 3, 525)

With this disadvantage to begin with, a double -*ing* is virtually impossible:

> You can convince them just by seeming disgusted
> (*)You can convince them just by seeming suffering.[3]

The meaning of the -*ing* itself may be a disadvantage. A point action is often hard to see in slow motion, and this reduces the chances of an -*ing* on the corresponding verb. Add that to a double -*ing* and the result is bad:

> She was waking
> She woke thinking she was at home
> (*)She was waking thinking she was at home

A construction may be too difficult to process. Multiple embeddings are avoided on this account in interrogative and relative clauses. Though the following are normal:

> I sat watching the children play(ing)
> I was sitting there watching the children play(ing)

when *the children* becomes the focus of a question the result is unacceptable:

> (*)Who were the children you sat watching play(ing)?

A triple -*ing* here is grotesque:

> (*)Who were the children you were sitting watching playing?

If a construction can go under because it already has a strike against it, it can be rescued by a supporting context. In the following, the doubtful *keeping going* is in parallel with the less objectionable *getting going*, and the accents on the auxiliaries reduce that on *going*:

> When you have something you don't like to do, the problem is
>   simply getting going and keeping going

Double -*ing*s are distracting because they imply an intention that is not there. Anyone who hears a conversation like:

> Was his the stolen token? – Yes, his was the token taken

---

[3] *By seeming ailing* is barely possible, but *ailing* is probably an adjective; witness *Look how he suffers!* versus **Look how he ails!*

knows that the interlocutors are spoofing – this kind of repetition is used deliberately as a joke: *handy Andy*, *legal eagle* (*legal beagle*), *funny money*, *double trouble*, *Swervin' Mervin* (the erratic race track driver). The unwanted joke of the double *-ing* is all too easy to blunder into because of the nature of the English verb, but it is no different from other such doublings, except in its frequency: (?)*Can something be sodden frozen*?

Doubling may be tolerated when it is less noticeable. This occurs when something intervenes, whether lexical material or a prosodic (or grammatical?) break, when one or both of the *-ing*s is de-accented or not in a prominent position in the sentence, and when one or both of the *-ing*s is lexicalized as a non-verb (and processed directly). It is also tolerated in some highly colloquial colligations. It seems that when the urge to say something is powerful enough, the niceties of prosody can be disregarded.

The syntax is only one factor in a long gradient, and most likely an indirect one, at that.

POSTSCRIPT

Pullum (1974) came to my attention after the foregoing was submitted for publication. It is a further attempt to explain the double *-ing* restrictions in grammatical terms, and does not affect the claims I make beyond providing some additional examples. Pullum's (8), which I hyphenate, can be compared with a sentence in which the second *-ing* has the same grammatical status but spoils the prosody:

> (8)Is my smoking making-you-feel-sick?
> Are my struggles failing?
> (*)Is my struggling failing?

His (9) similarly:

> (9)Was the man who was watching enjoying-what-he-saw?
> (*)Was the man who was watching talking?

His (12) is especially pertinent, as it shows the effect of the comma separation between successive coordinate adjectives, which I contrast here with successive non-coordinate adjectives that lack a prosodic separation:

(12) Three policemen dragged the screaming, struggling girl away
They found the striking employees who were missing
(*)They found the missing striking employees

Pullum states his rule (18) as: 'Any sequence v_i [V + ing] v_i – v_j [V + ing] v_j in surface structure is ungrammatical if v_j is in the complement of v_i. The three examples I have asterisked are all permitted by this rule. Trying to explain jingles as direct reflections of grammar is simply wrongheaded.

SUMMARY

Verb phrases containing repetitions of the suffix *-ing* in close proximity are restricted in occurrence. The restriction is eased by the following, approximately in order of importance:
(1) Degree of separation by intervening words, pauses, and possibly grammatical boundaries.
(2) Familiarity. In the second of the two *-ings* this generally reflects relative lexicalization – especially true of recognizable adjectives and nouns. In the first *-ing* it reflects prepositional status (e.g. *including*) or highly colloquial auxiliary status (especially *getting* and *going*).
(3) Prosody. First, a following close juncture magnifies the effect of a preceding wider juncture, enhancing the separation at the latter. Second, avoidance of accentual prominence on both *-ings* makes the repetition less noticeable. Third, broken rhythm and avoidance of additional alliteration and rhyme mitigates the attention-getting effect.
The problem is basically phonological – the *-ings* are repeated. The same occurs with other suffixes: *It was rotten that Otten had gotten forgotten.* It should be expected that additional aggravating factors are more apt to be phonological than grammatical.

Modes of meaning and modes of expression: types of grammatical structure, and their determination by different semantic functions

M. A. K. HALLIDAY

1. Preamble

Let us say that a code is a system of signs having a content and an expression; for example, a traffic control code (Fig. 1).

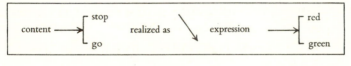

Fig. 1

The relation between the content and the expression is one of realiza-tion. Then, a semiotic, or semiotic system, is a code having two or more realizational cycles in it, so that the expression of content$_1$ (call it expression$_1$) is itself a content (content$_2$) that in turn has its own expression (expression$_2$). Hence there will be at least three levels, or strata, in such a system:

level one:	content$_1$	
two:	(realized as)	expression$_1$ = content$_2$
three:	(realized as)	expression$_2$ . . .

A semiotic, in other words, is a stratified, or stratal, system, in which the output of one coding process becomes the input to another.

In this sense language is a semiotic. It consists (at least) of three strata with, therefore, two realizational cycles; these are set out in Fig. 2, (i) in everyday and (ii) in technical terminology. The formulation 'at least' is intended to allow for the addition of further strata above the semantic system, since the semantic system itself can be regarded as the realization of some higher level semiotic. In principle this may be

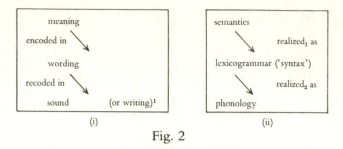

Fig. 2

associated with any of a number of different orders of meaning, cognitive, social, aesthetic and other things besides. At any particular time, attention is likely to be focussed on one or other of these higher orders.

It follows from this that as far as the elements of a semiotic system are concerned, we may in principle consider the organization of any one part of the system from three different aspects:

(1) at its own level – its relation to other elements identified at the same level as itself
(2) from above – its relation to elements at the next (or some) higher level
(3) from below – its relation to elements at the next (or some) lower level

Now it is typical of semiotic systems that the different strata are not isomorphic; there is no relation of biuniqueness (one–one correspondence) between one level and the next. This is bound to be the case in a system such as language, where the coding not only converts elements of one kind into elements of another kind – meanings into wordings into sounds – but also reduces both the size and the inventory of the basic components. By any usual definition of linguistic units, units of speech sound are both smaller than and fewer than units of form; and units of form are both smaller than and fewer than units of meaning. Hence when one organizational system is represented in terms of another there will be mismatches of various kinds: what Sydney Lamb called 'interlocking diversifications' in the realizational process. This means that we cannot simply operate with a schema of definitions and say, for example, that the elements of this system are defined 'from above'; it is not possible ever to derive the structure fully

---

[1] Written language may be (i) an alternative coding of meanings (ideograms); (ii) an alternative coding of wordings (characters, as in Chinese); or (iii) an alternative coding of sounds (syllabaries and alphabets).

from statements of this kind. The description of any part of the system involves an interpretation of all three sets of relations into which it enters, 'upward', 'downward' and 'across'.

This will be true no matter whether we are concerned with the most detailed specifics of the system, or with the broadest generalizations. Whatever is said in interpretation of one level has implications not only for that level but also for what is above and what is below. This provides the context for the present discussion.

2. *Functional modes of meaning*

Let us focus first on the semantic system, and introduce a broad generalization along the following lines. The semantic system of a natural language is organized into a small number of distinct components, different kinds of 'meaning potential' that relate to the most general functions that language has evolved to serve. Here are the headings we shall use:

The first of these is language as representation: the semantic system as expression of experience, including both experience of what is round about us in the outside world and experience of the world of consciousness that is inside us. This we are calling the ideational component. There are two subcategories: an experiential, where we represent experience 'directly' in terms of happenings (actions, events, states, relations), entities that participate in these happenings (persons, animate and inanimate objects, institutions, abstractions) and circumstantial features (extent, location, time and space, cause, manner and so on); and a 'logical', where we represent experience 'indirectly' in terms of certain fundamental logical relations in natural language – 'and', 'namely', 'says', 'is subcategorized as' etc. – which are not those of formal logic but rather are the ones from which the operations of formal logic are ultimately derived. These two, the logical and the experiential, together make up the ideational component in the semantic system: that of meaning in the reflective mode.

The second main component, the interpersonal, is language as interaction: it is meaning in the active mode. Here the semantic system expresses the speaker's intrusion in the speech event: his attitudes, evaluations and judgments; his expectations and demands; and the nature of the exchange as he is setting it up – the role that he is taking on himself in the communication process, and the role, or rather the role choice, that he is assigning to the hearer. This component is therefore both speaker- and hearer-oriented; it is interpersonal – what Hymes called 'socio-expressive' – and represents the speaker's own intrusion into the speech situation.

All discourse involves an ongoing simultaneous selection of meanings from both these components, which are mapped into a single output in the realization process. But there is also a third component, which we are calling the 'textual', whereby the meanings of the other two kinds take on relevance to some real context. Here the semantic system enables the speaker to structure meaning as text, organizing each element as a piece of information and relating it significantly to what has gone before. If the ideational component is language as reflection (the speaker as observer of reality), and the interpersonal component is language as action (the speaker as intruder in reality), the textual component is language as relevance (the speaker as relating to the portion of reality that constitutes the speech situation, the context within which meanings are being exchanged). The textual component provides what in modern jargon we might refer to as the ecology of the text.

For example, when the Carpenter says to the Walrus

Cut us another slice!

the ideational meaning is the representation of a material process, cutting, in which three entities participate, the one who cuts, the thing that is cut, and the one that the thing is cut for; also the place of *cut* in the taxonomy of actions and of *slice* in the taxonomy of things. The interpersonal meaning is a demand for goods-and-services, 'I want you to do something for me', embodied in the selection of the imperative mood, direct, explicit and without any special modulation. The textual meaning is the internal organization of this as a message with the focus on what is demanded, together with its relation to the preceding text through presuppositions – a slice of something, of which I have already had at least one.

3. *Above and below the semantic system*

Since this functional interpretation is a generalization about language it can be examined from all three angles of approach: from above, from below and from its own level. Presumably, if it is valid, it has some implications for all three.

The main concern of this paper is with its implications for what is below; the hypothesis will be that (i) EACH OF THESE SEMANTIC COMPONENTS TYPICALLY GENERATES A DIFFERENT KIND OF STRUCTURAL MECHANISM AS ITS OUTPUT, OR REALIZATION; and that (ii) THESE DIFFERENT TYPES OF STRUCTURE ARE NON-ARBITRARILY RELATED TO THE KINDS OF MEANING THEY EXPRESS.

However, let us focus briefly on the other two levels at which this generalization is significant: the semantic level itself, and the level above.

(1) If we represent the semantic system as a meaning potential through the use of system networks, which are networks of options each with its condition of entry, these functional components appear as relatively independent sets of semantic options.

WITHIN each component, the networks show a high degree of internal constraint: that is, of interdependence among the various options involved. The selections made by the speaker at one point tend to determine, and be determined by, the selections he makes at another. For example, within the interpersonal component, there is a high degree of interdependence of this kind between the systems of mood and modality, both in terms of what can be selected and in terms of the meaning of whatever is selected. To cite one particular instance of what is a complex and quite general phenomenon, the meaning of the modality 'probable' is different in interrogative mood from what it is in declarative, and it cannot combine at all with imperative.

But BETWEEN one component and another, there is very little constraint of this kind: little restriction on the options available, and little effect on their interpretation. For example, the choice of modality (in the interpersonal component) is quite independent of the choice of transitivity (in the ideational component): the speaker can always contribute his own judgment of probability no matter what the nature of the process he is talking about or what participants are associated with it.

Hence the categories of ideational, interpersonal and textual appear clearly in the semantic system itself, as system networks each having a high degree of internal dependence but a very low degree of external dependence. Choices made within one component have a great deal of effect on other choices within the same component but hardly any effect on choices in the other components.

(2) If we now look above the semantic system, to the social contexts in which meanings are exchanged, it seems to be the case that these functional components have considerable significance for the way in which the social context acts as the determinant text.

Every act of meaning has a 'context of situation', an environment within which it is performed and interpreted. For communication to take place at all, it is necessary for those who are interacting to be able to make intelligent and informed guesses about what kinds of meanings are likely to be exchanged. They do this on the basis of their interpretation of the significance – the semiotic structure – of the situation.

Let us postulate that the relevant features of a situation in which language has some place are the FIELD of social process, the TENOR of social relationships, and the MODE of discourse itself: that is, (i) what is going on, (ii) who are involved, and (iii) what part the text is playing – whether written or spoken, in what rhetorical mode and so on.

We shall then find a systematic relationship between these components of the situation and the functional components of the semantic system. It appears that, by and large, the field – the nature of the social activity – determines the ideational meanings; the tenor – the social statuses and roles of the participants in the situation – determines the interpersonal meanings; while the mode – the part assigned to the linguistic interaction in the total situation – determines the textual meanings.

In the example in §2, the activity going on is that of having a meal; the Walrus and the Carpenter are dining off the oysters, accompanied with slices of bread and butter, and this is what the Carpenter takes as the ideational content of his utterance. In this context the two of them are collaborators, since both have shared in the preparation of the meal; this is reflected in the interpersonal meaning as an instruction from one to the other. The text is language-in-action, directed towards furthering the activity in question; hence selection of the textual meanings makes 'exophoric' (situational) reference to the processes and the objects involved, as well as internal reference to an earlier occurrence *a loaf of bread* through the collocational potential of *slice*.

Hence the categories of ideational, interpersonal and textual appear to have implications for what is 'above', in that they represent different components of the meaning potential which are activated by different components of the social context (cf. Halliday 1977). This appears to be the basis on which interactants make predictions about the meanings that will typically be exchanged in any particular situation with which they find themselves confronted.

4. *The experiential mode*

For the rest of this paper we shall be concerned with what is 'below' the semantic system: with the question of what kinds of structural mechanism are typically involved in the REALIZATION of these various components of meaning. The suggestion will be that here too the same categories are relevant, since they tend to be expressed through fundamentally different types of structural organization (cf. Mathesius 1911: 24–5).[2]

Let us consider the experiential function first. Here we are concerned with the semantic (linguistic) encoding of experience; particularly our experience of the processes of the external world and of the internal world of our own consciousnesses. We tend to encode such experience in terms of configurations of elements each of which has a special and distinct significance with respect to the whole. Typically, we recognize a process itself, and various more or less specialized participants and circumstantial elements.

For example, suppose there is a flock of birds flying overhead. We represent this in language as something like *There are birds flying*; that is, a process of 'flying' and, separated out from this, an entity that is doing the flying, namely 'birds'. This is, certainly, one valid way of encoding it; but it is not the only one – we might have said, instead, *It's winging*. If we did say this in English we would be treating the phenomenon as a single unanalysed process, not as a process plus a participant; this is, after all, what we do with *It's raining* (although not, for some reason, with *The wind's blowing*). No doubt it is useful to be able to talk about birds doing other things than flying, and about flying being done by other things than birds. Some languages feel the same about rain: in Chinese one says, liberally translated, 'There's rain

---

[2] Mathesius's observation relates to 'functional styles' (orientation towards different functions in the use of language), not to functionally derived components of the system; but it is pertinent nevertheless: 'The influence of functional styles on the lexical and semantic aspects of speech was stressed especially by Gröber, . . . [who] distinguishes the subjective expression . . . and the objective expression . . . . The subjective expression differs from the objective both quantitatively (inasmuch as it expresses by a pause, by tone or by gesture what the latter expresses by words; and further, as *it repeats what could be expressed only once*) and qualitatively (by choosing other words than factual names of the things referred to), and, finally, locally (by *placing sentence elements into positions not pertaining to them in objective speech*). Both ways of expression are often combined in actual speech.' (My italics throughout.)

falling'; and in one south Chinese dialect, a variety of Cantonese, there are usually two participants in the pluvial process, which is encoded as 'The sky is dropping water'.

So there is no reason for assuming that each particular process will always be encoded as just this or that particular configuration of elements. But we can formulate the general principle that this is how processes are represented in languages. This means that a STRUCTURE which represents experiential meanings will tend to have this form: it will be a configuration, or constellation, of discrete elements, each of which makes its own distinctive contribution to the whole.

We usually represent this kind of structure linguistically as a functionally labelled constituent structure as shown, for example, in Fig. 3.

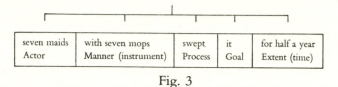

seven maids	with seven mops	swept	it	for half a year
Actor	Manner (instrument)	Process	Goal	Extent (time)

Fig. 3

There is no particular reason at this stage why the representation should have to be linear; that is no doubt the form of the final output, after the other structures have been mapped on to it, but experiential structures are not in fact sequential and we could just as well represent this as in Fig. 4. If ordering is to be introduced into the representation,

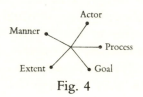

Fig. 4

there is the possibility of using a dependency construct having the Process at the centre, as in Fig. 5. But a more appropriate ordering would have a nucleus consisting of Process plus Goal, with the other elements clustering around it, as in Fig. 6. (We will leave aside

Fig. 5   Fig. 6

here the question of the appropriateness of the functional labels themselves.)

Each one of these elements may have a substructure of the same
general type, with different labels as, for example, in Fig. 7. This again
can be reinterpreted as Fig. 8. The layers introduced into the structure in

Fig. 7   Fig. 8

this way are the source of the linguist's classic mode of representation of
constituent structure in the form of trees, or labelled bracketings. But
the appropriate bracketing for functionally labelled structures is minimal, not maximal ('many ICs' rather than 'few ICs', in the terms of
Hudson 1967). Maximal bracketing imposes too much structure for a
functional grammar; for example, in *four young oysters* it is reasonable
to recognize *young oysters* as a constituent provided the labelled
elements are classes, since it is a nominal group, but in no way does
this correspond to any meaningful functional constituent. The non-
linear representation implies more of a molecular model of structure,
with a taxonomy similar to cell : molecule : atom : subatomic particle.

Experiential meanings are typically realized as elemental structures
of this type. The basic structural mechanism is that of constituency,
with larger units constituted out of layered clusters or bracketed
strings of smaller units, each part having its own specific function with
respect to the whole. We could call this 'segmental', except that it is
better perhaps to reserve the term 'segment' for an element in the final
output – the syntagm – that serves as input to the next realizational
cycle. So let us say that experiential meanings are realized through
some kind of constituent structure.

This expresses the particular way in which we order our experience
of reality when we want to turn it into meaning. The bounded entities
that enter into constituent structures with specific functions like Process, Actor, Goal, Extent, or Manner, offer a presentation of reality in
terms of 'things' – doings by, and happenings to, persons and objects,
in the environment of other persons and objects, with yet other
persons and objects, and also times and places and so on, as attendant
circumstances; and including various 'metathings' (facts and reports),
which are complex things that have already been encoded in language

and so acquired a status which enables them to participate in certain types of process as objects in their own right. Such elements naturally form constituent-like structures which allow us to isolate them and continue to refer to them as discrete entities.

5. *The interpersonal mode*

Now let us consider interpersonal meanings. These are expressed through very different structural devices.

Think of an example such as the following, uttered when somebody is sick: *I wonder if perhaps it might be measles, might it d'you think?* The experiential meaning is: Attribute 'measles' plus Time 'now'. With this the speaker has combined an interpersonal meaning of 'I consider it possible', together with an invitation to the hearer to confirm the assessment.

This interpersonal meaning, however, is strung throughout the clause as a continuous motif or colouring. It appears as *I wonder, perhaps, might, might* and *d'you think*; each of these expresses the same modality, and each one could occur by itself. When they all occur, the effect is cumulative; with each one the speaker reaffirms his own angle on the proposition.

The intonation contour is another mode of the realization of interpersonal meanings. It expresses the 'key', the particular tone of assertion, query, hesitation, doubt, reservation, forcefulness, wonderment, or whatever it is, with which the speaker tags the proposition. This too is continuous; and in this case there is no possibility of associating it with any segments – it is simply a melodic line mapped on to the clause as a whole, running through from beginning to end.

We shall refer to this mode of realization as 'prosodic', since the meaning is distributed like a prosody throughout a continuous stretch of discourse (cf. Mitchell 1958). It is characteristic of interpersonal meanings that they are expressed in this prosodic fashion. Mood and modality, tone and key, intensity and other attitudinal meanings are typically realized through this kind of structural pattern. Swearwords and obscenities, also, may occur at any or all points in the clause; it does not matter what segments they are attached to – many writers have noted that such elements readily occur even in the middle of a word. The speaker who says

Christ they beat the hell out of those bastards

is in fact using a very regular and well-established resource for the expression of meanings of this kind.

It is not difficult to see the rationale behind this mode of realization. The interpersonal component of meaning is the speaker's ongoing intrusion into the speech situation. It is his perspective on the exchange, his assigning and acting out of roles. Interpersonal meanings cannot easily be expressed as configurations of discrete elements. They may be attached, as connotations, to particular lexical items, like *bastards* above meaning 'people' plus 'I'm worked up'; but connotations do not enter into constituent-like structural relations. The essence of the meaning potential of this part of the semantic system is that most of the options are associated with the act of meaning as a whole. Even when the meaning is realized in a single word or a phrase, this can be interpolated at more or less any point in the clause; and even when two or more such elements are present at the same time, they still do not go together to form constructions.

It is much more difficult to know how to represent prosodic structures in a description of language. Usually they are either ignored or forced to fit into the constituency mould. It may be more effective to treat them like prosodies in phonology, that is as contrasting features having no place in the constituent structure (which is, after all, an experiential structure) but which are specified separately and then mapped on to the constituent structure as a distinct step in the realizational process.

6. *The textual mode*

The 'textual', or text-forming, resources in the semantic system generate structures of still another kind.

Consider the example:

Why did you let the big one get away?

This clause has, in effect, two points of prominence. It is a WH-question, which means a demand for a particular piece of information; and this demand is enunciated at the beginning, through the word *why*. The word *why* proclaims the theme of the discourse; the speaker begins by announcing 'What I'm on about is this: I want to know something.' This is what we call thematic prominence, and in English it is associated with first position in the clause; in fact it is REALIZED by first position, since putting something first is what gives it the status of a theme.

But there is also another point of prominence here, at the end. To be aware of it we have to consider the clause in its spoken mode, since this takes the form of tonic prominence; that is, the location of the tonic accent, which is the dynamic centre of the pitch contour, the place where the greatest pitch movement takes place. (This may be a falling movement or a rising movement or some kind of complex move-ment, depending on which kind of melody it is. It corresponds to what is sometimes called 'primary stress', although it is not, in fact, a stress feature.) Suppose we represent the intonation unit (the 'tone group') as bounded by double slash, and intermediate rhythmic units (the 'feet') by single slash, with tonic prominence as bold type; the likely form of the utterance would be:

// why did you / let the / big one / get a/**way** //

The meaning of tonic prominence is the focus of information; it signals the climax of what is new in the message. This kind of focal prominence can be assigned at any point in the clause; it is not REALIZED by final position, in the way that thematic prominence is realized by initial position. But it is TYPICALLY located at the end, and any other focus is 'marked' and so explicitly contrastive. In the typical form of the message, in other words, the speaker puts what is new at the end.

So there is a peak of prominence at the beginning, which is the Theme; and another peak of prominence, usually at the end, which is the focus of information or, simply, the New. The two are different in meaning. The Theme is speaker-oriented; it is the speaker's signal of concern, what it is that he is on about – he may even make this explicit, by starting 'as far as . . . is concerned'. The New is hearer-oriented (though still, of course, SELECTED by the speaker); it is the speaker's presentation of information as in part already recoverable to the hearer (the Given) and in part not recoverable (the New). These two types of prominence are independent of each other. But both contribute to the 'texture', to fashioning the fabric of the text.

What these text-forming systems do is to organize discourse into a succession of message units, quanta of information such that each has its own internal texture, provided by the two systems of prominence just mentioned. The message unit corresponds, typically (i.e. in the unmarked case), to a clause. Hence it is possible in such instances to represent both thematic and focal prominence as constituent–like structures of the clause, by recognizing the functional significance of the non-prominent part. So Theme contrasts with Rheme, and New contrasts with Given, as in Fig. 9. In fact, the information unit is not always coextensive with the clause; to return to 'The Walrus and the Carpenter', in *The moon was shining sulkily* (following the earlier *The*

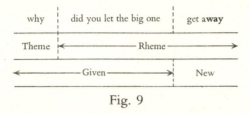

Fig. 9

sun was shining on the sea, shining with all his might) we should presumably have the structure shown in Fig. 10. But because a clause is TYPICALLY one information (focal) unit, and the focus in the information unit is TYPICALLY at the end, final position in the clause carries a potential for prominence which highlights it in the same way that initial position is highlighted by prominence of a thematic kind.

the **moon**	was shining	**sulkily**
Theme	Rheme	
New	Given	New

Fig. 10

The structures that realize options in the textual component are what we may call 'culminative' structures. They are not configurations or clusters of elements such as we find in the ideational component; nor are they prosodic chains of the interpersonal kind. What the textual component does is to express the particular semantic status of elements in the discourse by assigning them to the boundaries; this gives special significance to 'coming first' and 'coming last', and so marks off units of the message as extending from one peak of prominence to the next.

The effect of this is to give a periodicity to the discourse. The clause, in its status as a message, begins with prominence of one kind, thematic prominence, and ends with prominence of another kind, prominence due to information focus. The latter is expressed through the assignment of the tonic accent to a particular place in the tone group; so the prominence is also in part phonological – and can be heard. The periodicity is further reinforced by the use of conjunctives to link one sentence with another; these contribute to the texture by relating a clause cohesively to what went before it, and they also occur at the boundaries – usually the beginning, but sometimes, especially in casual speech, at the end.

Perhaps the clearest instance of the periodicity of texture is to be found in poetic forms. The metric regularity of the structures that have evolved in poetry – lines with a fixed number of feet, and stanzas or genres with a fixed number of lines – expresses in symbolic fashion the regularity of the structure of discourse as an exchange of messages. This is not to suggest, of course, that the structural unit of any particular genre, such as the iambic pentameter line, functions directly as the realization of any unit in the structure of the text. On the contrary, there is usually a tension set up between the two types or modes of structure, with the periodicity of the message, deriving from the theme and information systems (Theme–Rheme and Given–New), cutting across that of the metric form. But the impact of this tension on the reader, and especially on the listener, is one of the clearest indications of the reality of the two kinds of periodic movement.

7. Particle, field and wave

Fig. 11 summarizes the three types of structure we have recognized so far. It is important to stress that when we associate each of these structural types with one of the functional semantic components, we are talking of a tendency not a rule. Experiential structures tend to be more elemental in character, interpersonal structures tend to be prosodic, and textual structures tend to be culminative or periodic.

Furthermore this is a statement about the description of English. The functional categories themselves are universals; but the structural tendencies, though clearly non-arbitrary – we can see why it is that each should take this form – may differ very considerably from one language to another.

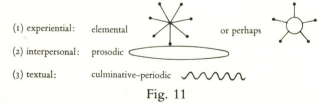

(1) experiential: elemental   or perhaps

(2) interpersonal: prosodic

(3) textual: culminative–periodic

Fig. 11

Given structures of these very general kinds, it is clear that each can be reduced to some form of constituency; but not all with the same success. Experiential structures are quite constituent-like; whereas interpersonal ones are not, and the attempt to represent them in constituency terms involves idealizing them to an extent that is tantamount to a form of reductionism. An example of this is the attempt to reduce an intonation contour to a sequence of pitch phonemes (which are then attached to specific places in a string).

Figs. 12 and 13 represent an English clause first in non-constituency terms and then in constituency terms. The clause is:

On Sunday perhaps we'll take the children to the circus, shall we?

If we consider the major traditions in linguistic thought, we find, not at all surprisingly perhaps, that those in the psycho-philosophical tradition, who are firmly committed to language as an ideational system, have usually worked with constituency models of structure: American structuralist and transformationalist theories, for example. By contrast, linguists in the socio-anthropological tradition, like Firth,

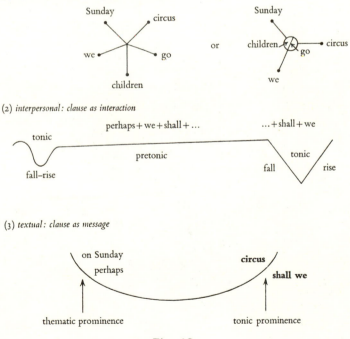

(1) *experiential: clause as representation (of process)*

(2) *interpersonal: clause as interaction*

(3) *textual: clause as message*

Fig. 12

experiential:

interpersonal:

textual:

on | Sunday ||| perhaps ||| we ||| 'll | take | the children | to | the circus || shall | we

Loc: Time — Agent — Process — Medium — Loc: Place

Modality | Subject | Finite — Key₂ — Subject | Finite | Key₃
Mood → — Mood →
Key₁

Theme₁ | Theme₂ | Theme₃
Theme

New₁ — New₂ — New₃

|| 4 ∧ on / **Sunday** per // ¹ haps we'll / take the / children to the / **circus** // ² **shall** we //

Key to phonological (prosodic) notation: || tone group boundary / foot boundary **Bold** tonic prominence ('focus')

∧ proclitic foot ¹ falling tone ² rising tone ⁴ fall-rise tone

Fig. 13

who are interested in speech functions and stress the interpersonal aspect of language, have tended to develop prosodic models. Those in the literary tradition, concerned primarily with texture and text structure, have developed models of a periodic kind: the structure of the paragraph (topic sentences, etc.), generic structures of various kinds, and of course the whole theory of metrics.

It is interesting to recall here Pike's (1959) important insight into language as particle, wave and field. Although Pike did not conceive of these in quite the same way, it seems very clear that this is what we have here:

constituent (experiential) structures are particulate
prosodic (interpersonal)   ,,   ,, field–like
periodic (textual)   ,,   ,, wave–like

8. *The logical mode*

There is one functional component that we have omitted to take into consideration so far, and that is the 'logical'. This is perhaps the most difficult to interpret.

As far as its origin at a higher level is concerned, the logical is a subcategory of the ideational, since it is language in the representation of reality. But there are two distinct modes of representing reality in semantic terms. In the experiential mode, reality is represented more concretely, in the form of constructs whose elements make some reference to THINGS. The linguistic structures actually stand as metaphors for the relations between things; and the elements that enter into and are defined by these relations are identified as Process, Actor, Goal, Extent, Manner and the like. These in turn are interpreted as 'roles' 'occupied by' various classes of phenomena, and these classes of phenomena themselves have NAMES, names like *moon* and *shine* and *sulky*.

In the logical mode, reality is represented in more abstract terms, in the form of abstract relations which are independent of and make no reference to things. No doubt these relations, which taken all together constitute what we might call the logic of natural languages, have evolved by a process of generalization out of relations between things; and some of them, for instance 'and', are not hard to interpret in concrete terms (one can lay a set of objects side by side). But unlike experiential structures, logical structures present themselves in the semantic system as independent of any particular class or classes of phenomena. They are not the source of rules about what goes where.

Again we have to deal with a distinction whose boundaries are fuzzy; there are the usual doubtful cases. More interesting, however, is the question whether languages differ as to what relations they are going to TREAT AS logical. It seems to me that they do, although this argument will depend on our being willing to accept evidence 'from below' – that is, to argue that, because we can identify a particular type of structure as characteristic of the expression of logical meanings, wherever we find that type of structure we shall assume it derives from the logical component. Since we are claiming these structural manifestations are only tendencies, such an argument is only tenable on the grounds that the type of structure that is generated by the logical component is in fact significantly different from all the other three.

The principle is easy to state: logical structures are recursive. But we immediately encounter a difficulty here, a difficulty that is associated with the use of the term 'embedding' to cover two different types of structure-forming process.

In one type – which I have referred to as 'rank shift' – the output of one network (by the application of realization statements) produces an element of structure which is a point of entry into the same (or some higher rank) network. A typical instance of rank shift is nominalization, where a function in the structure of a clause may be filled, not by a nominal group (the congruent form) but by something that itself has the structure of a clause, e.g. *to come and spoil the fun* and *That you have wronged me* in:

> It's very rude of him to come and spoil the fun
> That you have wronged me doth appear in this

Another example of rank shift is a restrictive relative clause, e.g. *the lights went out* in:

> The day the lights went out

These are not true recursive structures. The recursion-like effect that is produced is an incidental outcome of the selection, at a particular place in structure, of an item from the same rank or from a higher rank in the constituent hierarchy. Clearly, this effect may appear more than once, as in a 'house that Jack built' routine; but it is strictly a non-event – there is no function involved that we could identify as a recursive function.

True recursion arises when there is a recursive option in the network, of the form shown in Fig. 14, where A:x,y,z . . . n is any system and B is the option 'stop or go round again'. This I have called 'linear recursion'; it generates lineally recursive structures of the form $a_1 + a_2 + a_3 + \ldots$ (not necessarily sequential).

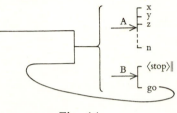

Fig. 14

These are of two kinds: paratactic, and hypotactic. The paratactic involve relations like 'and' and 'equals', which are logically transitive (A '&' B, and B '&' C, implies A '&' C; A '=' B, and B '=' C, implies A '=' C). The hypotactic are logically non–transitive; these include relations such as 'if' and 'says', where *a* 'if' β and β 'if' γ does not imply *a* 'if' γ, nor does *a* 'says' β and β 'says' γ imply *a* 'says' γ.

In paratactic structures, because they are transitive, recursive ORDER is expressed by structural (linear) SEQUENCE: there is no other way in which it can be expressed – no way, that is, in which a SEQUENCE *A and B and C* could realize an ORDER 'A & C & B'. The only departure from this strict sequence is nesting, where a sequence *A and B and C and D* represents an order 'A & (B & C) &D'. These are typically signalled in the phonological structure, e.g.:

// 3 **soup** // 3ʌ/ ham and / **egg s** // 3ʌ/apple/**pie** // 1ʌ and / tea or / **coffee** //
i.e. A 'and' (B 'and' C) 'and' D 'and' (E 'and' F)

In hypotactic structures there is no such restriction; recursive order is not always signalled by the sequence, which may reverse it (β before *a*) or modify it in other ways (β inside *a*, for example).

In English the principal instances of 'recursive structures' (i.e. structures deriving from recursive options) are as set out in Table 1.

We should distinguish structures of this kind from those which happen to be realized as lists, like counting. Counting *1 2 3 4 5 6* . . . is NOT a recursive operation, linguistically; it is simply the enumeration of a list, like *Sunday Monday Tuesday Wednesday Thursday Friday Satur-*

TABLE 1

(1) Paratactic

Symbol	Structural relation	Example
&	coordination (and/or)	a,b,c and d
C	conjunction (yet/so/then)	So they got thrown out to sea. So they got their tails stuck in their mouths. So they couldn't get them out again
=	apposition (equals)	Big Bill, the boxer, the one with the broken nose [with tone concord]
. . .	repetition	Hello hello hello hello hello!
"R"	quotation*	A says: 'B says: "C says . . ." '

(2) Hypotactic

Symbol	Structural relation		Example (sequence $\alpha\,\beta\,\gamma$ . . . except where indicated)
C	condition (if)		It won't be surprising if people protest if they don't punish him if he's guilty
=	modification	(logical	Those two splendid old electric trains
	subcategorization	structure of taxonomy of things)	$\zeta \qquad \varepsilon \qquad \delta \qquad \gamma \qquad \beta \qquad \alpha$
T	tense (serial contextualization in time)		had been going to be playing
			$\alpha\ \beta \qquad\qquad \gamma \qquad\qquad \delta$
"R"	report		A said that B said that C said that . . .
&	non-restrictive relatives (coordination as hypotaxis)		He told it to the captain, who told it to the mate

* Note that the quoting relation is transitive; at the level of wording, A does say: "C says" as part of his quotation 'B says . . .'.

day, but one which happens to be endless because there is a (non-linguistic) recursive mechanism for generating the items in the list. In the same way, the days of the week do not form a closed system, in the linguistic sense; they form a lexical set whose members happen to be limited and fixed. In both instances, the infiniteness of the set of natural numbers and the finiteness of the set of days of the week are properties not of the language but of the social system.

Logical structures are different in kind from all the other three. In the terms of systemic theory, where the other types of structure – particulate (elemental), prosodic and periodic – generate simplexes (clauses, groups, words, information units), logical structures generate complexes (clause complexes, group complexes etc.) (Huddleston 1965). The apparent exception is the sentence, which is generated by logical structures; but this is merely a terminological exception – the sentence is, in fact, simply a name for the clause complex. While the point of origin of a non–recursive structure is a particular rank – each one is a structure 'of' the clause, or of the group etc. – recursive structures are in principle rank–free: coordination, apposition, sub-categorization are possible at all ranks. The more restricted ones, like tense and report, are also the ones that are nearer the borderline; they are only just logical structures. Tense is particularly interesting because it has only come into this category within the last two to three centuries, and English appears to be unique in treating tense in this way.

9. *Postscript*

As a postscript, it should be noted that what is conceptually one and the same kind of relation may be coded in the semantic system in more than one way, i.e. may be realized through more than one of the functional components. The 'and' relation, for example, may be coded in a logical system, expressed as coordination; or in a textual system, expressed as conjunction. The same is true of 'yet', 'so' and 'then'; these are much more weakly represented in the logical mode, but on the other hand they can also be coded experientially. Table 2 shows different codings of the temporal 'then' relation.

Although the distinct types of structure discussed in this paper appear at all ranks throughout the grammar, in English at least it is at the rank of the clause that they are most clearly in evidence.

As an experiential construct, the clause is the locus of transitivity: it is the representation of the processes, participants and circumstances that constitute our experience of the real world. As an interpersonal construct it is the locus of mood and modality: the speaker's adoption and assignment of speech roles and his judgment of the validity of the proposition. As a textual construct it is the locus of theme and, typically, of information structure: the message as expression of the speaker's concern and his presentation of what is 'news'.

TABLE 2

Functional mode	Example
logical: paratactic	He sang, then people applauded, then. . .
logical: hypotactic	After he had sung, people applauded
textual	(First) he sang. Afterwards, people applauded
experiential	Applause followed his song. / His song was followed by applause

The clause, therefore, is a multiply structured concept; it is clause as representation, clause as interaction and clause as message. And each of these provides its characteristic contribution to the total, characteristic in terms of the kinds of structure we have been talking about. The clause is orchestrated as melody (the experiential component, constellations of different notes), as harmony (the interpersonal component, an ongoing modal progression) and as rhythm (the textual component, the beat which organizes the sound into a coherent whole).

This seems to support an interpretation of grammar which is structurally neutral, not based on the concept of constituent structure as the norm to which all grammatical patterns are expected to conform. In a systemic interpretation, language is treated as a resource, a potential; the various kinds of structure are the different means of expression of this potential. 'Structure' is then no longer the basic organizing concept; instead, structural representations are derived from a more abstract conceptual framework that is paradigmatic rather than syntagmatic, according to which the semantic system of a language is comprised of sets of options in meaning, each of which makes some contribution to the expression in its final shape.

SUMMARY

If we study the semantic system of a language we find that it consists of three major functional components: an ideational, an interpersonal and a textual; with the ideational further subdivided into an experiential and a logical.

This pattern appears clearly at the semantic level itself: within each component, the networks of systemic options are closely interconnected, whereas between one component and another there are relatively few connections. In other words, choices made in one component affect other choices within the same component but hardly at all affect the choices in other components.

It also appears clearly at a higher level, in the relation between language and situation. Broadly speaking, ideational meanings reflect the field of social action, interpersonal meanings reflect the tenor of social relationships, and textual meanings reflect the mode of operation of the language within the situation.

But it is at the lower level, that is in their grammatical realization, that these functional components are made manifest in the linguistic structure. In English, experiential options tend to generate constituent-like structures, actually constellations of elements such as can be fairly easily represented in constituency terms. Interpersonal options generate prosodic structures, extending over long stretches (e.g. intonation contours) which are much less constituent-like. Textual options generate culminative structures, elements occurring at the boundaries of significant units, and give a kind of periodicity to the text, which is part of what we recognize as 'texture'. Logical options generate recursive structures, paratactic and hypotactic, which differ from all the other three in that they generate complexes – clause complex, group complex, word complex – and not simple units.

Systemic theory takes the system, not the structure, as the basis of the description of a language, and so is able to show how these types of structure function as alternative modes of the realization of systemic options. They are then mapped on to each other to form the syntagm, which is the 'output' of the lexicogrammatical system.

On the logic of relations[1]

STEPHAN KÖRNER

The purpose of this essay is to argue for the revision of a widely accepted account of relations by combining some of the technical achievements of mathematical logic, as embodied in the lower predicate calculus, with some philosophical insights of Brentano's analysis of relations. The result is meant to be a logical theory which would be compatible with ontological positions as divergent as the theses of Aristotle that relations are less real than quality or quantity, of Leibniz that they are *entia rationis* or of Russell that they are not. Brentano took no serious notice of mathematical logic. Had he done so, many papers by his successors on intentional relations, opaque contexts, identity and related topics need not have been written.[2]

The main step which has to be taken in order to arrive at the revised theory of relations is quite simple. It starts from Brentano's account of *relativa* as connecting a *fundamentum relationis*, which occurs in *modo recto*, with a *terminus relationis*, which occurs in *modo obliquo*. And it consists in interpreting this account by adding so-called 'relational expressions' to the predicates of the lower predicate calculus. The interpretation will be elaborated in part I which after a preliminary comparison of directly and obliquely occurring expressions (§1) proceeds to a discussion of relational expressions, including compound predicates with names, predicates and sentences as their internal components, as well as relations in the narrow sense of the term (§2). The purpose of part II is to show the relevance of the preceding general discussion to some questions about extensionality, intentionality and

---

[1] This paper was first delivered to the Aristotelian Society on 21 February 1977, and is reprinted by courtesy of the Editor of the Aristotelian Society © 1976, The Aristotelian Society.
[2] Among them is this essay, which grew out of work with R. M. Chisholm on an edition of some of Brentano's posthumous papers. See Brentano (1976).

modality (§3); about various constraints on the substitution of equivalent expressions for each other (§4); and about different ways of 'rectifying' obliquely occurring expressions (§5).

I

1. *On the direct and oblique occurrence of names, predicates and sentences*

The difference between the direct and indirect mode of a linguistic expression may manifest itself in its form or in the form of wider expressions in which it occurs as a part. It may also manifest itself in the manner in which the users of the expression behave. In sketching a logical theory one must naturally put the main emphasis on exhibiting, or indeeed on instituting, formal differences between the direct and the oblique OCCURRENCE of linguistic expressions in contexts which themselves are texts, rather than on exhibiting non-formal differences between the direct and indirect USE of expressions in non-linguistic contexts.

A name occurs directly or referentially if, and only if, it occurs as naming, or referring to, a real particular, i.e. a particular in the actual world. Thus in the statements that Mr Healey is parsimonious and that Mr Micawber is parsimonious only the first name occurs directly. The nature of real particulars is here not in question. They could be – and have been assumed to be – material objects, persons and material objects, Whiteheadean events, Platonic forms etc. The real particulars acknowledged by a person may, moreover, fall into two classes, namely particulars which exist independently (e.g. horses or men in Aristotle's ontology) and particulars which exist only as aspects or features of independent particulars (e.g. numbers in the ontology of Aristotle). Our characterization of the direct or referential occurrence of names thus presupposes a differentiation of experience into particulars and attributes, but does not presuppose that there is or can be only one such differentiation.[3]

A name occurs obliquely if, and only if, it occurs as an internal component of a predicate, e.g. *is less-parsimonious-than-Mr Healey* or *is more-parsimonious-than-Mr Micawber*. Whenever it is convenient to indicate explicitly that an expression occurs as an internal component of a predicate, the expression will be preceded by a hyphen or con-

---

[3] For details see Körner (1970), the ontological pluralism of which is however not shared by Brentano.

nected by hyphens with the other parts of the predicate. Some names, like that of Mr Healey, occur both directly and obliquely. Names which, like that of Mr Micawber, occur only obliquely, are fictitious names. That a name occurs only obliquely is in ordinary discourse often tacitly understood, that is to say, without the explicit application of some such predicate as *x imagines-in-accordance-with-Dickens's-novel-that-Mr Micawber* . . . This compound predicate in which the name of Mr Micawber occurs obliquely, i.e. as an internal component, is, of course, applicable to real particulars, especially readers of Dickens's novel. If a name occurs non-referentially one normally has a more or less clear idea of what it would be like if the name had also a referential occurrence. The idea may, however, be so confused that it cannot even be consistently expressed. This familiar fact does not preclude the adoption of normative standards requiring that the idea SHOULD be capable of a formulation which is consistent and, perhaps, in addition possesses other features. (See §5, where this 'rectification' of obliquely occurring expressions is discussed.)

A monadic predicate – for the moment we need consider no others – occurs directly or applicatively if, and only if, it occurs as applying to one or more real particulars. Thus the predicate *x is human* occurs applicatively in *Mr Healey is human*, but not in any sentence in which the fictitious Mr Micawber is characterized as human. A monadic predicate occurs obliquely if, and only if, it occurs as an internal component of a predicate, as does the predicate *x is a woman* in *x-is-lover-of-all (some)-women*. Some predicates occur both directly and obliquely. Predicates which occur only obliquely, are fictitious predicates. That a predicate occurs indirectly is in ordinary discourse often tacitly understood. For example, in the statement that Mr Micawber is human not only the name *Mr Micawber* but also the predicate *x is human* is used indirectly, since in this sentence it does not apply to a real particular, but is understood to be an internal component of some such predicate as *x imagines-in-accordance-with-Dickens's-novel-that-Mr Micawber-is-human-and-* . . . If a predicate occurs obliquely one normally has a more or less clear idea of what it would be like if the predicate had also an applicative occurrence. The idea may be so confused that it cannot be consistently expressed.

A sentence occurs directly or implicatively if, and only if, it occurs as expressing a true proposition and, hence, as materially implying any other sentence expressing a true proposition. Thus, looking back at the preceding examples, whenever a predicate occurs applicatively the corresponding sentence occurs implicatively. A sentence occurs obliquely if, and only if, it occurs as an internal component of a predicate, e.g. *x believes-that-Mr Micawber-is-human*. Some sentences, such as *Mr Micawber-is-human* occur only obliquely. In ordinary discourse the direct and the indirect occurrence of sentences are often only tacitly distinguished. Again, if a sentence occurs obliquely, one usually has a more or less clear idea of what it would be like if the sentence also occurred implicatively. That the idea may not admit of being consistently expressed does not – as has been pointed out already – preclude the adoption of normative standards requiring that it be capable of a formulation which satisfies various conditions of acceptability.

2. *Relational expressions and their species*

As our examples show, the difference between directly and indirectly occurring expressions corresponds to a structural difference between predicates which do and predicates which do not contain a name, predicate or sentence as an internal (synsemantic, syncategorematic) component. For the purpose of a more systematic treatment of these and cognate distinctions it is useful to introduce the notion of relational expressions of which relations in the narrow sense of the term are merely one species. In doing so it will be sufficient to consider expressions of the form $x\,[Ry]$ in which x and y will respectively be called the 'external' and the 'internal' variable. What will be said about expressions containing one internal variable can be easily generalized to expressions containing two or more internal variables.

An expression $x\,[Ry]$ is a (dyadic) relational expression if, and only if, the external variable x can be replaced by some directly occurring expression and the internal variable y can be replaced by some DIRECTLY OR INDIRECTLY occurring expression in such a manner that the result is a true sentence. Relational expressions may be subdivided into three classes, namely:

(1) relations (in the narrow sense), i.e. relational expressions which yield true sentences, only if y is replaced by a directly occurring expression
(2) compound monadic predicates, i.e. relational expressions which yield true sentences, only if y is replaced by an indirectly occurring expression

(3) impure relational expressions which are neither relations nor compound monadic predicates but yield true sentences, both if y is replaced by some directly occurring expression or if it is replaced by some indirectly occurring expression.

In order to indicate these distinctions in a formal language one might, for example, represent relations by xRy, compound monadic predicates by $xR-y$ and impure relational expressions by $xR?y$. Each of these classes of relational expressions can be subdivided according to whether the external and internal variables range over names, predicates or sentences.

In order to indicate explicitly the type of expression by which the internal and the external variable must be replaced if a true sentence is to result from the replacement, a, b, c, will be used for variables ranging over names of particulars; F, G, H for variables ranging over predicates; and f, g, h for variables ranging over sentences. For constant names, predicates and sentences the same letters will be used and provided with a subscript. Examples of relations are *a collides with b* (where a and b range over names of material objects); *f logically implies g* (where f and g range over sentences); *a knows f* (where a ranges over names of persons and f over sentences). Examples of compound, monadic predicates are *a desires − b* (where a ranges over names of persons and b over names of particulars; and *a believes −f* (where a ranges over names of persons and f over sentences).

An example of an impure relational expression is *a is taller than ?b* where a and b range over the names of entities which have or are imagined to have a certain size. The substitution instances of this and other impure relational expressions resemble either the substitution instances of relations, as with *The Empire State building is taller than the Eiffel Tower*; or they resemble the substitution instances of compound, monadic predicates, as with *Mr Healey is-taller-than-the-first-inhabitant-of-Lilliput-seen-by-Gulliver-in-accordance-with-Swift's-tale*. In a formal language, which our sketch is meant to suggest, the difference between directly and obliquely occurring expressions can be read off from a difference in their form. (Although the analysis of impure relational expressions into combinations of pure ones seems feasible, it is by no means straightforward.)

The need for relational expressions other than relations in the narrow sense manifests itself especially in the analysis of intentional phenomena, i.e. of the connexion between a *res cogitans* and its *cogitata*.

Compound monadic predicates containing indirectly occurring names, predicates or sentences as components are clearly intentional since the oblique occurrence of an expression involves a thinker's idea of what it would be like if the expression also occurred directly. On the other hand, not all intentional predicates are compound monadic predicates since, as Brentano well knew, some intentional predicates are relations (in the narrow sense). Yet, all intentional predicates logically imply compound monadic predicates. More precisely, the applicability of any intentional predicate logically implies the applicability of a compound, monadic predicate of the form $aR - b$, $aR - F$ or $aR - f$. A few examples must here suffice.

A clear example of a predicate which is both intentional, and a relation (in the narrow sense) is the relation of imagining each other. Whereas *John imagines – Venus* does not express a relation because it does not imply that each of the names occurring in it occurs referentially, *John and Venus imagine each other* does express a relation – be it because it has to be understood in the light of an ontology which acknowledges goddesses as real particulars, be it because the woman whom John imagines and who imagines John was christened *Venus*. It is furthermore clear that the applicability of *a and b imagine each other* to John and Venus logically implies the applicability of the compound monadic predicate *a imagines – Venus* to John and of the compound monadic predicate *b imagines – John* to Venus.

Another clear example of a predicate which is both intentional and a relation is the relation of correct belief. Whereas *John believes-that-Columbus-discovered-America* or, more briefly, *John believes-f_1* does not express a relation because it does not imply that the name and the sentence occurring in it occur directly (the name referentially, the sentence implicatively), *John correctly believes f_1* does express a relation between John and the sentence f_1. It is furthermore clear that the applicability of the relation *a correctly believes f_1* to John and f_1 logically implies the applicability to John of the compound monadic predicate *a believes – f_1*. As against this the applicability of a non–intentional relation, e.g. *a is to the left of b* does not logically imply the applicability of a compound monadic predicate.

II

3. *On compound monadic predicates, extensionality and modality*

By admitting relational expressions, in particular compound monadic predicates of the form $aR - b$, $aR - f$ and $aR - F$, into the lower predicate calculus one increases, of course, its expressive power. But in doing so one does not in any way affect the referential occurrence of names, the applicative occurrence of predicates or the implicative occurrence of sentences. The enlarged theory is in particular no less 'extensional' than the original: monadic predicates – whether compound or not – are applicable only to real particulars; any sentence resulting from such an application to a real particular is WITH RESPECT TO THIS PARTICULAR existentially quantifiable (e.g. $a_0R - b_0$ implies $(\exists x) (xR - b_0)$); any sentence formed by the application of a predicate to a real particular or by existential or universal application has a truth value and contributes in the usual manner to the truth value of any truth-functional compound of which it is a truth-functional component.

The intentional or non-intentional character of a sentence must be distinguished from its modal character. More precisely, whether a sentence is logically necessary, ontologically necessary, contingent, logically possible etc. does not depend on whether or not it contains a compound monadic – or more complex – intentional predicate. While we are only concerned with alethic or, as I shall say, implicative modalities which can be expressed in the language or metalanguage of the lower predicate calculus, it is important not to underestimate its power to express even subtle modal differences.

The fundamental implicative necessity is logical necessity whose syntactical and semantical definition is here taken for granted. Because classical quantification theory is sound and complete we shall indicate the logical necessity of a sentence f by $\vdash f$ (and not distinguish between $\vdash f$ and $\vDash f$). In terms of logical necessity we can define various kinds of relative necessity with respect to various conjunctions of non-logical principles N, which may be ontological principles, physical principles etc. If, for example, N is a conjunction of ontological principles to which, as Kant put it, every judgment must conform 'if it is not to lose all its content', then the definition of ontological necessity takes the form:

(1a) f is ontologically necessary $\overset{=}{\mathrm{D}} f \wedge (N \vdash f)$

or,   (1b) $\overset{=}{\mathrm{D}} f \wedge \vdash (N \rightarrow f)$

or, briefly (1c) $\overset{=}{\mathrm{D}} \vdash_N f$

If one were to introduce the stronger notion of physical necessity one would have to replace the conjunction N by, say $M \wedge N$ where M

is a conjunction of physical principles. In a similar manner one defines:

$$(2)\ f \text{ is logically possible } \overset{=}{\text{D}} \ \neg(\vdash \neg f)$$

and $$(3)\ f \text{ is ontologically possible } \overset{=}{\text{D}} \ f \mathbf{V} \neg(N \vdash \neg f)^4$$

The implicative necessity – or other modality – of a sentence can also be formulated as the applicative necessity of a predicate. In the Kantian ontology, for example, the ontological necessity of the second analogy can be expressed either by characterizing the sentence *Every event is caused* as ontologically necessary or by characterizing the predicate *being caused* as applicable with ontological necessity to any real particular to which the predicate *being an event* is applicable. Yet either formulation conforms to our formal definitions and can be expressed in terms of the logical validity of sentences and of logical implications between sentences within the framework of the lower predicate calculus.

The defined modalities thus are, or are included in, the so-called modalities *de dicto*. They must be distinguished from the so-called modalities *de re* which cannot be expressed in the lower predicate calculus. It is sufficient to consider *de re* necessity, which expresses a necessary connexion – not between one sentence and another or between the applicability of one predicate and the applicability of another – but between a predicate and an individual *qua* individual. For example, to assert the *de re* necessity of *Socrates is mortal* would be to assert that Socrates *qua* Socrates – and not, e.g., *qua* human being or *qua* animal – is necessarily mortal.

It is by no means obvious how the distinction between an individual's necessary predicates (those which it necessarily possesses *qua* individual) and its other predicates can be implemented by a formal theory. One way of achieving this implies the assumption that individuals can be given names of which they remain the recognizable bearers 'in all possible worlds'. Theories of this kind have been adumbrated by Isaiah (LVI: 5) who ascribes to God the power of conferring 'an everlasting name which cannot be cut off'. One such theory is a corner-stone of Leibniz's *Theodicée*. Others have been elaborated by contemporary modal logicians.[5] It may well be that the impression of a need for such theories arises from underestimating the power of the lower predicate calculus – and its metatheory – to cover a much wider

---

[4] For details see Körner (1973).
[5] See especially Kripke (1971).

spectrum of modalities than the protagonists of *de re* modalities would have us believe.

4. *Equivalence and substitutivity*

The equivalence of two expressions in virtue of which one may be substituted for the other – e.g. as leaving the rhythm of a poem or the force of an insult intact – depends on their function. In logic one is concerned with the co-reference of names, the co-implication of sentences, the co-application of predicates and lastly the co-designation of names on the one hand and predicates on the other. If one rejects the *de re* necessity of a thing's possessing a certain name, then a statement asserting the reference of a name to a thing or the co-reference of two names to it, say:

(4) *a* coref *b*

is contingent. In the case of the co-implication of sentences one can distinguish between different modes of co-implication, namely logically necessary, ontologically necessary and contingent (where we again ignore the possibility of interpolating, say physical necessity between ontological necessity and contingency). Of the following statements of co-implication:

(5) $\vdash f \leftrightarrow g$, $\vdash_N f \leftrightarrow g$, $f \leftrightarrow g$

each unilaterally implies its successor.

To the different modes of co-implication between two sentences *f* and *g* there correspond analogous modes of co-application, which may be represented by, say:

(6) $\vdash (\forall x) (F(x) \leftrightarrow G(x))$, $\vdash_N (\forall x) (F(x) \leftrightarrow G(x))$, $(\forall x) (F(x) \leftrightarrow G(x))$

In the case of co-designation a name, say, *a* and a predicate, say, $F(x)$ designate the same particular, the name by naming it, the predicate by applying to it and only it. Co-designation, which may be represented by, say:

(7) *a* codes $F(x)$

is always contingent because the statement that a name names a particular is contingent.

Since there can be no co-reference between two names unless both occur referentially it would be a mistake to deduce from the premisses (i) John believes-that-Cicero-denounced-Catilina and (ii) *Tully* coref *Cicero* the conclusion (iii) John believes-that-Tully-denounced-Catilina. The mistake arises, as Brentano pointed out long ago, from confusing the direct or referential occurrence of a name with its oblique occurrence.

Just as there can be no co-reference of two names unless either occurs referentially – and hence no referential equivalence or intersubstitutivity of a referentially and a non referentially occurring name – so there can be no co-implication of an implicatively and a non-implicatively occurring sentence; no co-application of an applicatively and a non-applicatively occurring predicate; and no co-designation of a predicate and a name if the predicate is used applicatively and the name non-referentially or the name referentially and the predicate non-applicatively. The rule might be briefly summarized by the slogan 'No direct co-signification without direct signification' and justly be called Brentano's rule.

Because co-implication and co-application may be of different strength, the application of Brentano's rule must be combined with that of another rule which might be called the rule of Theophrastus. According to it the conclusion of a deductive inference has the modal strength of the weakest premiss – assuming, of course, that the premiss is essential i.e. cannot be dropped without affecting the validity of the inference. As has been noted, logical necessity is stronger than ontological necessity, which is stronger than contingency which in turn is stronger than logical possibility. The interpolation in this sequence of other modalities, such as physical necessity or ontological possibility presents no difficulty.[6]

Having exemplified the application of Brentano's rule in resolving a typical paradox which arises from a conflation of the direct and oblique mode of an expression's occurrence, we seem to be obliged to exemplify the application of Theophrastus's rule in resolving some characteristic paradoxes which arise from conflating modalities of different strength. Our first example is due to Kneale & Kneale (1962: 611) who use it in an attempt at discrediting the rule of Theophrastus: from (a) *It is logically possible that the number of apostles is not smaller than 13* and (b) *The number of apostles =12*, there seems to follow (c) *It is*

---

[6] See Kneale & Kneale (1962: 102), where a Latin version of the rule is given as *Sectetur partem conclusio deteriorem.*

logically possible that 12 is not smaller than 13 which is indeed 'ridiculous'. But the paradox disappears if in (b) the identity sign is properly interpreted and (b) replaced by (b') *The class of apostles is contingently co-designative with the numeral 12 (i.e. happens as a matter of contingent fact to have 12 members).* The conclusion then has to be reformulated by (c') *It is logically possible that a class which is contingently co-designative with the numeral 12 should not be smaller than 13* (that a class which as a matter of contingent fact has 12 members should have a number of members which is not smaller than 13).

Similar remarks apply to the apparent paradox that from the premisses (a) *It is logically necessary that if there is life on the evening star, then there is life on the evening star* and (b) *The evening star = the morning star* there follows (c) *It is logically necessary that if there is life on the evening star, then there is life on the morning star.* However, since (b) must be interpreted as expressing the merely contingent co-application of *evening star* and *morning star* (c) must be replaced by (c') *It is contingently true that if there is life on the evening star then there is life on the morning star.* The paradox arose once again from ignoring the different modal strengths of the premisses and, hence, the correct modal strength of the conclusion.

From co-reference, co-implication, co-application and co-designation, which are equivalences between linguistic expressions, one must distinguish the equivalences between temporally or otherwise distinct aspects of things, in virtue of which two different aspects of a kind of thing – such as a table or a person – are judged to be aspects of the same particular thing and as representing this thing and each other in certain contexts and for certain purposes, defined by law, social practices, etc. Equivalences of this kind play an important role in the constitution and individuation of things, rather than in the designation of already constituted and individuated things, in the application of predicates to them and in making statements about them.[7]

Just as modal statements *de dicto* allow for the substitution of equivalent expressions if the rules of Brentano and Theophrastus are satisfied, so under the same conditions do they allow for existential quantification. Thus the logically necessary statement of the arithmetical theorem that $9 < 10$ implies that there exists an x such that the predicate $x < 10$ is with logical necessity applicable to it; and the contingent statement that the number of planets < 10 implies that there exists an x such that the predicate $x < 10$ is contingently applicable to it. In all such

[7] See, e.g., Körner (1975).

cases the applicability of the predicate has the same modality as the assertion of the sentence which has been subjected to existential quantification.

5. *On the normative rectification of obliquely occurring expressions*

The oblique occurrence in a compound monadic predicate of a name, a predicate or a sentence makes some distinctive, though indefinite, contribution to the meaning of the compound predicate. For although the oblique occurrence of an expression is associated with SOME idea of what it would be like if the expression had a direct occurrence, this idea – as has been noted earlier – may not even be internally consistent. (To deny this would be to deny, for example, that a scientist or mathematician who believed a certain theory to be true could not have believed the theory to be true, if it later turned out to be internally inconsistent.)

There are various ways of making the correspondence between obliquely and directly occurring expressions more definite by imposing standards of acceptability on the obliquely occurring expressions or, briefly, by rectifying them. Among the rectifications, which have been proposed, one can distinguish two main types, namely, logical rectifications, which impose purely logical requirements (expressible in terms of logical consequence and other metalogical notions of the lower predicate calculus); and ontological rectifications, which require conformity to certain supreme principles which, though non-logical, are regarded as necessary conditions of all acceptable ('meaningful', 'coherent', etc.) thinking. Here it will be sufficient to exemplify both types of rectification very briefly by considering indirectly occurring sentences expressing beliefs.

One method of logically rectifying them consists in a stipulative definition of the correctness of a sentence expressing a belief. Consider the following:

(8) Columbus correctly believed $-f_1$ (that he discovered America)
(9) Columbus incorrectly believed $-f_2$ (that he discovered India)
(10) Cagliostro incorrectly believed $-f_3$ (that he discovered the elixir of eternal youth)

If Columbus correctly believed $-f_1$, it must be the case that f_1 is true and that he believed at least some of the logical consequences of f_1. A strong, but rather unrealistic, definition of correct belief would require him to believe ALL logical consequences of f_1, so that – with obvious abbreviations – (8) can be formalized as:

(11) Columbus bel $-f_1.\wedge.$ Columbus bel-Cn $(f_1).\wedge.f_1$

The analogous formalization of (9) is:

(12) Columbus bel $-f_2.\wedge.\urcorner$ (Columbus bel-Cn $(f_2).\wedge.f_2$)

If we assume that to the obliquely occurring sentence $-f_3$ there corresponds no directly occurring sentence and if we indicate this assumption by adding the superscript zero to it, then (10) can be formalized as:

(13) Cagliostro bel $-f_3^0$

One could, without going beyond the extended lower predicate calculus, also formalize various weaker notions of a sentence expressing a correct belief, e.g. by requiring that Columbus did not believe the negation of any logical consequence of f_1.

All these stipulative definitions presuppose that whereas simple and compound predicates are syntactically distinct, semantically they are both alike interpreted as monadic predicates which are applicable to real particulars. (Thus the set determined by, e.g., *x believes* $-f_3$ is a proper subset of the set determined by *x is human*.) It is, moreover, worth emphasizing that the obliquely occurring $-f_1, -f_2, -f_3$ and any other obliquely occurring sentence is NOT a meaningless expression, a true or a false sentence, a sentence without a truth value or a sentence with a truth value other than truth or falsehood. It is none of these, but a syncategorematic part of a compound monadic predicate. Similar remarks apply to logical rectifications which are global in that they concern the whole system of the sentences expressing a person's beliefs, e.g. the requirement that this system be internally consistent. Further examples of actually adopted, merely proposed or as yet only conceivable, logical rectifications could be easily produced.

It is even more obvious that there is a great variety of ontological rectifications since every metaphysical doctrine proposes some overriding constraints on the system of a person's beliefs. A recently revived example of such a metaphysical doctrine implies the assumption of *de re* modalities, expressing necessary connexions between individuals *qua* individuals and some of their predicates and the assumption of 'rigid' names, which allow the identification of individuals in different possible worlds. It is sometimes argued[8] that the

[8] E.g. by Linsky (1971: 100).

possibility and, indeed, the ontological necessity of such transmundane identification follows from the fact that, say, *I did not miss this morning's lecture, but I might have* and *I did not miss this morning's lecture, but there is a possible world in which I did* are full paraphrases of each other. Yet, once a person is identified in the actual world and the fact established that he did not miss this morning's lecture, one can – without assuming *de re* necessities about him and without assuming his transmundane identifiability – assert that the false statement to the effect that he missed the lecture is logically possible, ontologically possible or possible with respect to still more specific assumptions (compare the definitions 1–3 in §3).

It is not a task of this essay to argue either for the rectification of indirectly occurring expressions or for leaving the correspondence between indirectly and directly occurring expressions in its naturally indefinite state. Nor is it among its tasks to argue for or against any particular kind of rectification. However, the analysis of the correspondence between directly and obliquely occurring expressions would be incomplete if it did not exhibit the difference between unrectified and rectified correspondence, between logical and ontological rectification and if it did not indicate different – including mutually exclusive – versions of either.

Idealization of ordinary language for the purposes of logic

CZESLAW LEJEWSKI

Originally, logicians made use of ordinary language for the purpose of formulating the principles or theses of their discipline. Thus, Aristotle formulated his syllogism in terms of ordinary language, which he had supplemented with variables. The use of variables within the framework of ordinary language was by no means a minor innovation, but its significance had remained unrecognized until the reappraisal of the ancient logic in the last sixty years by the historians of the subject. The variables introduced into ordinary language by Aristotle were NOMINAL variables. They stood for general names, or common nouns as the traditional grammarians call them. Now, the credit for introducing, into ordinary language, PROPOSITIONAL variables must be given to Theophrastus and to the Stoics. However, neither Aristotle nor Theophrastus nor Chrysippus fully realized that the use of variables involved the notion of quantification. They appear to have felt that in connexion with the variables something else was implicitly used, and both Aristotle and Theophrastus were on the brink of articulating it, the former in his proofs by ecthesis and the latter in his proleptic syllogisms, but, in fact, the task of establishing quantification on a firm basis was left to be accomplished, over two thousand years later, by Frege and Peirce. By that time the logician's language as used in his written work had become symbolic. This development, however, is not the kind of idealization of ordinary language I have in mind. The use of symbolism is like the use of shorthand. It facilitates the idealization but does not predetermine it.

Idealizing ordinary language may go in two directions. First, it can be said that logicians idealize part of the vocabulary of ordinary language. They 'borrow' certain expressions from ordinary language, distinguish various meanings which are attached to them in common usage, decide which meaning they wish to preserve, and finally determine that meaning with the aid of axioms or definitions. Propositional connectives such as 'and', 'or', 'if. . . then' and 'if-and-only-if' have been idealized in this way to become truth functors. In concatenation with propositional arguments they form compound propositions, whose truth depends exclusively on the truth or falsity of the arguments. Secondly, idealization of ordinary language may consist in rationalizing its grammar and constructing an artificial language, which as a means of articulation is better suited for the purposes of logic.

Several different artificial languages have been constructed by logicians. The most advanced of them are the languages of the 'growing' systems of logic.

A deductive system of logic can be said to grow in more senses than one. It can be said to grow in the sense that we can keep on adding to it new theses by taking advantage of the rules of inference. However, by applying rules of inference to theses already available in the system we do not contribute to the growth of its vocabulary or to the growth of its grammar. If we want our deductive system of logic to grow in these two latter respects, we have to equip it with appropriate rules of definition. For it is by adding definitions to the system what we enrich its vocabulary. Now, a definition may introduce into the system a term, which belongs to a semantical category (substitution class, part of speech) already acknowledged in the system or it may introduce into the system a term which represents a new semantical category, not represented by any expression to be found in any of the theses preceding the definition in the system. This latter case exemplifies the categorial (grammatical) growth of the system and its language.

The notion of semantical category does not have exactly the same connotation in every artificial language because artificial languages differ from one another as regards the choice of expressions whose role is to refer, or to purport to refer, directly to objects outside the language. However, forgetting these differences for the time being, the notion of semantical category in a more general sense, namely in relation to the class of unspecified expressions, call them *as*, can be defined, recursively, as follows:

D1 (i) The class of propositions, i.e. the class of declarative sentences is a semantical category with respect to *as*; the class of *a*s is a semantical category with respect to *a*s; it differs from the class of propositions.

(ii) If every member of the sequence $c, c_1, \ldots, c_n$ is a semantical category with respect to *a*s then so is the class of functors, each of which, in concatenation with expressions $e_1, \ldots, e_n$ where $e_{1 \leq k \leq n}$ belongs to $c_{1 \leq k \leq n}$, forms an expression belonging to c; the semantical category of these functors differs from every member of the sequence $c, c_1, \ldots, c_n$.

The semantical category of propositions is called basic because propositions can never be used in a language as functors; it is assumed that the semantical category of the unspecified expressions referred to in D1 as *a*s is also basic. Note that members of the sequence $c, c_1, \ldots, c_n$ in D1 need not differ from one another as regards the semantical categories to which they belong. Note also that the availability of the functors mentioned in D1 (ii) is secured by the rules of definition operative in the system of logic whose language is under consideration.

Among the noun expressions of ordinary language we can distinguish (i) singular names, e.g. *Socrates, the husband of Xanthippe, Pegasus, the winged horse of Bellerophon*; (ii) general names, e.g. *philosopher, inhabitant of Athens, mermaid, daughter of Mnemosyne*; alternatively, we can distinguish (iii) referential names, that is to say, names that name or designate or denote or refer to objects outside the language, e.g. *Socrates, the husband of Xanthippe, man, inhabitant of Athens*; and (iv) non-referential names, that is to say, names that purport to name or designate or denote or refer to objects outside the language but fail to do so, e.g. *Pegasus, the winged horse of Bellerophon, mermaid, daughter of Mnemosyne*.

Now, by specifying '*a*s' in D1 we get different definitions of different notions of semantical category applicable to different artificial languages. In Lejewski (1967) I mention four artificial languages. With reference to D1 they can be characterized as follows:

In L_1, which I call Aristotelian language, the class of general referential names is the second basic semantical category in addition, of course, to the semantical category of propositions. L_2, which bears the name of Frege–Russellian language, has the semantical category of singular referential names as its second basic category. In L_3, which is Leśniewskian language, the second basic semantical category is that of general names. And in L_4, in terms of which my theory of non-reflexive identity is formulated, the second basic semantical category is the semantical category of singular names.

The notion of semantical category as used above appears to be applicable to classes of constant expressions only. In fact, it is meant to be understood in a wider sense. Thus, for instance, the semantical category of propositions is meant to comprise not only constant propositions, simple or compound, but also propositional variables, for which constant propositions can be substituted, and propositional functions, i.e. expressions which contain free variables and turn into constant propositions once the free variables have been replaced by appropriate constant expressions. Similarly, the semantical category of singular names is meant to comprise not only constant singular names but also variables whose substituends include constant singular names, and nominal functions which turn into singular names once the free variables occurring in them have been replaced by appropriate constants. Analogous qualifications apply to any other semantical category.

In connexion with propositional functions, mention should be made of the quantifiers. Concatenated with a propositional variable, or with a propositional function, a quantifier produces a constant proposition or a propositional function with fewer variables than in the original function. However, as linguistic expressions, quantifiers remain outside the scheme of semantical categories.

Now, how do the four artificial languages compare with ordinary language? In all of them, as has already been pointed out, the class of propositions is a semantical category, and the same can be said about propositions in ordinary language. In the four artificial languages, and indeed in all artificial languages, we have the semantical category of proposition forming functors for two arguments each of which is a proposition ('and', 'or', 'if . . . then', 'if-and-only-if'). And we have, or can have if we want to, the semantical category of proposition forming functors for one propositional argument ('It-is-not-the-case-that'). Rules of definition in systems of logic formulated in any of the four artificial languages make it possible for us to introduce, into the system and thus into its language, several other semantical categories of proposition forming functors for propositional arguments, but these semantical categories do not seem to have counterparts among the parts of speech or among the substitution classes of ordinary language.

In each of the four languages a subclass of noun expressions is assumed to be a semantical category. For instance, in L_1 the class of general referential names is a semantical category. Non-referential names are not to be found in L_1. They are replaced by appropriate verbs or verb expressions, that is to say, by functors which require a general referential name as the only argument to form a proposition. Singular referential names are treated in L_1 as if they were general referential names that happen to designate only one object each.

In L_2 the class of singular referential names is a semantical category. Non-referential names and general names have no status of their own. They are regarded as integral parts of verbs or verb expressions (*Pegasizes, is-Pegasus, is-a-philosopher*).

In L_3 the class of all names (singular, general, referential, non-referential) is a semantical category. *Prima facie* the semantical category of names in L_3 coincides with the notion of SUBSTANTIVE or NOUN. Indeed, the traditional grammarian may say that the grammar of L_3 approximates to the grammar of ordinary language to a much greater extent than does the grammar of any other artificial language, but the general linguist is likely to disagree. He may point out that substantives or nouns do not form a substitution class. If in a meaningful context we replace a singular name by a general name then by doing so we may destroy the meaningfulness of the context. Sequences of words such as *Socrates is a Socrates, philosopher is a philosopher*, or *philosopher is a Socrates* cannot be described as well constructed propositions. Nor can they be dismissed as solecisms. They should rather be treated on a par with such meaningless conglomerations of words as *and is or if* or *every but then or*.

L_4, in which the class of singular names is a semantical category, resembles L_2 in that it uses verbs instead of general names. On the other hand, it comes nearer to ordinary language by including within one semantical category both singular referential and singular non-referential names.

In each of the four artificial languages the semantical category of proposition forming functors for one nominal argument, and the semantical category of proposition forming functors for two nominal arguments, coincide with a subclass of intransitive verbs and with a subclass of transitive verbs respectively, but in the case of L_2 and L_4 the area of coincidence is somewhat smaller than in L_1 or L_3. The L_2 or L_4 analogues of such intransitive verbs as *exist* (in one of its senses) or *intermarry* belong to the semantical category of proposition forming functors for one argument, which itself is a proposition forming functor for one nominal argument. And transitive verbs like *outnumber* have to be rendered in L_2 and in L_4 by expressions belonging to the semantical category of proposition forming functors for two functorial expressions as arguments. Each of these latter belongs, in turn, to the semantical category of proposition forming functors for one nominal argument.

The overlap between, on the one hand, the semantical categories of artificial languages as exemplified by L_1, L_2, L_3, and L_4, and the substitution classes or parts of speech of ordinary language, on the other, does not amount to much. But can it be extended? In the view of some logicians it can. Kazimierz Ajdukiewicz was the first to note that one could have an artificial language with the hierarchy of semantical categories based on the semantical category of propositions and, not just one, but two other basic semantical categories coinciding with the class of singular names and the class of general names respectively (see Ajdukiewicz 1934).

In some earlier papers of mine (e.g. Lejewski 1974), I referred to an artificial language whose semantical categories form a hierarchy based on the semantical category of propositions, and ONE other basic semantical category, as UNICATEGORIAL, and to a language which complies with Ajdukiewicz's proposal, as BICATEGORIAL. Now, we have seen that there are, in fact, several different unicategorial languages, and, similarly, we can have several different bicategorial languages, but the notion of semantical category for a bicategorial language can be comprehensively defined as follows:

D2 (i) The class of propositions, i.e. the class of declarative sentences is a semantical category with respect to as and bs; the class of as is a semantical category with respect to as and bs, and it differs from the semantical category of propositions; the class of bs is a semantical category with respect to as and bs, and it differs from the semantical category of propositions and from that of as.

   (ii) If every member of the sequence $c, c_1, \ldots, c_n$ is a semantical category with respect to as and bs then so is the class of functors, each of which, in concatenation with expressions $e_1, \ldots, e_n$ where $e_{1 \leqslant k \leqslant n}$ belongs to $c_{1 \leqslant k \leqslant n}$, forms an expression belonging to c; the semantical category of these functors differs from every member of the sequence $c, c_1, \ldots, c_n$.

By pointing out that ordinary language lends itself to a unicategorial idealization or to a bicategorial idealization, Ajdukiewicz tried to show that certain arguments concerning the existence of universals appear to be valid if formulated in a unicategorial language, but they appear to lose their cogency if one reformulates them in terms of a language that is bicategorial. However, Ajdukiewicz did not go as far as to use his bicategorial language for the purpose of constructing a deductive system of logic.

I benefited from Ajdukiewicz's ideas when in 1973 I tried to work out a system of logic that would be acceptable to those ontologists who maintain that there are two different kinds of entity: individuals, and classes of individuals (see Lejewski 1974). The language which I used on that occasion was bicategorial but it differed from the one suggested by Ajdukiewicz. Ajdukiewicz's assumption was that noun expressions of ordinary language fell into two subclasses, one being the class of singular names and the other the class of general names. According to him either class would be regarded as a distinct semantical category. I began by assuming that singular names of ordinary language fell, in fact, into two separate semantical categories, the semantical category of singular names, by which I meant singular names that referred, or purported to refer, to individual objects, and the semantical category of singular class expressions (*the class of philosophers, the class of lions*) which referred to, or purported to refer, in a somewhat different sense of referring, to classes. Thus, the notion of semantical category in the artificial language I needed was derived from D2 by specifying *a*s as singular names, in the sense explained just now, and *b*s as singular class expressions.

It seems to me that if one wants to discuss a bicategorial ontology one has to have a logic formulated in terms of a bicategorial language. But one can have a logic formulated in terms of a bicategorial language without necessarily being committed to a bicategorial ontology. The reason for wishing to have such a logic may be this: its language, artificial as it is, appears to approximate to ordinary language more closely than an artificial language that is unicategorial.

In the remaining part of my paper I propose to outline a system of logic, system **S**, whose language is, in fact, the one originally suggested by Ajdukiewicz. I shall refer to it as L_5. Contrary to Ajdukiewicz's intentions, L_5 is meant to serve the purpose of unicategorial ontology. The notion of semantical category applicable to L_5 can be derived from D2 by specifying *a*s as singular names and *b*s as general names.

System **S** presupposes protothetic, i.e. the logic of propositions. The axioms of **S** characterize two primitive terms: the functor of singular identity '=' and the functor of inclusion 'ε_1'.

The former occurs in expressions of the form '$A = B$' where 'A' and 'B' are variables which count singular names among their substituends. '$A = B$' means the same as 'A is the same object as B'. Thus, '=' is a proposition forming functor for two arguments, each of which is a singular name in the wider sense of the term.

The latter occurs in expressions of the form '$A \, \varepsilon_1 \, a$' where 'A' is a singular name in the wider sense of the term and 'a' is a general term also in the wider sense. '$A \, \varepsilon_1 \, a$' means the same as 'A is an a'. Thus 'ε_1' turns out to be a proposition forming functor for two arguments of which the first belongs to the semantical category of singular names while the second is a general name; both in the wider sense, of course.

The following two theses serve as axioms of **S**:

SA1 $[AB] : A = B . \equiv . [\, \exists C] . C = A . C = B$
> for all A and B, A is-the-same-object-as B if-and-only-if for some C, (C is-the-same-object-as A and C is-the-same-object-as B)

SA2 $[Aa] :: A \, \varepsilon_1 \, a . \equiv . : . [\exists b] . : . \, A \, \varepsilon_1 \, b : [B] : B \, \varepsilon_1 \, b . \equiv . A = B . : . [B] : B \, \varepsilon_1 \, b . \supset . \, B \, \varepsilon_1 \, a$
> for all A and a, A is-an a if-and-only-if for some b, (A is-a b and (for all B, B is-a b if-and-only-if A is-the-same-object-as B) and for all B, if B is-a b then B is-an a)

Further theses can be added to the axioms by applying the directives or rules of procedure. They are of three kinds. First we have three rules of inference, namely, substitution, quantification, and detachment. Secondly, we have three rules of definition, and finally, three rules of extensionality.

The rules of inference operative in **S** are equivalent to the rules of inference made use of in the traditional systems of logic, and call for no explication.

The rules of definition can be outlined as follows:

RD1. On the assumption that a thesis T is, at a given stage, the last thesis of **S**, the rule of definition RD1 allows us to add to the system a new thesis of the form:

(1) $[\ldots] : a \, (\ldots) . \equiv . \beta$

provided the following conditions are fulfilled: the definiendum which in (1) is represented by '$a(\ldots)$' is either (i) a constant proposition, which does not occur in T or in a thesis preceding T in the system; or (ii) a simple propositional function or a many-link propositional function; its constant functor, represented by 'a', occurs neither in T nor in any thesis preceding T in the system, and the arguments of the function are all variables, none of which occurs in the definiendum more than once; the definiens, which in (1) is represented by 'β' is, with respect to T, a meaningful propositional expression, i.e. every constant term and every variable occurring in the definiens occurs in T or in a thesis preceding T in the system or in protothetic, and every variable occurring in 'β' belongs to a semantical category already available in the system or in protothetic; every variable occurring in the definiendum occurs in the definiens as a free variable, and every free variable in the definiens occurs in the definiendum; a universal quantifier binds all free variables occurring in the definitional equivalence.

RD$_{\text{II}}$. On the assumption that a thesis T is, at a given stage, the last thesis of **S**, the rule of definition RD$_{\text{II}}$ allows us to add to the system a new thesis of the form:

$$(2)\ [A\ldots]\ \therefore A = X(\ldots).\ \equiv:\ A = A\colon [B]\colon \Phi(B).\ \equiv .A = B$$

provided the following conditions are fulfilled: the expression represented in (2) by '$X(\ldots)$' is (i) a constant singular name, which does not occur in T or in a thesis preceding T in the system; or (ii) a simple singular name function or a many-link singular name function; its constant functor, represented by 'X', does not occur in T or in a thesis preceding T in the system or in protothetic, and the arguments of the function are all variables none of which occurs in the function more than once or is equiform with 'A'; the definiens, i.e. the expression represented in (2) by '$A = A\colon[B]\colon \Phi(B).\ \equiv .A = B$', is, with respect to T, a meaningful propositional expression; every constant term occurring in the definiens occurs in T or in a thesis preceding T in the system or in protothetic, and every variable occurring in the definiens belongs to a semantical category already available in the system; every variable occurring in the definiendum, i.e. in the expression represented in (2) by '$A = X(\ldots)$', occurs in the definiens as a free variable, and every free variable in the definiens occurs in the definiendum; a universal quantifier binds all free variables occurring in the definitional equivalence.

RD$_{\text{III}}$. On the assumption that a thesis T is, at a given stage, the last thesis of **S**, the rule of definition RD$_{\text{III}}$ allows us to add to the system a new thesis of the form:

(3) $[A. \ldots] : A \; \varepsilon_1 \; \mathrm{x}(. \ldots). \; \equiv \; . \; A = A. \; \Phi(A)$

provided the following conditions are fulfilled: the expression represented in (3) by 'x(. . .)' is (i) a constant general name, which does not occur in T or in a thesis preceding T in the system; or (ii) a simple general name function or a many-link general name function; its constant functor, represented by 'x', does not occur in T or in a thesis preceding T in the system or in protothetic, and the arguments of the function are all variables none of which occurs in the function more than once or is equiform with 'A'; the definiens, i.e. the expression represented in (3) by '$A = A. \Phi(A)$', is, with respect to T a meaningful propositional expression; every constant term occurring in the definiens occurs in T or in a thesis preceding T in the system or in protothetic, and every variable occurring in the definiens belongs to a semantical category already available in the system; every variable occurring in the definiendum, i.e. in the expression represented in (3) by '$A \; \varepsilon_1 \; \mathrm{x}(. \ldots)$' occurs in the definiens as a free variable, and every free variable in the definiens occurs in the definiendum; a universal quantifier binds all free variables occurring in the definitional equivalence.

The rules of extensionality obtaining in **S** can be outlined as follows:

REI. On the assumption that a thesis T is, at a given stage, the last thesis of **S**, the rule of extensionality REI allows us to add to the system a new thesis of the form:

(4) $[\varphi \psi] \; \therefore [. \ldots] : \varphi(. \ldots) \; . \; \equiv \; . \; \psi(. \ldots) : \; \equiv : [\Phi] : \Phi(\varphi). \; \equiv \; .\Phi(\psi)$

provided every variable occurring in the new thesis belongs to a semantical category already available in the system, and provided the following further conditions are fulfilled: the two expressions represented in (4) by '$\varphi(. \ldots)$' and '$\psi(. \ldots)$' respectively are simple propositional functions or many-link propositional functions; they are equiform with each other except for the variable functors 'φ' and 'ψ'; their arguments are all variables, none of which occurs in either function more than once.

REII. On the assumption that a thesis T is, at a given stage, the last thesis of **S**, the rule of extensionality REII allows us to add to the system a new thesis of the form:

(5) $[\varphi \psi] \; \therefore [A. \ldots] : A = \varphi(. \ldots) \; . \; \equiv \; . \; A = \psi(. \ldots) : \equiv : [\Phi] : \Phi(\varphi).$
$\equiv \; .\Phi(\psi)$

provided every variable occurring in the new thesis belongs to a semantical category already available in the system, and provided the following further conditions are fulfilled: the two expressions represented in (5) by '$\varphi(\ldots)$' and '$\psi(\ldots)$' respectively are either (i) singular name variables different from 'A' and from each other (in that case 'φ' and 'ψ' in '$[\Phi]:\Phi(\varphi). \equiv .\Phi(\psi)$' stand for these variables); or (ii) simple singular name functions or many-link singular name functions, which are equiform with each other except for the variable functors 'φ' and 'ψ'; the arguments of the two functions are all variables, none of which is equiform with 'A' or occurs in either function more than once.

RE$_{III}$. On the assumption that a thesis T is, at a given stage, the last thesis of **S**, the rule of extensionality RE$_{III}$ allows us to add to the system a new thesis of the form:

$$(6)\ [\varphi\psi] \therefore [A]:A\ \varepsilon_1\ \varphi(\ldots). \ \equiv\ . \ A\ \varepsilon_1\ \psi(\ldots): \equiv :[\Phi]\ \Phi(\varphi). \ \equiv\ .\Phi(\psi)$$

provided conditions analogous to those stipulated by RE$_{II}$ are fulfilled, with '$\varphi(\ldots)$' and '$\psi(\ldots)$' in (6) standing now for general name variables or general name functions.

It is evident from D2 that as regards the variety of semantical categories L_5 is richer than L_3, which is the language of Leśniewski's system of logic. In fact it can be shown that every thesis obtainable within the framework of the standard system of Ontology – this is the name Leśniewski gave to his logical theory, see Leśniewski (1930) and Lejewski (1958) – is obtainable in **S**. The proof involves the following deductions within the framework of **S**.

We begin by making use of RD$_I$ in order to add to the system a thesis which defines in **S** the primitive terms of Leśniewski's system of Ontology. The thesis reads thus:

SD1 $[ab]::a\ \varepsilon\ b . \ \equiv \therefore [\exists A] \therefore A\ \varepsilon_1\ a \therefore [B]:B\ \varepsilon_1\ a. \ \equiv .A=B \therefore [B]:$
$B\ \varepsilon_1\ a . \ \supset . \ B\ \varepsilon_1\ b$

Definition SD1 expresses formally what was said earlier informally, namely that in L_3 singular names are treated as general names that happen to designate at most one object.

We continue our deductions as follows:

ST1	$[AB]:A = B. \ \equiv .B = A$	(follows from SA1)
ST2	$[ABC]:A = B.C = A. \ \supset .C = B$	(from SA1)
ST3	$[ab]:a\ \varepsilon\ b. \ \supset .a\ \varepsilon\ a$	(SD1)
ST4	$[ab]:a\ \varepsilon\ b. \ \supset .[\exists c].c\ \varepsilon\ a$	(ST3)
ST5	$[ABa]:A\ \varepsilon_1\ a.A = B. \ \supset .B\ \varepsilon_1\ a$	

Proof:

[ABa] : :
    (1) $A \ \varepsilon_1 \ a.$
    (2) $A = B. \supset.$
        $[\exists b] \therefore$
    (3) $[C] : C \ \varepsilon_1 \ b. \equiv .A = C \therefore$ $\Big\}$ (SA2, 1)
    (4) $[C] : C \ \varepsilon_1 \ b. \supset .C \ \varepsilon_1 \ a \therefore$
    (5) $B \ \varepsilon_1 \ b \therefore$ (3, 2)
        $B \ \varepsilon_1 \ a$ (4, 5)

ST6 $[abcdB] : a \ \varepsilon \ b.c \ \varepsilon \ a.d \ \varepsilon \ a.B \ \varepsilon_1 \ c. \supset .B \ \varepsilon_1 \ d$
      $[abcdB] \therefore$
    (1) $a \ \varepsilon \ b.$
    (2) $c \ \varepsilon \ a.$
    (3) $d \ \varepsilon \ a.$
    (4) $B \ \varepsilon_1 \ c. \supset :$
    (5) $B \ \varepsilon_1 \ a :$ (SD1, 2, 4)
        $[\exists C] :$ $\Big\}$ (SD1, 3)
    (6) $C \ \varepsilon_1 \ d.$
    (7) $C \ \varepsilon_1 \ a.$ (SD1, 3, 6)
          $[\exists A] .$ $\Big\}$
    (8) $A = B.$ (SD1, 1, 5, 7)
    (9) $A = C :$
    (10) $C = B :$ (SA1, 9, 8)
        $B \ \varepsilon_1 \ d$ (ST5, 6, 10)

ST7 $[abcd] : a \ \varepsilon \ b.c \ \varepsilon \ a.d \ \varepsilon \ a. \supset .c \ \varepsilon \ d$
      $[abcd] : :$
    (1) $a \ \varepsilon \ b.$
    (2) $c \ \varepsilon \ a.$
    (3) $d \ \varepsilon \ a. \supset \therefore$
        $[\exists A] \therefore$ $\Big\}$
    (4) $A \ \varepsilon_1 \ c:$ (SD1, 2)
    (5) $[B] : B \ \varepsilon_1 \ c. \equiv .A = B \therefore$
    (6) $[B] : B \ \varepsilon_1 \ c. \supset .B \ \varepsilon_1 \ d \therefore$ (ST6, 1, 2, 3)
        $c \ \varepsilon \ d$ (SD1, 4, 5, 6)

ST8 $[abcB] : a \; \varepsilon \; b.c \; \varepsilon \; a.B \; \varepsilon_1 \; c. \supset .B \; \varepsilon_1 \; b$
$[abcB] :$
    (1) $a \; \varepsilon \; b.$
    (2) $c \; \varepsilon \; a.$
    (3) $B \; \varepsilon_1 \; c. \supset .$
    (4) $B \; \varepsilon_1 \; a.$ (SD1, 2, 3)
        $B \; \varepsilon_1 \; b$ (SD1, 1, 4)

ST9 $[abc] : a \; \varepsilon \; b.c \; \varepsilon \; a. \supset .c \; \varepsilon \; b$
$[abc] : :$
    (1) $a \; \varepsilon \; b$
    (2) $c \; \varepsilon \; a. \supset \therefore$
        $[\exists A] \therefore$
    (3) $A \; \varepsilon_1 \; c :$ (SD1, 2)
    (4) $[B] : B \; \varepsilon_1 \; c. \equiv .A = B \therefore$
    (5) $[B] : B \; \varepsilon_1 \; c. \supset .B \; \varepsilon_1 \; b \therefore$ (ST8, 1, 2)
        $c \; \varepsilon \; b$ (SD1, 3, 4, 5)

ST10 $[Aa] \therefore A \; \varepsilon_1 \; a. \supset : [\exists b] : b \; \varepsilon \; a : [B] : B \; \varepsilon_1 b. \equiv .A = B$
$[Aa] : :$
    (1) $A \; \varepsilon_1 \; a. \supset \therefore$
        $[\exists b] \therefore$
    (2) $A \; \varepsilon_1 \; b :$ (SA2, 1)
    (3) $[B] : B \; \varepsilon_1 \; b. \equiv .A = B \therefore$
    (4) $[B] : B \; \varepsilon_1 \; b. \supset .B \; \varepsilon_1 \; a \therefore$ (ST5, 1, 3)
    (5) $b \; \varepsilon \; a:$ (SD1, 2, 3, 4)
        $[\exists b] : b \; \varepsilon \; a : [B] : B \; \varepsilon_1 \; b. \equiv .A = B$ (5, 3)

ST11 $[aAB] : : [cd] : c \; \varepsilon \; a.d \; \varepsilon \; a. \supset .c \; \varepsilon \; d \therefore A \; \varepsilon_1 \; a.B \; \varepsilon_1 \; a \therefore \supset .A = B$
$[aAB] : :$
    (1) $[cd] : c \; \varepsilon \; a.d \; \varepsilon \; a. \supset .c \; \varepsilon \; d \therefore$
    (2) $A \; \varepsilon_1 \; a.$
    (3) $B \; \varepsilon_1 \; a \therefore \supset \therefore$
        $[\exists b] \therefore$
    (4) $b \; \varepsilon \; a:$ (ST10, 2)
    (5) $[C] : C \; \varepsilon_1 \; b. \equiv .A = C \therefore$
        $[\exists c] \therefore$
    (6) $c \; \varepsilon \; a:$ (ST10, 3)
    (7) $[C] : C \; \varepsilon_1 \; c. \equiv .B = C \therefore$

(8) $b \varepsilon c.$ (1, 4, 6)

$[\exists D].$

(9) $D \varepsilon_1 b.$ $\Big\}$ (SD1, 8)

(10) $D \varepsilon_1 c.$ (SD1, 8, 9)

(11) $A = D.$ (5, 9)

(12) $B = D.$ (7, 10)

$A = B$ (ST2, **ST1**, 11, 12)

ST12 $[abA] : : [d] : d \varepsilon a. \supset .d \varepsilon b \therefore A \varepsilon_1 a \therefore \supset .A \varepsilon_1 b$

$[abA] : :$

(1) $[d] : d \varepsilon a. \supset .d \varepsilon b \therefore$

(2) $A \varepsilon_1 a \therefore \supset \therefore$

(3) $A = A \therefore$ (SA2, 2)

$[\exists d] \therefore$

(4) $d \varepsilon a:$ (ST10, 2)

(5) $[B] : B \varepsilon_1 d. \equiv .A = B \therefore$ $\Big\}$

(6) $A \varepsilon_1 d.$ (5, 3)

(7) $d \varepsilon b.$ (1, 4)

$A \varepsilon_1 b$ (SD1, 7, 6)

ST13 $[abc] : : c \varepsilon a : [de] : d \varepsilon a.e \varepsilon a. \supset .d \varepsilon e \therefore [d] : d \varepsilon a. \supset .d \varepsilon b. \therefore \supset$
$.a \varepsilon b$

$[abc] : :$

(1) $c \varepsilon a:$

(2) $[de] : d \varepsilon a.e \varepsilon a. \supset .d \varepsilon e \therefore$

(3) $[d] : d \varepsilon a. \supset .d \varepsilon b \therefore \supset \therefore$

$[\exists D] \therefore$

(4) $D \varepsilon_1 c.$ (SD1, 1)

(5) $D \varepsilon_1 a:$ (SD1, 1, 4)

(6) $[B] : B \varepsilon_1 a. \equiv .D = B \therefore$ (ST11, 2, 5,
                                                               ST5, 5)

(7) $[B] : B \varepsilon_1 a. \supset .B \varepsilon_1 b \therefore$ (ST12, 3)

$a \varepsilon b$ (SD1, 5, 6, 7)

ST14 $[ab] : : a \varepsilon b. \equiv \therefore [\exists c]. c \varepsilon a : [cd] : c \varepsilon a.d \varepsilon a. \supset .c \varepsilon d \therefore [c] :$
$c \varepsilon a. \supset .c \varepsilon b$ (ST4, **ST7**, **ST9**, **ST13**)

By proving **ST14**, which is the only axiom of the standard system of
Leśniewski's Ontology, we have shown that any thesis obtainable in
Ontology in virtue of the rules of inference is also obtainable in system

S. We now go on to show that any thesis obtainable in Ontology in virtue of the ontological rule of nominal definition is also obtainable in **S**. But, first of all, note that on the assumption that a thesis T is the last thesis of the system the rule of nominal definition in Ontology allows us to add to the system a new thesis of the following form:

$$(7) \; [a \ldots] : a \; \varepsilon \; x(\ldots). \equiv .[\exists c] . a \; \varepsilon \; c . \varphi(c)$$

provided conditions analogous to those stipulated by RDɪɪɪ are satisfied by the definiendum and by the definiens, i.e. by the expression represented in (7) by '$a \; \varepsilon \; x(\ldots)$' and '$[\exists c] . a \; \varepsilon \; c . \varphi(c)$' respectively.

In order to accomplish our objective we deduce:

ST15 $[ab\varphi] :: [A] : A \; \varepsilon_1 \; b. \equiv .A = A. [\exists c] . A \; \varepsilon_1 \; c. \; \varphi(c) \therefore a \; \varepsilon \; b \therefore$
$\supset . [\exists c]. a \; \varepsilon \; c. \; \varphi(c)$
$[ab\varphi] ::$

(1) $[A] : A \; \varepsilon_1 \; b. \equiv .A = A. [\exists c] .A \; \varepsilon_1 \; c. \; \varphi(c) \therefore$

(2) $a \; \varepsilon \; b \therefore \supset \therefore$
$\qquad [\exists A] \therefore$

(3) $\qquad A \; \varepsilon_1 \; a :$

(4) $\qquad [B] : B \; \varepsilon_1 \; a. \equiv .A = B \therefore \quad \Big\}$ (SD1, 2)

(5) $\qquad [B] : B \; \varepsilon_1 \; a. \supset .B \; \varepsilon_1 \; b \therefore$

(6) $\qquad A \; \varepsilon_1 \; b \therefore$ (5, 3)
$\qquad [\exists c] \therefore$

(7) $\qquad A \; \varepsilon_1 \; c. \quad \Big\}$ (1, 6)

(8) $\qquad \varphi(c) \therefore$
$\qquad [\exists d] \therefore$

(9) $\qquad A \; \varepsilon_1 \; d :$ $\Big\}$ (SA2, 7)

(10) $\qquad [B] : B \; \varepsilon_1 \; d. \supset .B \; \varepsilon_1 \; c \therefore$

(11) $\qquad [B] : B \; \varepsilon_1 \; a. \supset .B \; \varepsilon_1 \; d \therefore$ (ST5, 9,
$\qquad\qquad\qquad\qquad\qquad\qquad\qquad\qquad\qquad\qquad$ (4)

(12) $\qquad [B] : B \; \varepsilon_1 \; a. \supset .B \; \varepsilon_1 \; c \therefore$ (11, 10)

(13) $\qquad a \; \varepsilon \; c$ (SD1, 3, 4, 12)
$\qquad [\exists c] .a \; \varepsilon \; c. \; \varphi(c)$ (13, 8)

ST16 $[abd\varphi] :: [A] : A \; \varepsilon_1 \; b. \equiv .A = A. [\exists c] . A \; \varepsilon_1 \; c. \; \varphi(c) \therefore a \; \varepsilon \; d. \; \varphi$
$(d) \therefore \supset .a \; \varepsilon \; b$
$[abd\varphi] ::$

(1) $[A] : A \; \varepsilon_1 \; b. \equiv .A = A. [\exists c] .A \; \varepsilon_1 \; c. \; \varphi(c) \therefore$

(2) $a \; \varepsilon \; d.$

$$(3) \quad \varphi(d) \therefore \supset \therefore$$
$$[\exists A] \therefore$$

$$(4) \qquad A \, \varepsilon_1 \, a :$$
$$(5) \qquad\quad [B] : B \, \varepsilon_1 \, a. \equiv .A = B \therefore$$
$$(6) \qquad\quad [B] : B \, \varepsilon_1 \, a. \equiv B \, \varepsilon_1 \, d \therefore$$

$$\left.\begin{array}{}\\\\\\\end{array}\right\} \text{(SD1, 2)}$$

$$(7) \qquad\quad A = A. \hspace{4cm} (5, 4)$$
$$(8) \qquad\quad A \, \varepsilon_1 \, d . \hspace{3.9cm} (6, 4)$$
$$(9) \qquad\quad A \, \varepsilon_1 \, b : \hspace{3.6cm} (1, 7, 8, 3)$$
$$(10) \qquad [B] : B \, \varepsilon_1 \, a. \supset .B \, \varepsilon_1 \, b \therefore \hspace{1.4cm} \text{(ST5, 9, 5)}$$
$$\qquad\qquad a \, \varepsilon \, b \hspace{4cm} \text{(SD1, 4, 5, 10)}$$

ST17 $[b\varphi] :: [A] : A \, \varepsilon_1 \, b. \equiv .A = A. \, [\exists c]. A \, \varepsilon_1 \, c. \, \varphi(c) : \supset : [a] : a \, \varepsilon$
$b. \equiv . [\exists c] .a \, \varepsilon \, c. \, \varphi(c)$ \hspace{2.5cm} (**ST15**, **ST16**)

The import of **ST17** is that any thesis which satisfies the conditions of the ontological rule of nominal definition can be derived immediately from a thesis which satisfies the conditions of RDiii.

The ontological rule of nominal extensionality allows us to add to the standard system of Ontology a new thesis of the form:

$$(8) \quad [\varphi\psi] \therefore [c] : c \, \varepsilon \, \varphi(\ldots). \equiv .c \, \varepsilon \, \psi(\ldots): \equiv :[\Phi] : \Phi(\varphi). \equiv .\Phi(\psi)$$

always assuming that a thesis T is, at a given stage, the last thesis of the system, and that the new thesis complies with conditions analogous to those set out in REiii.

It is easy to see from **ST19** that ontological theses of nominal extensionality can be derived from appropriate theses of **S** introduced into **S** by making use of REiii. Now, **ST19** can be proved as follows:

ST18 $[abA] :: [c] : c \, \varepsilon \, a. \equiv .c \, \varepsilon \, b \therefore A \, \varepsilon_1 \, a \therefore \supset .A \, \varepsilon_1 \, b$
$[abA] ::$

$$(1) \quad [c] : c \, \varepsilon \, a. \equiv .c \, \varepsilon \, b \therefore$$
$$(2) \quad A \, \varepsilon_1 \, a \therefore \supset \therefore$$
$$\qquad [\exists c] \therefore$$

$$(3) \qquad A \, \varepsilon_1 \, c:$$
$$(4) \qquad [B] : B \, \varepsilon_1 \, c. \equiv .A = B \therefore$$
$$(5) \qquad [B] : B \, \varepsilon_1 \, c. \supset .B \, \varepsilon_1 \, a \therefore$$

$$\left.\begin{array}{}\\\\\\\end{array}\right\} \text{(SA2, 2)}$$

$$(6) \qquad c \, \varepsilon \, a. \hspace{3.2cm} \text{(SD1, 3, 4, 5)}$$
$$(7) \qquad c \, \varepsilon \, b: \hspace{3.5cm} (1, 6)$$

(8) $[B] : B \, \varepsilon_1 \, c. \supset .B \, \varepsilon_1 \, b \; \therefore$ (SD1, 7)

$A \, \varepsilon_1 \, b$ (8, 3)

ST19 $[ab] \; \therefore \; [c] : c \, \varepsilon \, a. \; \equiv \; .c \, \varepsilon \, b : \supset : [A] : A \, \varepsilon_1 \, a. \; \equiv \; .A \, \varepsilon_1 \, b$ (**ST**18)

This completes my outline of the proof that the standard system of Leśniewski's Ontology is a part of **S**. As regards the variety of semantical categories L_5, i.e. the language of **S** is richer than L_3, which is Leśniewski's language, but this has no logical or philosophical significance. For to every statement in L_5 there corresponds a statement in L_3, and the truth conditions of the two statements are the same. Thus, if one values economy of expression, one will opt for L_3 rather than L_5. However, if one uses the grammar of an artificial language as a set of coordinates on which to plot grammatical features of ordinary language then L_5 appears to be preferable to any other artificial language (see Lejewski 1975). The differences which the grammar of ordinary language draws between singular names, general names and intransitive verbs are reflected in the differences between certain semantical categories of L_5, whereas in L_1 and L_3 the categorial difference between singular names and general names is obliterated while L_2 and L_4 try to squeeze general names into the mould of intransitive verbs. It is for these reasons that L_5 may prove to be of interest to the general linguist.

Knowledge and truth: a localistic approach

JOHN LYONS

G. K. Chesterton once remarked that the highest compliment that one could pay to an author was to misquote him. Faithful to the spirit, rather than the letter, of this typically Chestertonian paradox, I will correctly (but selectively) quote one of the sentences that appears in Professor Haas's generous and constructive review of one of my own works and show that I have taken it to heart by turning it to my own advantage: 'Every serious methodological commitment which refers specifically to language implies an ontological one: the method is assumed to yield ADEQUATE descriptions' (Haas 1973b :92). I shall have nothing to say about linguistic methodology in this article. But ontological commitment will be very much to the fore; and the question of adequacy – in particular, of explanatory adequacy, in a non-Chomskyan sense of this notoriously Chomskyan term – will also come up for consideration.

It is obvious, not only from the review from which I have just quoted, but from the many works that Professor Haas has devoted to fundamental theoretical and methodological issues in linguistics and the philosophy of language, that he and I differ in what he aptly refers to as 'metaphysical temper'. He may not feel as strongly as I do 'the pull of an old and powerful tradition' (cf. Haas 1973b: 91). But he understands and takes seriously the very traditional question with which I shall be concerned (in a rather untraditional way) in this essay: the interdependence of ontology, grammar and epistemology. And I have no doubt that he will be as tolerant of its almost inevitable failure to meet his own high standards of explicitness and empirical valida-tion as he was of my burgeoning views on semantics when I first came to him for informal advice and discussion about my PhD research some twenty years ago. My essay is speculative rather than empirical;

and, as I have already remarked, it is shot through with ontological commitment. It takes up, and develops in some detail, a thesis that is no more than hinted at in my recent book on semantics: the thesis that the proposition 'X knows *p*' is comparable with, and perhaps derivable from, 'X has *p*' and thence – by virtue of the localistic derivation of 'X has Y' from 'Y is at X' (where Y, unlike *p*, is not restricted to expressions referring to propositions) – from '*p* is at X' (cf. Lyons 1977: 724).

This thesis, in the form in which I have just put it, has one of its sources in the work that I did for my PhD dissertation, when I was struck by the fact (which I found intriguing, but simply recorded without comment) that there were syntactic and semantic parallels in Platonic Greek between 'know' and 'have' and that one of the verbs meaning 'know', *epístasthai*, was synonymous in certain contexts with the word for 'have', *ékhein* (cf. Lyons 1964: 152ff).[1] At the time I was totally unaware of both the more general and the more specific tenets of what has come to be called localism (cf. Anderson 1971, 1973; Lyons 1977: 718ff). But, having been brought up in 'an old and powerful tradition', I was familiar with, and fascinated by, some of the philosophical discussion that there has been, in this tradition, of the concepts of existence, truth and knowledge (not to mention meaning) and of their interconnexions. It was only after I had come to the view, by no means independently (cf. Benveniste 1960; Allen 1964; Kahn 1966; Lyons 1967), that, in some languages at least, there are parallels between existential and locative expressions, on the one hand, and between locative and what are traditionally, but ineptly, referred to as possessive expressions, on the other, that I began to think a little more deeply, and in a localistic frame of mind, about the connexion between knowing and having. I then discovered that others, having come by a different route, were thinking similar thoughts (cf. Anderson 1971: 100). Ultimately, if not finally ('tout se tient'!), I came to see that a case might be made for an intuitively appealing localistic interpretation of truth and epistemic modality.

The purpose of this purely autobiographical preamble is not merely to relate the contents of this essay to the circumstances in which I first

---

[1] I use italics throughout for both forms and expressions (including lexemes) and for both sentences and utterances. I use quotation marks for direct quotation, for meanings and for propositions. To save unnecessary circumlocution, I have also used a representation of the meaning of an English lexeme to stand for a lexeme or set of lexemes in other languages. In all cases the context should make it clear what I am referring to.

met and became intellectually indebted to Professor Haas. I also wish to acknowledge, by inserting such a preamble, the indubitable fact that much of what seems to me either clear or intuitively appealing will not seem so to others, unless their linguistic and philosophical background (and their 'metaphysical temper', which is, in part at least, a product of their own academic history) coincides sufficiently with mine. I cannot, in the space of one short essay, argue for, or even explain fully, all the points that I shall have to take for granted in what follows. Many of them are philosophically controversial; some of them are distinctly unfashionable; but none of them, I think, is untenable. Philosophically-minded linguists and linguistically-inclined philosophers will note, without it being necessary for me to inform them, what is either controversial or unfashionable. I shall be content to make it clear where I stand on any such issue that comes up, if it is directly relevant to the validity of the thesis that I am putting forward. Let us begin then by hacking ourselves a path through some of the philosophical undergrowth. And let us do so, moreover, with an avowed and almost brutal insensitivity to philosophical niceties that are not of immediate concern.

Philosophers often draw a distinction between knowing that something is (or is not) so and knowing how to do something: between propositional knowledge, on the one hand, and what is perhaps best described as performative knowledge (or, more colloquially, know-how), on the other.[2] Whether (and, if so, how) the latter kind of knowledge is reducible to the former (or conversely) is but the first of the many important philosophical issues that we will bypass.[3] As linguists, however, we will note that in many familiar languages there are two different verbs for 'know', one of which is used, in its most characteristic collocations, for propositional knowledge and the other for performative knowledge: e.g. Russian *znatj* and *umetj*. Another distinction that has been drawn by philosophers holds, at first sight at least, between knowing that something is so and knowing some person or thing, in the sense of being acquainted with that person or thing: knowledge-by-acquaintance, as we shall call it (borrowing the

---

[2] The term 'performative' is now more familiar in the sense in which Austin (1962) employed it in his more developed theory of illocutionary acts. There is of course a connexion between the contrast that Austin drew between the descriptive, or constative, and the performative function of language and the opposition that is drawn here between propositional and performative knowledge.

[3] The question whether linguistic competence of the kind that Chomsky (1965) postulates is performative or propositional, or neither, is one such issue.

term, though not the rather peculiar use that he made of it, from Bertrand Russell). Once again, it may be noted that the distinction between knowledge-by-acquaintance, on the one hand, and either propositional or performative knowledge, on the other, is lexicalized in several familiar languages. For example, whereas the most commonly used verb for knowledge-by-acquaintance in French is *connaître*, the most commonly used verb for both propositional and performative knowledge is *savoir*; in German, the lexical distinction between *kennen* and *wissen* corresponds, in what are perhaps their most typical uses, to the distinction between knowledge-by-acquaintance and propositional knowledge (and performative knowledge is subsumed under the more general *können*); in Polish, there is a tripartite lexical distinction, with *znać* being used, in what I take to be its most characteristic contexts of occurrence, for knowledge-by-acquaintance, *umieć* for performative knowledge and *wiedzieć* for propositional knowledge.

For convenience, I will distinguish the three kinds of knowledge by means of numerical subscripts as knowledge$_1$ (knowledge-by-acquaintance), knowledge$_2$ (performative knowledge) and knowledge$_3$ (propositional knowledge), so that the propositional formula 'X knows$_1$ Y' will be interpreted as 'X knows Y by acquaintance', 'X knows$_2$ Y' as 'X knows how to perform Y' and 'X knows$_3$ Y' as 'X knows that Y is so'. The assignment of these numerical subscripts is by no means arbitrary. The most typical objects of knowledge-by-acquaintance are what, in my naive realism, I refer to as first-order entities; and the most typical objects of propositional knowledge are third-order (i.e. intensional) entities (cf. Lyons 1977: 442ff). The ontological status of the most typical objects of performative knowledge is, in the context of the present essay, of less importance. On one fairly plausible view of the matter, however, they constitute that subtype of second-order entities that are commonly referred to as acts: hence my characterization of performative knowledge as knowledge$_2$. It is of course propositional knowledge with which we shall be mainly concerned. The intuitively asymmetrical connexion between propositional knowledge and knowledge-by-acquaintance, however, is not without interest: I take it for granted that, although first-order entities cannot in principle be the objects of knowledge$_3$, third-order entities can be the objects of knowledge$_1$. Whether 'X knows$_3$ p' entails 'X knows$_1$ p' – or, to put it in a more recognizably traditional way, whether all propositional knowledge must be overt and explicit – is a question that has much exercised philosophers.[4] As we shall see later, a more relevant question for our purposes is whether 'X knows$_1$ p' entails 'X knows$_3$ p'.

To forestall the possibility of misunderstanding, there are two points that should be made in connexion with our assignment of subscripts to the three kinds of knowledge. The first point is that, although there is ontological significance in the distinction of lower-order and higher-order entities, the former being regarded as more basic than the latter, no such significance is to be read into the distinction between knowledge$_1$, knowledge$_2$ and knowledge$_3$: it is not being suggested that knowledge$_1$ is more basic than knowledge$_3$. The second point has to do with the statements made above about the lexical recognition of two or three different kinds of knowledge in certain familiar languages. In making such statements, I do not wish to imply that the meaning of the lexemes which I cited can be fully accounted for in this way. Nor do I wish to imply that because, let us say, Latin *scire* and French *savoir* are both used for propositional and performative knowledge in characteristic contexts of occurrence, they are translational equivalents in all contexts. Full translational equivalence between the lexemes of any two natural languages, as far as their everyday vocabulary is concerned, is the exception rather than the rule (cf. Haas 1962b). It may very well be the case, however, that many everyday lexemes can be put into correspondence across languages by virtue of their more or less complete translational equivalence in what Haas (1964a, 1973a) has referred to as their most normal – i.e. their most distinctively normal, or focal – collocations.[5] That distinctive collocational normality, in this sense, can be established, if not wholly, at least partly, in terms of frequency of occurrence is a plausible suggestion (cf. Haas 1964a: 1069). There is at least one language – Platonic Greek – of which I can assert with some confidence, on the evidence of a very considerable and sufficiently homogeneous corpus of material, that the prediction implicit in this suggestion is borne out, as far as the verbs denoting the different kinds of knowledge are

[4] Many other questions can be formulated more precisely than they sometimes are in terms of the distinction between knowledge$_1$ and knowledge$_3$. For example, does 'X knows$_1$ Y' entail 'X knows$_3$ that X knows$_1$ Y'? And does 'X knows$_3$ p' entail 'X knows$_3$ that X knows$_3$ p' (but not 'X knows$_1$ that X knows$_3$ p')? The answers to these last two questions might very well be different, though they are both particular versions of the more general question whether one can know something without knowing that one knows it.

[5] There is a parallel between Haas's notion of focal collocations and the notion of focal denotation with which the proponents of so-called prototype semantics are currently operating. It is to be expected that the two notions would be mutually reinforcing.

concerned (cf. Lyons 1964: 182ff). And in their most distinctively normal collocations there is no doubt that *gignōskein* denotes knowledge$_1$; *epístasthai* denotes knowledge$_2$ and *eidénai* denotes knowledge$_3$.[6] It certainly does not follow from this fact, however, that the Greek *gignōskein* and the Polish *znać* (or the Greek *epístasthai* and the Polish *umieć*) are in all contexts translationally equivalent; and I very much suspect that they are not.

We turn now to the question of truth. There are several philosophical theories of truth. Two of these only need be mentioned here: the correspondence theory and the coherence theory. Roughly speaking, the former says that truth is a matter of correspondence between propositions (or statements) and the world that they purport to describe; the latter, that truth is wholly internal to a set of logically consistent propositions (or statements). It is some version of the correspondence theory of truth that the proponents of truth-conditional semantics have in mind when they say, as they commonly do, that to know the meaning of a sentence (or utterance) is to know what the world would be like if it (or the proposition that it expresses) were true (cf. Kempson 1977). Up to a point this view is both attractive and, it seems to me, tenable. But certain qualifications and reservations must be registered. First of all, I do not accept that all sentences have truth conditions; and I prefer to restrict the notion of truth (i.e. truth-by-correspondence) to propositions, allowing that sentences (and utterances) which have the same propositional content may nonetheless differ in meaning (cf. Lyons 1977). This point is important in the present connexion only in so far as I believe that the attempt that is currently being made by some formal semanticists to account for the whole of the meaning of natural-language sentences in terms of truth conditions involves a kind of unwarranted objectification and propositionalization comparable with the objectification and propositionalization of modality that some, but perhaps not all, natural languages make possible and may indeed encourage. The propositionalization of modality – and more especially of epistemic modality – is one of the topics that will be referred to though not discussed, in a localistic framework, in the present essay.

There is a second qualification that has to be made in connexion with the principle that to know the meaning of a sentence (or utterance) is to know what the world would be like if that sentence (or

[6] In fact, *epístasthai* denotes something narrower than knowledge$_2$ – roughly that part of knowledge$_2$ which is taught by another or comes as a result of systematic study (cf. Lyons 1964).

utterance) – or the proposition that it expresses – is true: it is obviously unreasonable to suppose that every sentence whose meaning is known to any arbitrary speaker of the language in question should be directly verifiable, in terms of correspondence with reality, by that person. It is not even necessary to assume, on Putnam's principle of the 'division of linguistic labour', that every such sentence should be verifiable, in terms of correspondence, by at least one member of the language community (cf. Putnam 1975: 227ff). And it is certainly unnecessary to assume that there is a determinate set of basic sentences, the propositional content of each of which is isomorphic, in some sense, with the state of affairs that it purports to describe. Some propositions (and not only those which express logical truths) may not be verifiable by anyone in terms of correspondence, but are indirectly verifiable in terms of coherence. A language system does not need to be anchored to the physical and social world in which it operates at all points. It suffices that it be so anchored to the world (in terms of the extension of its names and predicates) at a perhaps quite small number of publicly determinable points. This is all that is required for an empirically acceptable version of the correspondence theory of truth to be coupled with the ontology of naive realism and put to use in the construction of a theory of linguistic semantics. The only kind of truth that we are concerned with in this article is truth-by-correspondence. It was important, therefore, to make it clear that it is a rather restricted version of the correspondence theory of truth that is being postulated as valid. My purpose is to show how at least some natural languages enable us not only to make true statements, but also to say that certain statements (or propositions) are true.

In this connexion, it must be emphasized that, whatever the situation might be with respect to the formalization of propositional logic, linguists must treat '*p* is true' as being more complex than, and significantly different from, *p*. I agree with Austin: 'Affirmation and negation are exactly on a level, in this sense, that no language can exist which does not contain conventions for both and that both refer to the world: whereas a language can quite well exist without any device to do the work of "true" and "false" ' (1950).[7] Apart from anything else, it seems to me that whereas it is reasonable to assert both of a man and

---

[7] To be more precise, I would say that it is important to draw a clear distinction between the formulation of positive and negative statements, on the one hand, and the ascription to statements (or to the propositions that they express) of the properties of truth and falsity, on the other.

his dog that each knows that it is raining and that it is propositional knowledge that is involved in each case (cf. the absolutely normal, non-zeugmatic, statement *They both know that it is raining*), I should feel uncomfortable about saying of a dog – or, if we must be open-minded in these matters, of any dog that I have yet encountered – that it knows that 'It is raining' is true. It is my assumption that propositions are logically dependent upon language in that they cannot be said to exist unless they can be formulated in some language (whether natural or constructed) and that they cannot be known (i.e. known$_3$) to be true unless they are knowable (i.e. knowable$_1$) in the language in which they are formulable. Furthermore, although I am prepared to accept that for the formalization of epistemic logic it is reasonable to say that 'X knows$_3$ p' entails p, I am reluctant to say that it entails 'p is true', and still less that it entails 'X knows$_3$ that p if true'. Even if we take knowledge$_3$ to be tacit, rather than overt, I will assume that 'X knows$_3$ that p is true' cannot itself be true unless it is at least possible in principle (by virtue of X's knowledge – knowledge$_2$? – of the language in which p is formulated) for 'X knows$_1$ p' to be true.

I have made these several preliminary points about knowledge and truth for two reasons. First, I want to make it absolutely clear that the underlying structures that I shall be constructing for the localistic analysis of sentences expressing propositions like 'X knows$_3$ p' and 'p is true' are not being postulated as universal. I quoted earlier a short passage from J. L. Austin's famous paper on truth, including in my quotation his statement that a 'language can quite well exist without any device to do the work of "true" and "false" '. Not only do I think that such languages can (could?) exist, but I am inclined to believe that they do. A lot turns upon what is meant by 'do the work of "true" and "false" '. Part of the work of the words *true* and *false* in English is to enable interlocutors to express agreement and disagreement. I suspect though I do not know (and, unless it can be proved that what would seem to be – like the number of the planets – matter for empirical determination is in fact non-empirical, no-one does know) that all natural languages have, if not words, 'devices' of some kind or another (in the limiting case purely prosodic) by means of which interlocutors can indicate their acceptance or rejection of one another's statements, suggestions, proposals, etc.[8] But *true* and *false* in English (and their

[8] It is worth pointing out that *Yes* and *No* in English and the more or less equivalent expressions in other languages are often more satisfactorily analysed as meaning 'I accept/reject that' than as meaning 'That is true/false'.

congeners in certain other languages in comparable collocations) can also be used to assert that something is or is not so, in situations in which the concepts of agreement and disagreement are either inapplicable or of secondary importance. This function of *true* and *false* is what we are concerned with; and I see no reason to believe that it is universal. It may very well be that it is the product, in the historical development of the syntax and vocabulary of particular languages, of a perhaps culturally-determined style of logical discourse.

The second reason is that, although I do not share Professor Haas's conviction, or impression, that there 'cannot' be 'a universal semantic base of grammar', I do agree with him that there is a currently fashionable, but misguided, tendency for linguists to treat a very particular man-made formalization of logic as if it were God-given and universal (cf. Haas 1973b: 101). Many axioms that are eminently reasonable for the formalization of logical discourse are far from being self-evidently acceptable for the semantic analysis of other kinds of discourse and should not be built into the very structure of natural languages by metatheoretical and methodological decision. I reject the view that English (or any other natural language-system) is a formal language with respect to its semantic structure and hold rather to the opinion that the application of the techniques and concepts of standard formal logic to the semantic analysis of natural language-systems depends upon the regimentation, to a greater or lesser degree according to the kind of discourse that is involved, of ordinary language-behaviour (cf. Quine 1960). This prejudice of mine will be evident in various places and it informs the whole of this essay.

One or two other metatheoretical and methodological prejudices that have a bearing on the analysis that is to be presented should be laid bare at this point. Professor Haas, more than anyone else in recent years, has drawn attention to the diversity and incompatibility of the many theories of deep structure that have been, and are, competing for general acceptance and, no less importantly, has challenged the assumption, all too commonly made by the proponents of generative grammar, that surface structure is given, if not by simple observation, at least by the application of straightforward and uncontroversial analytical techniques (cf. Haas 1973b, c, 1975b). I appreciate the force of his criticisms. I nonetheless believe that it is reasonable to say, not only that the notion of surface structure is both less controversial than and logically independent of the notion of deep structure, but also that certain aspects of the surface structure of sentences are more or less indisputable. Furthermore, I see no reason to reject in advance the notion of deep structure itself or the principle that languages are more similar in their deep structures than they are in their surface structures. I will not operate with fully-specified deep structures but with skeletal deep structures containing no more than the information that is required for the present purpose. I do not deny that even these skeletal deep structures (in certain respects non-standard) might be challenged. I have given some justification of them elsewhere (cf. Lyons 1977: 467ff). All that need be said here is that they seem to me to be more perspicuous (in the sense of Strawson 1974) than some of the deep structures proposed by linguists working within a more orthodox transformational framework. I return briefly to the question of descriptive and explanatory adequacy at the end of this essay. Meanwhile I must ask the reader to take the skeletal deep structures on trust and evaluate them, in part, by the use that is made of them here.

In what follows, we shall be guided principally by two insights about the content of propositional knowledge. The first is the relatively unsophisticated observation that it is communicable by means of language and that the process of communication is naturally regarded as one in which information passes from the speaker, or illocutionary agent, to the hearer. This suggests that 'John told Peter that p', like 'John gave Peter the book', can be brought within the scope of the schema CAUSE (X, (Y HAVE Z)) and thus, by virtue of the localistic reduction of (Y HAVE Z) to AT(Z, Y), within the scope of CAUSE (X, (AT(Z, Y))). In so far as propositions are treated as the objects, not only of illocutionary acts, but also of such cognitive attitudes as knowledge and belief, 'Peter knows p' can be construed as saying that Peter is the location (or one of the locations) of p, regardless of whether p has been put there by someone's illocutionary act or not. The reader will see immediately that one of the points to which we shall have to address ourselves is the difference between knowledge$_1$ and knowledge$_3$ in this connexion. 'John told Peter that p' is plausibly analysed from a semantic point of view as having 'Peter knows$_1$ p', rather than 'Peter knows$_3$ p', embedded within it. And yet the most natural, and perhaps the only, interpretation of statements like *Peter knew that it was raining* in English involve 'know$_3$' (whether in addition to or independently of 'know$_1$'). Let us note this as a problem.

The second insight is a more distinctively philosophical one: that there is an intrinsic connexion between truth, reality and existence.

Existence is more general than either reality or truth. To say that something is real is to say that it exists in the actual world and not merely in some perhaps possible, but non-actual, world. The predicate 'real' applies to both first-order entities (persons, animals, things) and second-order entities (states, processes, events, etc.): i.e. to entities that are commonly held to exist (or, in the case of non-static second-order entities, to occur, take place, etc.) in the extensional world that we ourselves inhabit and can refer to. 'True' (in the sense that concerns us) applies only to propositions; and, in so far as propositions (third-order entities) are the intensional correlates of situations in the real world, truth is the intensional correlate of reality. Looked at from this point of view, truth is a higher-order concept than reality. But like reality it is a mode of existence: it is intensional, rather than extensional, existence.

Aristotle's classic formulation of what is generally taken to be a version of the correspondence theory of truth is interesting in this connexion: 'To say of what is that it is not, or of what is not that it is, is false while to say of what is that it is or of what is not that it is not, is true' (*Metaphysics* 1011b, 26–7). Though quoted with approval by Tarski (1944), it differs strikingly from the kind of formulation that a formal semanticist might give these days, in that it introduces the speech–act of assertion.[9] It was of course Austin's (1950) view that 'the primary forms of expression' are such statements as *It is true (to say) that the cat is on the mat*, *The statement that the cat is on the mat is true*, etc., rather than such more obviously metalinguistic statements as '*The cat is on the mat' is true* (which are rare in non-philosophical discourse). It is indeed arguable that the notion of speaking truly is more basic in everyday usage than is the notion of truth that is abstracted from it and incorporated in, say, Tarski's (1944) convention T: 'X is true if, and only if, p' (where 'p' is to be 'replaced by any sentence of the language to which the word "true" refers' and 'X' is to be 'replaced by a name of this sentence'). It may also be the case, as a matter of empirical fact, that many, and perhaps most, natural languages do not allow for the ascription of truth as a property of either sentences or propositions independently of the act of assertion; and that speaking truly may be not so much a matter of being true to the facts as of speaking honestly

[9] The quotation from Aristotle continues: 'And whoever says that [something] is or is not will speak truly (*alētheúsei*) or will speak falsely (*pseúsetai*).' Not only does this, once again, introduce the speech–act of assertion, but it makes use of the verbs *alētheúein* and *pseúdesthai*, which are commonly employed for 'tell the truth' and 'tell lies', respectively. There is of course a very considerable difference between saying what is true and telling the truth.

or in accordance with established opinion.[10] But, I repeat, we are concerned in this essay with the notion of truth which, whether it is basic or not, and whether it is universal or not, is rightly thought of in terms of correspondence between a linguistic entity, on the one hand, and the situation that it describes, on the other.

What is more important, from this point of view, about Aristotle's formulation is that it uses the verb 'to be' in its so-called absolute function (i.e. without a complement) in expressions which in Greek (*tò ŏn* and *tò mè̄ ŏn*) are much more obviously higher-order nominals in surface structure than are the corresponding expressions in the English translation. Now the expression *tò ŏn* is translatable equally well in this context, as very often in Greek, as *what is real* (or even *reality*); and, when it is used absolutely, the verb 'to be' can be used quite freely in Greek with either a first-order or a second-order nominal as its subject. But there are other contexts, in which the verb 'to be' can be used absolutely to ascribe the property of truth to what is said, rather than to ascribe reality to what is being described. Indeed, Aristotle himself points this out later in the same work (*Metaphysics* 1017a: 31–2). There is no reason to believe that what has been aptly referred to as the veridical use of the verb 'to be' involves the deletion of the adjective 'true' (*àlēthés*).[11] Indeed, there is no reason to believe that the verb 'to be' differs in meaning according to whether it is translatable in English as *to exist*, *to be real* or *to be true*. It is worth noting, at this point, that the very common expressions of assent and dissent *taûta ĕsti* (lit. 'These things are') and *ĕsti oûtōs* (lit. 'It is so') can be construed equally well (and more readily perhaps than can the English *That is so*) as either 'The situation is as you say it is/That situation does (indeed) exist' or

---

[10] Detienne (1967) argues that the Greek concept of truth was magical and religious in origin; and that its secularization and objectivization was the product of the secularization of language by the rationalizing philosophers of the sixth and fifth centuries BC. Whatever one thinks of the details of his account, one must surely agree that the notion of truth that is enshrined in the correspondence theory, coupled, as it usually is, with presuppositions of objectivity and immutability, is a product of social and cultural development and may not be found in all societies.

[11] The term 'veridical' is Kahn's (1973: 331ff). It is particularly apt in that it relates being true to the arguably more basic notions of speaking truly and telling the truth (see above, n. 9). Kahn points out that 'earlier authors who took notice of the veridical use generally grouped it with existential uses'. He himself objects to this (whilst admitting the undoubted similarities) on the grounds that 'in the veridical construction [the verb 'to be'] takes a subject which is sentential in form'. However, I believe that, if truth is treated as third-order existence, both the similarities and the differences that he notes between veridical and other kinds of existential constructions are accounted for. The development of my ideas on the relationship between existence, truth and reality, as well as my understanding of the Greek constructions, has been strongly influenced by Kahn's work.

'What you say is true'. It is only when it is clear that what is being referred to is a second-order entity or a third-order entity that the two interpretations 'be real' and 'be true' are semantically distinguishable; and in the context in question they are of course pragmatically equivalent. We can, for convenience, distinguish three uses of the verb 'to be' – 'be$_1$', 'be$_2$' and 'be$_3$' – according to whether its subject is a first-order, a second-order or a third-order nominal. But these are not three distinct meanings, as 'know$_1$', 'know$_2$', and 'know$_3$', are arguably different meanings of the English verb *know*.

It is at this point, if not earlier, that the nominalist is likely to start talking somewhat testily of Plato's beard and Occam's razor (cf. Quine 1948). But he would be wrong to do so, I believe, in the present instance. The thesis to which I subscribe, in so far as it rests upon the assumption that there are first-order entities (notably persons and animals) whose ontological status as individuals is independent of the existence or use of language, is obviously incompatible with the most extreme version of latter-day nominalism. It is perfectly compatible with traditional versions of nominalism and does not commit its adherents to Platonic, or even Aristotelian, realism.[12] Indeed, the thesis that I am developing is a characteristically nominalistic one, in that it holds that the domain of language-independent existence is greatly extended by language – and perhaps differently by different languages – by the transformational process of nominalization, on the one hand, and by the devices that particular languages make available for individuation and quantification, on the other. Nor is my unabashed postulation of propositions, as distinct from sentences and statements, in any way reprehensible within a nominalistic framework. For it is not being suggested that such intensional entities as propositions exist, or subsist, independently of the language or languages in which they are formulated. On the contrary, the whole tenor of my argument will be that propositions are created by language and that the process of propositionalization may have been carried further by some natural languages than it has been by others. Propositions (in the sense in which the term 'proposition' is being employed here) may be theoretically dispensable, as many have argued, in favour of sentences. But I find it terminologically conve-

---

[12] What is Aristotelian perhaps is the desire to relate the various uses of the verb 'to be' to a single basic function. But, as Kahn (1973: 3ff) points out, although this may be contrary to 'the Mill–Russell–Carnap tradition' in modern logic, it has its parallels in the work of Leśniewski (who did not blush to use the term 'ontology') and even of Quine.

nient, to say the least, to be able to draw a distinction between a sentence and its propositional content, to affirm that two sentences (of the same language or of two different languages) may be used, as statements, to assert the same proposition and so on.[13] Nothing of what follows, however, turns upon the irreducibility of the distinction between sentences and propositions. We shall return to the notion of propositionalization. But, first, let us develop the more specifically linguistic part of the thesis.

It is arguable that, although first-order entities – or, to be more precise, a distinguished subset of them (notably persons and animals) – are, as we have assumed, ontologically basic, second-order and third-order entities are partly, if not wholly, dependent for their essence and their existence upon the grammatical structure of particular languages. In some languages, if not all, one can nominalize the propositional content of sentences and use the resultant phrases (as second-order nominals) to refer to, to re-identify and to quantify overt situations in the real world. It is only because one can do this that one can treat any situation, should one wish to do so, as an individual and say that it exists (or that it occurs, is in progress, etc.). Similarly, and perhaps more obviously, with respect to such third-order entities as propositions, which serve as the objects of illocutionary acts and of knowledge. It is quite possible that not all natural languages provide the means for referring to propositions and distinguishing them clearly, as intensional entities, from the situations that they describe. But some natural languages do; and formal languages are readily provided with the means of doing so by introducing the simple technical device of quotation marks for the construction of metalinguistic names.[14] As far as English is concerned, there is little doubt, that the language-system permits the formation of both second-order and third-order nominals by means of productive rules of nominalization;

[13] It is important for a linguist to emphasize that it is no more than a contingent fact of English and of some, but not all, other natural languages that declarative sentences can be used, without variation of form, in three distinguishable functions: (i) to assert that something is so; (ii) to refer to themselves (or to the propositions that they express) in metalinguistic statements, and when they have this function, to be subjects of the predicate 'true' (*'Snow is white' is true*); (iii) to express the propositional content of the protasis of a conditional clause, of the complement of a verb of saying or knowing, etc. If declarative sentences did not have all three functions, Tarski's (1944) famous example *'Snow is white' is true if, and only if, snow is white* could not be formulated in more or less natural English to satisfy his convention T. This does not affect the principle underlying convention T; but it does make its formulation in terms of sentences, rather than propositions, less attractive for certain natural languages than for others.

[14] It is worth noting that this is a technical device, for which there is relatively little backing in the normal use of English. For example, sentences like *'Snow is white' is true* are decidedly odd, if

and there are many non-derived second-order or third-order nouns in the everyday vocabulary of the average native speaker (cf. Lyons 1977: 446). In the rules and schemata to be given and discussed in this essay first-order, second-order and third-order nominals will be symbolized (with superscript numerals) as NP^1, NP^2, and NP^3 respectively, regardless of whether they are derived by means of a productive syntactic transformation or not.[15]

If we assume that existential and possessive constructions are derivable, ultimately, from underlying locative structures such as:[16]

(1) NP (+ Cop) + Loc

and (if we admit the possibility of locative subjects, cf. Lyons 1977: 455ff):

(2) Loc (+ Cop) + N

and:

(3) Loc (+ Cop) + NP

it is obvious that the constructions that we are concerned with in this essay should be derived from the very same underlying locative structures; and, provided that we temporarily disregard the problem of the existence of false propositions (and the associated problem of communicating propositions which, whether true or false, are not accepted as true by the person to whom they are communicated) this is both straightforward enough from a formal point of view and intuitively satisfying.

Although sentences like *The book is on the table* and *John has the book* are very different in their surface structure, in that (i) *The book* is the subject-nominal in the former and (under standard analyses) the object-nominal in the latter and (ii) the former contains what is indisputably a predicative locative complement, *on the table*, and the latter

not actually ungrammatical, in non-philosophical English. A far more natural sentence is *It is true that snow is white*, in which the extraposed nominal clause is hardly to be thought of as the name of a sentence, though it is perhaps correctly said to refer to the proposition that is expressed by *Snow is white* (see above, n. 13).

[15] For some discussion of the degree to which nominalization is a productive syntactic process in English, cf. Chomsky (1970).

[16] 'NP' stands for 'noun phrase' (or 'nominal'), 'Loc' for 'locative phrase' (this term being construed broadly to include both positional and directional expressions) and 'Cop' for 'copula'. This symbol for the copula is put in parentheses to indicate that it is optional in some languages and perhaps eliminable from deep structures. For further details and discussion, cf. Lyons (1977: 455ff).

an entity-referring subject-nominal, *John*, there are good reasons for saying that both are analysable, at a deeper grammatical level, in terms of (1). Both sentences may be used to answer the question *Where is the book?* (which makes fewer presuppositions than *Who has the book?*, but may be used in situations in which *Who has the book?* is equally appropriate); and when they are used with this communicative function the prosodic contour that is superimposed upon the two sentences clearly indicates that *John* has the same role as *on the table*. It is of course possible for *John has the book* to be used in answer to the explicit or implicit question *What has John got?* (or some more general question about John), provided that the book that is being referred to is salient in the universe of discourse. But *John has the book* will then differ in prosodic structure; and its congener will not be *The book is on the table*, but rather *The table has the book on it*, which is perhaps to be derived from (3), rather than (1). The surface structure constraints of English render the following sentences ungrammatical: **The book is at John*, **The table has the book* (unless the table is personified: cf. Lyons 1977: 380, 442), **Where has the book?* and possibly (?)*Which place has the book?* And the fact that there is this distributional asymmetry, supported as it is by semantic and intonational parallelism, strongly suggests that both *John has the book* (in the appropriate interpretation) and *The book is on the table* are to be derived from a structure like (1), containing a first-order nominal: namely NP^1 (+ Cop) + Loc. The difference between the two sentences is to be accounted for, therefore, in terms of the difference between a locative which contains a person-referring (or animal-referring) nominal and one which contains a thing-referring nominal.

It follows from the more specific assumptions that we are making in this article that *John knows that Peter is ill* is to be derived from a structure like:

(4) NP^3 (+ Cop) + Loc

or:

(5) Loc (+ Cop) + NP^3

As Anderson (1971: 100ff) has pointed out, *know* is both syntactically and semantically comparable with the more obviously locative verb *contain*. Though *John contains many facts* is hardly more acceptable perhaps than **John has many facts*, there is nothing at all unusual about *This book contains many facts*, which (like *This book has many facts in it*) is derivable from (5).[17] The phrase *many facts* is patently a third-order nominal. The difference between *John knows many facts* and *This book contains many facts* is to be accounted for, therefore, in terms of the difference between personal and non-personal location. Hence Anderson's informal localistic gloss on *Many people know part of the truth* and what he refers to as its 'copular' version *Part of the truth is known to many people*: '(knowledge of) part of the truth is associated with ("located with respect to") many people'.

The 'copular' version is more directly relatable to (4) than it is to (5). That *John knows many facts* would probably be thought of as being more basic than *Many facts are known to John* is explicable in terms of the general principle, operative in English and many languages, whereby personal nominals tend to be put in subject-position. It is this principle which explains the origin and the differential development of a variety of 'have'-structures in the several Indo-European languages. Looked at from this point of view the stative passive evident in *Many facts are known to John* is comparable with the reflexive/middle *se habere* in Latin (cf. *Res ita se habent*, lit. 'Things have themselves thus'), the reflexive/passive *imetjsja* in Russian (cf. *Imeetsja u nego . . .*, lit. 'There is had at him . . .'), etc., which, though morphologically more complex than the corresponding active forms, are syntactically equivalent to forms of the copular verb par excellence: the verb 'to be'. In other words, it can be seen as a matter of historical accident that English has sentences like *Many facts are known to John*, but neither *This book is had to John*, on the one hand, nor *Many facts are at/to John*, on the other. It has often been pointed out that there is a sense in which 'have' is the passive equivalent (i.e. the converse) of the locative and existential copula. When 'have' or 'know' develops its own morphological passive, reflexive or middle voice we get back, as it were, to the starting point: the converse of the converse of the relation R is equivalent to R ($R'' \equiv R$).

Let us now suppose that, just as we have recognized lower-order and higher-order nominals, so we can recognize both higher-order and lower-order locatives. A first-order locative, whether predicative or purely referential, will relate to spatial location; a second-order locative will relate to temporal location; and a third-order locative will

[17] It is not difficult to construct a context in which *John has many facts* and *John's facts* are perfectly acceptable – John might have been collecting facts and listing them in a book or a filing case. Clearly a more careful treatment of the question would have to draw a distinction between this kind of possession or appurtenance and the kind of intensional location that we are concerned with in this article.

relate to what may be referred to as intensional location. The distinction between spatial and temporal locatives, and their characterization as first-order and second-order locatives (Loc^1 and Loc^2) respectively, need not be justified here (cf. Lyons, 1968: 348f; 1977: 719). It is the distinction between spatial and intensional, or third-order, location that concerns us most in the present connexion. Let us therefore split (4) and (5) into:[18]

(4a) NP^3 (+ Cop) + Loc^1
(4b) NP^3 (+ Cop) + Loc^3
(5a) Loc^1 (+ Cop) + NP^3
(5b) Loc^3 (+ Cop) + NP^3

It is obvious that *Many facts are known to John/Many facts are (contained) in this book* and *John knows many facts/This book contains many facts* are to be derived from (4a) and (5a), rather than from (4b) and (5b). For John and the book are first-order entities; and they serve to identify first-order locations. What then is the intensional correlate of a first-order location? The most obvious candidate, I would suggest, is what is formalized in modern modal logic in terms of the notion of possible worlds (cf. Allwood *et al.* 1977: 22, 108). One of the advantages of the notion of possible worlds is that it allows us to relativize truth (and knowledge) to a particular viewpoint or occasion and to treat absolute truth as a particular, and special, kind of relative truth. To say that a proposition is true in some possible world is to say no more than that it exists in that intensional world; to say that it is true absolutely is to say that it exists in the particular intensional world that is in correspondence with the extensional world of reality and, according to the concept of truth with which we normally operate in our culture, is eternal, objective and immutable. Truth, as we said earlier, is intensional existence. A sentence like *It is true that it is raining* or *That is so* (construed in such a way that *that* is held to refer to a proposition) is derivable from (4b), as *John exists* is derivable from:

(4c) NP^1 (+ Cop) + Loc^1

and *It is known that it is raining*, by means of extraposition, from (4a). What all these three sentences have in common, distinguishing them from *If . . ., (then) it is true that it is raining* (where the conditional clause

---

[18] The reader might find it helpful to interpret these schemata as follows: (4a) 'A third-order entity is in/at a first-order location'; (5a) 'A first-order location contains a third-order entity'; and so on.

sets an index to a set of possible worlds to which the optional deictic adverbial *then* refers), *John is (over) there* and *It is known to John that it is raining*, is the characteristic that the locative predicate, Loc^1 or Loc^3 as the case may be, is left unspecified.

This analysis, it will be noted, extends the localistic analysis of existence proposed in Lyons (1975; 1977: 723; etc.) in two directions. And it enables us not only to relativize truth, but also to objectify knowledge. The objectivization of knowledge by means of such propositions as 'It is known that p' (derived here from NP^3 (+ Cop) + Loc^1, with Loc^1 left unspecified) is something that Popper has written about in several of his recent essays (cf. Popper 1972). What he calls 'knowledge without a knowing subject' is objective; and, as he rightly points out, much of what counts as objective knowledge in the technological and literate society in which we live, may not be known subjectively to even a single member of society. It is stored in books, computer memories, etc. And yet, whether we treat objective knowledge in Popper's sense as corrigible (as he does) or incorrigible, there would seem to be an important semantic difference between 'It is known that p' and 'It is true that p'. Even if the former is held to entail the latter, the latter certainly does not entail the former. Our analysis preserves this distinction: in the contrast between an unspecified Loc^1 and an unspecified Loc^3.

Since we now have two kinds of intensional existence – the one being an abstraction from, and arguably an idealization of, subjective knowledge, the other being absolute truth construed as a special case, and arguably an idealization, of relative truth – we have, in part at least, solved the problem of both relating and distinguishing knowledge and truth at the intensional level.

We now come to the analysis of expressions for the communication of propositional knowledge. Once again, this is both formally straightforward and (provided that we continue to disregard the problems alluded to above) intuitively satisfying. As we saw earlier, communication can be thought of, like giving, as a process of causing some entity – in the case of communication, an intensional entity – to travel from its source, X, to its goal, Y (cf. Miller & Johnson-Laird 1976: 626ff). If X communicates p to Y, X thereby and therein makes p known to Y. *Peter told John that it was raining* is naturally accounted for, therefore, by assuming that *tell* is associated in the lexicon of English with a causative, or operative–factitive, valency-schema in which the innermost predicative structure is a first-order personal locative (cf.

Lyons 1977: 491ff). Under this analysis, the difference between *Peter told John that it was raining* and *Peter made (it) known that it was raining* is identical with the difference between *John knows that it is raining* and *It is known that it is raining*.

It might be thought that *Peter said that it was raining*, rather than *Peter made (it) known that it was raining* (*Peter told that it was raining* being ungrammatical), is the sentence which corresponds most closely to *Peter told John that it was raining*, differing from it solely in that Loc[1] is left unspecified. This is perhaps a defensible view. But I want to suggest a more interesting derivation of 'X says that *p*' below. In partial justification, I would here mention the fact that the English verb *say* can be construed, according to context, in two radically different ways: roughly, as meaning either 'assert' or 'utter' (cf. Lyons, 1977: 740ff). It is perhaps possible, though unusual, to employ *say* in the sense of 'assert' with an overt personal locative: namely *Peter said to John that it was raining*. But the truth conditions of *Peter said to John that it was raining* are arguably different from those of *Peter told John that it was raining*. In particular, the former, but not the latter, could be true even if John did not understand what was said to him. The point is subtle but, I think, valid. When the verb *say* occurs with an overt personal locative (e.g. *What did X say to Y?*) it is much more likely to be construed as (roughly) 'utter' (cf. Miller & Johnson-Laird 1976: 620ff). Furthermore, in such circumstances the locative phrase is less obviously a complement of *say* than it is of *tell* in superficially similar sentences. I would suggest that *Peter said that it was raining* carries no implication whatsoever of there being an addressee and that its truth, unlike that of *Peter said to John that it was raining*, but like that of *Peter told John that it was raining*, depends upon Peter's fulfilment of the felicity conditions for assertion. *Peter said to John that it was raining* can be construed as meaning 'Peter directed at John an utterance which would normally be used to assert that it is raining' and under this interpretation, which may or may not be rather forced, the proposition expressed would be true if Peter had said, for example, *Es regnet* or *Il pleut* regardless of whether John, or even Peter, understood German or French. And it is worth pointing out that, contrary to what is sometimes suggested in philosophical discussions of direct and indirect speech, *Peter said (to John) 'It is raining'* might well be held to be true if Peter had uttered *Es regnet* or *Il pleut*. Since the verb *say* in the sense 'utter' does not concern us here, I will disregard such sentences; and I will provide a different analysis for sentences containing *say* in the sense 'assert' from the one suggested for sentences containing *tell*.

We must now face the problem, which will no doubt have occurred to the reader, that, whereas in 'X knows that *p*' it is propositional knowledge (knowledge$_3$) that is involved, in 'X makes *p* known to Y' it is much more plausibly taken to be knowledge-by-acquaintance (knowledge$_1$) or something akin to it. The first point that must be made in this connexion is that the everyday use of the verb *know* with a *that*-complement frequently shows the connexion between knowledge-by-acquaintance and propositional knowledge. For example, the question *Did you know that the sun is over 93 million miles away from the earth?* – and it is important to note the past tense – is frequently employed in situations where *Have you heard/been told that . . .?* or *Are you aware that . . .?* is equally appropriate. The object of knowledge is certainly propositional, but the sense of *know* that is predominant here is surely 'know$_1$', rather than 'know$_3$'. It might be argued that *Did you know that . . .?* still commits the questioner to the truth of the proposition that is expressed by the complement of *know* and that it would be wrong for the respondent to reply (without qualification) *Yes, but it's not true* (or *Yes, but I don't believe it*). The fact remains that it is not always easy to draw a sharp distinction between 'know$_1$' and 'know$_3$' in the cases like this.[19] It is worth noting also that in some languages in which there is a morphological or periphrastic causative verb derived from a simpler verb meaning 'know$_3$', the causative may not carry the same presuppositions as the simpler verb. For example, *faire savoir* in French does not carry the same presuppositions in normal usage as *savoir: Je lui ai fait savoir qu'il pleuvait* (lit. 'I made him know that it was raining') does not commit the speaker to the truth of the complement of *savoir* and is more or less equivalent to the English *I informed him that it was raining*.

A second point is that it is quite possible to use the verb *know* in English with an object-expression referring to a proposition and for *know* to have the sense 'know$_1$', rather than 'know'$_3$. Indeed, if the referring expression names the proposition, this is the only interpreta-

---

[19] One could add many other instances of the use of *know* in English where propositional knowledge is involved, but where 'know$_1$' is also prominent. For example, *How do you know that it is raining?* is perhaps best interpreted, on many occasions of its use, as meaning 'By what means have you been made aware that it is raining?' and as being neutral with respect to factivity. Or again, if X mentions to Y some fact (or something that is presented as a fact) and Y responds with *I know*, Y's utterance will commonly sustain the interpretation 'I have (already) been informed (of that)', rather than 'I hold that to be true (and can justify my belief if necessary)'.

tion that *know* can sustain. For example, *Goldbach's conjecture* is the name of the proposition to the effect that every even number is the sum of two primes. This proposition is known$_1$ to many mathematicians, but so far, apparently its truth value has not been demonstrated (cf. Popper 1972: 118, 160). The statement *Many mathematicians know Goldbach's conjecture* is true. So too is *Many mathematicians know the proposition 'Every even number is the sum of two primes'*. But *Many mathematicians know that every even number is the sum of two primes*, which can only be interpreted as involving knowledge$_3$, would normally be held to be false by anyone who subscribes to the view that 'X knows$_3$ *p*' entails 'X knows$_3$ that *p* is true' or '*p* is true'.

It is quite possible then, to know propositions by acquaintance – and even to know them by name, if they are sufficiently portentous to have a name. Furthermore, this kind of knowledge seems to be at least as relevant as knowledge$_3$ when we think of the advance of science. For example, the statement *Pythagoras's theorem was known to the ancients* cannot but be interpreted as involving knowledge$_1$. So too for *The theorem that the square of the hypotenuse of a right angle is equal to the sum of the squares of the other two sides was known to the ancients*. But what about *It was known to the ancients that the square of the hypotenuse . . . the other two sides*? If pressed, we might say that this involves knowledge$_3$, and that, even in a case like this, 'X knows$_3$ *p*' does not entail 'X knows$_1$ *p*'. But it must be granted that what is referred to in our culture as scientific knowledge – i.e. a constantly growing (and not necessarily incorrigible) body of propositions – is frequently described by means of statements in which it makes very little difference whether we take the verb *know* as meaning 'know$_1$' or 'know$_3$'; and that, if we are forced, or inclined, to draw the distinction sharply, we have to rely upon the syntactic structure of the language to do so in particular instances.

Many philosophical problems have arisen as a consequence of the attempt to reconcile the subjectivity and corrigibility of personal knowledge and belief with the concept of eternal and immutable truth; and modern epistemic logic has inherited these possibly insoluble problems. As far as the communication and storage (in Loc^1) of propositional information is concerned, the objective truth of the information (its existence in Loc^3) is irrelevant. It is reasonable to assume that no proposition is stored unless it is held to be true. Provided that the language that is employed is rich enough to permit metalinguistic reference, whether by name or otherwise, to other propositions, it can be used to formulate and store not only p, but 'p is false' (i.e. the negative proposition, itself held to be true, 'p is not in Loc^3'). For example, having been told authoritatively, but perhaps wrongly, that Goldbach's conjecture is false, one might store the metalinguistic proposition 'Goldbach's conjecture is not in Loc^3' (and hold it to be true) without necessarily being able to formulate Goldbach's conjecture in propositional form. The existence of false propositions and negative propositions is no problem at all in so far as they constitute the content of personal knowledge and belief. Not only does it make perfect sense to say *People in the Middle Ages knew that the world was flat*, but it is arguable that, in saying this, one is making a true statement (cf. Miller & Johnson–Laird, 1976: 641).

Once we adopt this point of view, the connexion between 'know$_1$' and 'know$_3$' is at least pragmatically explicable. By communicating p to Y, X does no more than acquaint Y with p. But by virtue of the felicity conditions associated with the illocutionary act of assertion, X is himself committed to the truth of p; and he licenses Y to store p. For one reason or another, Y may refuse to accept the gift that is offered him. In the paradigm case, however, Y will accept p (i.e. hold it to be true) and store it (in Loc^1); and both 'X told Y that p' and 'Y (now) knows$_3$ p' (and not merely 'Y (now) knows$_1$ p') will be true. Since the purpose of acquainting someone with p is normally to get him to know$_3$ p, it is natural that, in many languages, the morphological or periphrastic causative of know$_3$ should be used to mean 'inform'.

It is also natural, though by no means inevitable, that, in a language in which the difference between 'know$_1$' and 'know$_3$' is lexicalized, the verb which means 'know$_1$' should come to be employed, in addition to, or in place of 'know$_3$', for that kind of propositional knowledge which comes by intuition or immediate observation, rather than by discursive reasoning or by means of another's communicative act. (This is true of *gignōskein* in Platonic Greek, but not of *connaître* in French). It is no less surprising that some languages, like English, should draw no lexical distinction between 'know$_1$' and 'know$_3$'. The semantic distinction between them is sharp enough in what we assumed to be their focal collocations at the very beginning of this essay. But, as has now become clear, the two senses tend to come together, at least pragmatically, in the paradigm instance of the communication of propositional knowledge.

We come finally to what is perhaps the most controversial part of our analysis. If 'X makes (it) known that p' is the causative correlate of

(4a) with Loc^1 left unspecified, what is the causative correlate of (4b) with Loc^3 left unspecified? The answer, I suggest, is simply 'X says that p'. This is tantamount to the proposal that the illocutionary act of assertion should be thought of as an act of creation (in the most literal sense). By uttering S under the appropriate conditions – S being an utterance-unit, and in the standard case a declarative text-sentence, which expresses p (cf. Lyons 1977: 633) – X puts p in Loc^3: i.e. he makes it true by giving to it the particular kind of intensional existence that we have associated with truth, rather than knowledge.

The thesis that saying p makes p true is at first sight highly counter-intuitive in two quite different respects: (i) the principle that assertion is a sufficient condition of truth would seem to run foul of the evident fact that we can express objectively false propositions no less readily that we can express true propositions; (ii) the principle that assertion is a necessary condition of truth would seem to exclude the possibility of there being any true, but so far unasserted, propositions. These objections, I would suggest, are misdirected. As far as (i) is concerned, we have already noted that the existence of false propositions is a problem to which we must address ourselves. Let us do so now.

We have related the notion of third-order location to the logician's concept of an intensional world. This is of course a very abstract and sophisticated concept. We may think of an intensional world, for our purposes, as a set of descriptive propositions which is constructed, in the course of a normal conversation, by the collaborative effort of the participants. Any such intensional world, provided that it is internally consistent, will truly describe a possible, though perhaps unreal, extensional world. Indeed, it is quite common for the participants in an everyday conversation to create a more or less elaborate imaginary or fictional world simply by saying that something is so. Provided that the notion of truth with which we are operating is that of relative, rather than absolute, truth, the alleged existence of false propositions is a pseudoproblem. For intensional existence and relative truth, as we saw earlier, are indistinguishable. The alleged existence of false propositions would be a genuine problem for the analysis only if it were being maintained that the very act of asserting p makes p objectively, or absolutely true; and that would indeed be an absurd thesis to maintain.

What then of the concept of absolute truth? It is undoubtedly the case that this concept is widely operative in our culture. But we can also think of the world of absolute truth, or at least of our access to it, as being partly dependent upon the notion of authoritative acts of assertion. *Who says/said so?* is a common challenge when the objective truth of a proposition is at issue. There are two ways of construing this. It may be taken as a straightforward enquiry as to the identity of whoever is assumed to have access to the independently existing intensional world of objective truth. But it may also be taken, I would suggest, as an enquiry as to the identity of the person who first placed the proposition in question in the constantly expanding, and in practice changing, body of propositions that we think of, at any one time, as objective and immutable truth. However that may be, it suffices for the thesis that is being maintained here that 'X says that p' should be plausibly analysable as 'X makes p (relatively) true'.

Less time need be spent in countering objections to the implication, or apparent implication, that a proposition cannot be true unless or until it has been asserted. Once again, there is no problem as far as relative truth is concerned. In posing or asking the question whether p holds, we do of course presuppose that p has a determinate (though perhaps undiscoverable) truth value, regardless of whether any assertion is made in response to the question or not. It is nonetheless reasonable to say that anyone who answers the question contributes to the construction of an intensional world (whether it is the world of objective truth or not) by putting either p or its contradictory in it. And this is all that is required by way of an intuitive justification of the thesis that truth is the product of assertion.

Mention has been made of Popper's notion of objective knowledge. It might be helpful to the reader if I now relate the ontological and epistemological part of what I have been saying more explicitly than I did earlier to Popper's theory of the three Worlds – World 1 being the real world of persons, animals and physical objects (and of the situations in which they are involved), World 2 being the subjective world of human beliefs, expectations, intentions, etc. and World 3 being the World of objective and autonomous knowledge (cf. Popper 1972). It is of course Popper's view of World 3 which constitutes the most original part of his theory. As physical entities (first-order entities in my terminology) we human beings are part of the furniture of World 1. As knowing subjects, we create World 2 (partly no doubt by virtue of the species-specific innate ideas, or expectations, with which we are endowed); as creatures that possess language – i.e. a communication system which, in addition to its expressive and instrumental functions, has both a descriptive and an argumentative function – we are capable of formulating objective, World 3, knowledge. 'With the descriptive function of human language', Popper says, 'the regulative idea of truth emerges, that is, of a description which fits the facts' (Popper 1972: 120).

It is important to realize that the distinction between World 2 and World 3, in so far as knowledge is concerned, is a distinction between subjective and objective knowledge. Construed as psychological entities, propositions are, in Popper's scheme, denizens of World 2; as non-psychological entities – the product of the process of objectification – they inhabit World 3. Furthermore, whereas World 3 knowledge is necessarily propositional, World 2 knowledge is only partly propositional. The creation of World 3 knowledge therefore involves, not only objectification, but also, in many cases, what I will refer to as propositionalization.

Now there are several points that can be made, and brought into sharper focus, in relation to Popper's scheme. First of all, Popper is clearly right to emphasize, as he does, that the word *knowledge* is frequently employed, both in scientific discourse and in everyday conversation, in its objective sense and that traditional epistemology, taking knowledge to be a certain kind of belief, fails to give proper recognition to this fact (Popper 1972: 110, 122). He is also right, no doubt, to make the notion of regulative truth by correspondence dependent upon language. It seems to me quite likely, however, as I said earlier, that this particular notion of truth is culturally restricted. Furthermore, although all natural languages provide their users, presumably, with the means of making descriptive statements (with or without epistemic or evidential qualification) and thus of expressing propositions which, if held to be sufficiently authoritative, come to be part of World 3 knowledge for the society in which the statements are made, languages will differ considerably in respect of the means that they provide, grammatical and lexical, for the objectification and propositionalization of World 2 beliefs, feelings and attitudes. I think it very probable that in many, and perhaps most, languages that have not been used extensively for more or less dispassionate philosophical and academic discussion, it is not possible to express and distinguish 'X knows p', 'p is known (objectively)' and 'p is true'. But we certainly can express and distinguish all three – and, in particular, we can distinguish 'p is known (objectively)' from 'p is true' – in many languages. In this article, I have been concerned to show how a language may, but of course need not, create a set of proposition-referring expressions by nominalization and enable its users to say such things as 'X knows p', 'p is known' and 'p is true' by embedding third-order nominals in locative constructions. One cannot infer from the analysis that has been provided some of the more particular implications of 'know$_3$' and 'true': that 'X knows$_3$ p' entails 'p is true' (or, as I should prefer to put it, that one would not say 'X knows$_3$ p' unless one held p to be true); that if p is true, it is eternally true; and so on. There is perhaps no good reason to believe that these more particular implications are universally associated with what we should otherwise regard as the translational equivalents of *X knows that p*, *It is known that p* and *p is true*.

We can now take up, albeit briefly, the question of epistemic modality. At one point, Popper criticizes epistemic logic for its perpetuation of the traditional view of knowledge as being necessarily subjective (1972: 140ff). His criticism depends of course upon his distinction between World 2 and World 3 knowledge. There is a sense, however, in which epistemic logic objectifies and propositionalizes what Popper regards as World 2 knowledge. An English utterance like *It may rain* can certainly be construed on occasion, as it is treated in epistemic logic, as a statement which contains, not only the simple non-modal proposition 'It rains' (or 'It will rain'), but also a more complex modal proposition, true or false, which is a function of it. That this is so is evident from the fact that it is possible to make such statements in everyday English as *The fact that it may rain does not deter me*, *John knew that it might rain* and even (though the use of epistemically interpretable modal verbs in the protasis of a conditional sentence is less common) *If it may rain, why don't you take your umbrella?*. But I have argued elsewhere, in accordance with what has surely been the standard view among linguists until recently, that what we have now learnt to call epistemic modality in the everyday use of English and other languages is usually subjective, not just in Popper's sense that it relates to World 2 knowledge, but in the more particular sense that it directly reflects the illocutionary agent's involvement in the utterance-act and is not part of the propositional content of his utterance-signal (cf. Lyons 1977: 793ff). And current epistemic logic gives a very unsatisfactory account – or rather gives no account at all – of this kind of non-propositional modality.

All languages may very well provide their users with the means – grammatical, prosodic or lexical – for the subjective epistemic qualification of their utterances. Relatively few languages, I would surmise, have developed the means for the propositionalization of epistemic modality. However, in so far as objective epistemic modality can be formalized in terms of an accessibility relation holding between possible worlds (cf. Allwood *et al.* 1977: 113), it would seem to have an intuitively natural interpretation within a localistic framework of the kind that has been outlined here. Different specifications, personal or non-personal, of Loc^1 enable us to distinguish between different members of a set of intensional worlds indexed in terms of the location of the propositions that comprise them. For example, given that $B_a p$ formalizes '*a* believes (that) *p*', which under our analysis is seen as having the structure '*p* is at *a*' (no distinction being drawn between knowledge and belief as far as the first-order location of intensional entities is concerned), this is converted, in straightforward fashion, to $Loc^1_a p$: namely '*p* is a member of the set of propositions that are held in store at *a*'. We can relate Loc^1_a (the contents of *a*'s store of propositional knowledge) either to the world of absolute truth, i.e. an unspecified Loc^3, or to a particular member, or subset, of logically possible worlds, indexing or quantifying Loc^3, appropriately. But this is a big topic whose further development must be left for another occasion.[20]

It now remains to say something about descriptive and explanatory adequacy and, in doing so, to bring this essay to its conclusion. As Chomsky (1965: 27ff) has explicated these notions, a descriptively adequate grammar of any natural language is one that not only generates, in the ideal, all and only the sentences of that language, but assigns to each a structural description that is in accord with the linguistic competence of the native speaker, and an explanatorily adequate general theory of the structure of natural languages is one that 'provides a principled basis for selecting a descriptively adequate grammar on the basis of primary linguistic data by the use of a well-defined evaluation measure'. I take roughly the same view of descriptive adequacy as Chomsky does, except that I have little faith in the native speaker's intuitions of grammatical relatedness and would place more emphasis on the necessity of integrating the phonology, morphology, syntax and semantics as systematically as possible. As far as explanatory adequacy is concerned, I would echo one of Chomsky's earlier pronouncements: 'We should like the syntactic framework of the language that is isolated to be able to support semantic description, and we shall naturally rate more highly a theory of formal structure that

---

[20] Something has been said along these lines in Lyons (1977: 793ff). But it will be evident to the careful reader that there are gaps in the development and possibly inconsistencies.

leads to grammars that meet this requirement more fully' (Chomsky 1957: 102). This requirement is not strong enough, or sufficiently precise, to serve as the sole criterion of explanatory adequacy. But it is nonetheless an important criterion that must be satisfied. And I submit that, as I have argued elsewhere, it is well satisfied by a theory which permits the formulation of the underlying syntactic structures that have been postulated in this article (cf. Lyons 1977: 467ff). Both traditional grammar and Chomskyan generative grammar can be fairly criticized for their failure to recognise the semantic and syntactic importance of locative expressions, whether deictic or non–deictic, in many, and perhaps all, languages.

I remarked earlier that, although I agree with Haas that surface structure is as much a theoretical construct as deep structure is, certain aspects of the surface structure of sentences seem to me to be more or less indisputable. For example, I take it for granted that *John has something on his mind* and *John has something on his desk* are, apart from the lexical difference between *mind* and *desk*, either identical or almost identical in surface structure. Given that the surface structure description that is assigned to them by our grammatical model is formalized in terms of a labelled bracketing, no-one, I imagine, would wish to argue that they differ in their bracketing (whatever it is) or with respect to the labelling of *something*, of *on*, of *mind/desk*, of *his mind/desk* or of *on his mind/desk*. But there are clear, and independently determinable, semantic differences, in terms of the ontological status of their potential referents, between the sets of referring expressions that can be substitutes for *something*, especially if we give priority to focal collocations, in the two syntactically identical (or near-identical) contexts. To put it crudely, the potential reference of *something*-substitutes in *John has something on his mind* is more abstract than in *John has something on his desk*; and *on his mind* refers to a more abstract kind of location than *on his desk* does. Surface structure similarities like this, between spatial and non–spatial locative expressions, are found in many unrelated languages throughout the world. It seems natural to assume that the spatial locative expressions are psychologically basic and serve as the structural templates, as it were, for the more abstract expressions. The whole of this article has been predicated upon the localistic assumption that a general theory which takes account of so pervasive a phenomenon in language as the structural similarities between spatial expressions and more abstract, non-spatial, expressions has a higher degree of explanatory adequacy than one which does not.

The expressions that have been brought together and derived from underlying locative structures in this essay are far from being as similar in their surface structure (whatever it is) as the two sentences cited in the previous paragraph. The thesis that I have been defending rests implicitly upon several metatheoretical assumptions, not all of which would be accepted by all linguists. The first is that there is some validity in the distinction between surface structure and a deeper level of syntactic analysis and that sentences which are very different in their surface structure (e.g. *John exists* and *The fact is that it is raining*) can be shown to be almost identical, or at least very similar, in their deep structure. Given the power of transformational grammars, as they are currently formalized, it is of course possible to postulate almost any arbitrary deep structure for any sentence and successfully derive the required surface structure from it. It is for this reason that many generative grammarians, after a period of enthusiasm for the universal base hypothesis, have become sceptical about its empirical status (cf. Bach 1974; Sampson 1975). I am myself committed, if not to the strongest version of the universal base hypothesis, at least to the proposition that languages are more similar at the level of deep structure than they are at the level of surface structure. And I believe that the problem of the excessive power of transformations is alleviated by the application of the principle (to which I have manifestly adhered throughout) that nothing should be postulated as part of the deep structure of any language unless it is found as part of the surface structure of some language – and preferably of many unrelated languages.

The only transformational process to which extensive appeal has been made is nominalization. There are many formal difficulties attaching to the notion of nominalization, and more especially to the decision as to where the boundary should be drawn between the grammar and the lexicon (cf. Chomsky 1970). But no-one, I think, would dispute the fact that there are productive grammatical processes of nominalization in many, if not all, languages. As to the distinction drawn here, on semantic grounds between second-order and third-order nominals, this corresponds, at least partly, with the distinction that has been drawn by transformationalists between action and factive nominalizations (cf. Lees 1960; Vendler 1968). The distinction is not so obvious in English, as far as the internal structure of the resultant nominals (NPs) is concerned, as it is in, say, Turkish (cf. Lees 1965). But in so far as it is independently determinable it both supports and is supported by the distributional differences between first-order, second-order and third-order nominals (in their focal collocations) and the clear ontological differences between their referents. The purely grammatical (i.e. distributional) facts that are accounted for by the analysis that has been proposed in this essay are many and disparate. I have done no more than hint at them. My main concern has been to construct a partly philosophical and partly linguistic case for the coherence and explanatory value of a localistic treatment of an important set of expressions in English, and by implication in other languages. I have made it clear at several points that I do not assume that all languages have developed the same range of expressions; and I am willing to concede, if it is shown to be the case, that there are languages for which a non-localistic treatment is either preferable or equally satisfactory. This remains to be seen.

Grammatical function

ANDRÉ MARTINET

It may not be superfluous to stress once more that the use of 'function', in 'grammatical function', is much older than that of the adjective 'functional' in reference to a specific approach to the study of language and that, at first sight, there seems to be no connexion between the two.

A linguistic functionalist is one who tries to determine how speakers manage to reach their communicative ends by means of a language and who is ready to classify and hierarchize facts accordingly, even at the expense of formal identities.

The best illustration of functional practice is the way speech melody is analysed in a so-called tone language. Observation, either direct or through recordings, yields a melodic curve, with rises and falls, troughs and peaks, slurs and gaps. A pure phonetician – and many linguists still are, in that respect, pure phoneticians – will be satisfied with a bare description of the formal accidents of the curve, irrespective of their possible relations to the content of the message. A functionalist will, as a first step, check whether some of those accidents contribute to the identification of minimal significant units ('morphemes' or, better, 'monemes'). Those that do will be called 'tones' and placed with the phonemes of the language in the arsenal of distinctive units. The next step will be to check what features of the melodic curve participate in establishing the prominence of one given syllable in contradistinction to – and at the expense of – its neighbours in the spoken chain, a prominence which we call accent, stress being only one of its possible physical constituents. What remains, when tones and accent have been taken care of, is intonation proper, and functional analysis will not be complete before intonational features have been identified as either syntactically relevant, indicative of the speaker's mood, dialect markers, or sheer physiological necessities.

Relevancy is, of course, the functionalist's password; relevancy on the phonological plane, relevancy on the plane of significant units where phonological likeness or difference must be forgotten as soon as the identity of the units has been secured. Morphology, the study of forms, is just one step in the process of linguistic analysis, one that has to be ignored as soon as its products have been stored. Why should one be concerned about the sounds of a given Latin ablative, when what is at stake is its syntactic function? If, at a later stage, the dynamics of the language are put in the foreground, phonological likeness, as a possible source of confusion, will naturally reappear. Deliberate change of viewpoint is the functionalist's daily practice, and it is no wonder that this is confusing for the untrained scholar.

Grammatical function has a much more restricted domain. It is a purely syntactic phenomenon, which, in the framework of a certain approach to linguistic description, practically exhausts the field of syntax proper. Recently, some linguists have been tempted to discard this traditional phrase and have proposed the term 'case' instead. But the various implications of 'case' would seem to rule out this proposition. The polysemy of 'function' is, after all, no worse than that of many terms which have been used without serious drawbacks: context will as a rule make clear what sort of function we have in mind and, in case of danger, the specification 'grammatical' is always available.

If we try to see how the term 'function' came to be used for the relation between two items in the chain, we find that it was originally meant to distinguish between the value of a given significant unit (a 'word') by itself, irrespective of its context, and the additional value which accrued to it through the context. The former was called its NATURE, the latter its FUNCTION. What is common to that operation, and the practice of functional linguistics, is the analytic procedure whereby a single linguistic item is analysed, not in successive material segments, but according to its different contributions to the message. As a matter of fact, our distant predecessors, insofar as they managed to avoid the pitfalls of logicism, were far more functionally minded than some more recent generations of linguistic scholars.

Retaining 'grammatical function' does not imply that we should adopt its counterpart 'nature'. We shall see below how we should define 'function' which, when we try to oppose it to 'nature', remains fairly nebulous. But 'nature' itself is by no means unambiguous; what is the nature of, say, *pen* when we consider it out of its context? Is it the meaning of the item *pen*, or is it its belonging to the noun class? Linguists and grammarians of a prestructural age would probably have answered that there is no need to make such a distinction, since the meaning of *pen* implies its belonging to the noun class, so that it is just a matter of degree of specification. We are a bit more exacting because we are apt to question the existence of a semantic feature common to all the members of the noun class. For us, a moneme does not belong to the noun class because it shares some shade of meaning with the other units of that class, but because it has the same syntactic compatibilities, such as determination by articles, possessives, and the like.

What this amounts to is that if 'nature' means belonging to a given class, 'nature' depends on the various functions assumed by the units of that class. And there goes the clear-cut opposition of 'nature' and 'function'. Now, if by 'nature' we mean the specific semantic content of a given unit, the concept becomes a purely lexical one which we must disregard in a grammatical approach.

Having thus got rid of 'nature', we are left with function as the only tool for the identification of our classes of monemes. But should we accordingly call 'function' any direct relation between two monemes in an utterance, so that we should identify a function between *the* and *book* in *the book* or between *white* and *stone* in *white stone*? Whatever terms they use, some linguists are tempted to posit, in, for example, *the book*, three units: *the*, *book*, and the relation between the two monemes. They would argue that, when we hear *He put the book on the shelf*, we identify, between *the* and *book*, a connexion we miss between *book* and *on*. A functionalist's interpretation is of course different since, when the speaker has chosen to say *book* and to determine it by means of the definite article, he has made two choices, not three, and *the* and *book* will automatically appear as *the book*. *The* and *book* belong to their respective classes, each characterized by a set of definite compatibilities, among which is the compatibility of articles with nouns with all its formal implications in the chain.

This means that there is no need to speak of a function in the case of the combination of an article with a noun, because, when the speaker has chosen to use the definite article in connexion with a given noun, he has no choice among different ways of connecting them. The relationship between article and noun can be nothing but determination of the latter by the former, and if we want to make that determination different, our only recourse will be the use of another article or determinant.

The condition for mentioning a function is the possibility of several different relationships between two significant units such as are found in English between noun and verb. Two items, like *cat* and *kill(s)*, may stand in two different relations as in . . . *cat kill(s)* or in . . . *kill(s) cat*, so that it becomes necessary to have designations for them. The former, of course, is called subject function, the latter object function.

Now, some people will be tempted to argue that if we distinguish among different functions when there is a choice, there will still be a function when there is no choice. That explains why the relation between *the* and *book* in *the book* is sometimes presented as unifunctional, while that between noun and verb is said to be plurifunctional. It does not make much difference what formulation is chosen. The second one enables the linguist to define syntax, in its narrower sense, as the examination and presentation of plurifunctional relations, whereas the determination of the different moneme classes on the basis of respective compatibilities belongs to a previous section called the Inventory.

To say, as we have done so far, that a function is a relation between two monemes, by themselves or as representatives of their respective classes, is a very loose way of presenting the actual situations we want to describe. In the case of . . . *cat kill(s)*, for instance, the relation between the two units is of a definite type, but not on account of *kill(s)*. When passing to . . . *kill(s) cat*, the killing as such is not affected, but its effect on the cat is; the function of *kill(s)* is just the same; that of *cat* is different. In other words, the function is not that of a relation, but that of a given unit in its relation to another more central unit. A function is a specific type of determination characterizing a determinant, not the nucleus it determines.

Accordingly, it is perfectly justified to say that a given noun or a pronoun HAS a subject function, or FUNCTIONS as a subject. As a matter of fact, few people would object to such formulations, although some would probably remark that it is easier to say that the noun or pronoun in question IS the subject. It would be a waste of time to discuss here the various implications of the copula. When we say that *cat* IS the subject, we are after all referring to a state of affairs which is not so very different from the one to which we allude when we say that Mr Jones IS the chairman. Using the copula in such cases does not necessarily imply a permanent identification of the subject and the predicate.

Since it does not coincide with the determinant to which it is attached, the function is a linguistic unit or, in Saussurian terms, a linguistic sign with meaning, i.e. an implication for the message and form, i.e. a perceptible mark of its existence. In the case of the subject and object functions in English, that perceptible mark is the respective position of noun and verb. Similar functions in other languages may be indicated by case endings or unamalgamated particles. Speakers of English or French – two languages where the most frequent functions, subject and object, are economically marked by position – are apt to set them apart, with the dative function reluctantly added because of the occasional absence of its specific mark. But the material form of functional indication is syntactically irrelevant. In Spanish, the object is marked by a preposition wherever ambiguity might arise. It is true that such functions as involve the participants in the action are likely to be more frequent than those implying more peripheric conditionings. Being more frequent, they are apt to be expressed more economically. But dynamically we find, in all languages, a constant trend towards using the markers of concrete relations for a more explicit character-ization of the participants in the action.

Accordingly, there is no reason, in a general linguistic approach to the problem, to set aside once and for all the so-called participants, and to treat circumstances as quasi-adverbial phrases: there is no doubt that, e.g., *with pleasure* plays a role similar to that of an adverb, but as long as *pleasure* is a noun, we shall have to reckon here with a function marked by *with*.

Budding functionalists often suggest that since functions are ling-uistic signs, with meaning and form, they should be considered monemes, since monemes, in contradistinction to morphemes, need not appear as distinct segments. There are several reasons which justify the retention of a distinction between functions and monemes. The most decisive one is the fact that, in many instances, a given preposition or case, for which both formal identity and semantic unity are secured, is found to correspond to different functions. Let us consider the preposition *to*. Whether we have it with a dative value, in *I gave it to him*, or in an allative sense, in *He went to London*, the notion of 'direction towards' is there. But dative and allative are two formally and semantically distinct functions in English as shown by the fre-quent absence of *to* as a dative mark (*I gave him the book*), as opposed to its permanency as the indication of the allative except, of course, with adverbs like *home* or adverbial phrases like *downtown*. We have here a case of partial homonymy for the two functions, a case of stable identity for the preposition.

In a case language, such as Latin, we may posit a 'circumstantial' moneme, the so-called 'ablative case', which corresponds to a number of distinct functions, such as the proper ablative function where it is regularly supplemented by *ab*, or the agent function where the addition of *ab* is limited to animates. This, together with the opposition of *in* + accusative to *in* + ablative in Latin (*in* + dative in German), illustrates the frequent use of discontinuous functional indicators where both a case ending and a preposition are needed, a feature parallel to a compound preposition like *into* or such a complex function marker as *on to*.

Grammatical functions are generally illustrated by reference to the behaviour of units of the nominal classes in their relations to verbs. But, of course, grammatical functions are to be posited wherever plurifunctionality is attested, between clauses for instance, between an adjectival nucleus and its nominal determinant (*good* OF *you, good* FOR *you*).

The main point about functions, that which basically sets them apart from all other significant units in language, is their establishing a one-way relation between other significant units. There are, no doubt, other relational units, the coordinators, such as *and, or, nor*. But, by definition, coordination only exists between two syntactically equal elements and never between a determinant and its nucleus.

Extracting grammatical functions from a corpus of utterances is not always an easy task. In the older Indo-European languages, we find them amalgamated with the monemes of number. In many cases, we may hesitate to identify a segment as a determinant of the verb or the functional marker of the noun: Latin *equō dē-jectus* 'dismounted', 'thrown down from his horse' and *dē equō* 'down from his horse'. Note the ambiguous status of *on to* in English. Elsewhere, we may wonder whether we are faced with a verb meaning 'to give to' or an indication of the dative function. But all this of course is no reason why we should revert to the traditional practice of letting form alone, irrespective of the communicative aims of language, dictate the form of our analysis.

Deep structure

P. H. MATTHEWS

In Chomsky's latest work, the 'extended standard theory' of the early 1970s (EST) is already going the way of both the 'standard theory' of the middle 1960s (also called the '*Aspects*-model') and the model of *Syntactic structures* in the 1950s. For it is now being superseded by yet another attempt to get the role of the semantic component right. At first the grammar did not have such a component; that was in Chomsky's earliest and still essentially Bloomfieldian phase (Chomsky 1957). Then it acquired one, which assigned interpretations to a set of deep or underlying structures. By definition, these comprised the aspects of syntactic descriptions which determined the semantic representation of a sentence, just as surface structures comprised the aspects which determined its phonetics (see especially Chomsky 1966: 7). But that was soon said to be wrong; semantic interpretations were to be determined not by underlying structure alone, but by deep and surface structures together (Chomsky 1972). Now that too appears to be wrong; the meaning and the phonetics are both to be determined from the surface structures alone (see, for example, Chomsky & Lasnik 1977: 428). At the time of writing Chomsky is still calling this the EST. Strictly speaking it is a new 'revised extended standard theory' (REST), which raises a fresh set of problems for both the transformational grammarian and his critics.

Among these problems, the status of deep structure is especially puzzling. In the *Aspects*-model it was seen as quite uncontroversial (cf. Chomsky 1966: 8). The grammar had to specify semantic representations and there had to be syntactic structures from which they were determined; the only 'substantive assertion' was that they were distinct from surface structures. In the EST that was no longer so; if the meaning was determined from both levels in the syntax, the postulation of such levels seemed to need some independent justification. But perhaps they determined different 'aspects' of the meaning (cf. especially Jackendoff 1972). In that case they might still be established *a priori*, and it is conceivable that even the terminology ('deep' or fundamental versus 'surface' or contingent) might not be entirely tendentious. But none of this can hold for the REST. About the term itself Chomsky is becoming understandably sheepish (Chomsky 1976; more recently Chomsky & Lasnik 1977: 6n); it is presented as no more than a technical label, with none of its original motivation. But the distinction is assumed as confidently as ever. A syntactic description still has two parts, and the syntactic rules are still divided into two major components, assigning two successive structures. The reason is not explained. This is just part of the EST, or the REST, and we must either take it or leave it.

I confess that I would like to know why I should be expected to take it. For if the deep structure no longer does what it was originally defined as doing, and does not even have the partial semantic role assigned to it by the 'extended' theory, one is bound to wonder what it is supposed to be for. The answer cannot be found in a discussion of 'methodological preliminaries' (Chomsky 1965: ch. 1), or in any other arguments that have been current in the past fourteen or fifteen years. We are therefore forced back to the very beginnings of transformational syntax, in the decade before the terminology of 'deep' and 'surface' was introduced. The latest Chomsky is perpetuating a distinction which has no direct semantic relevance, of a type which only the earliest Chomsky has ever sought to validate.

Let us start with the notion of a 'transformational component'. In the *Aspects*-model, a syntactic transformation was simply a rule which helped to relate two different levels of structure. The levels themselves were defined independently; so, provided they were distinct (the 'only substantive assertion'), the positing of such rules required no further justification. But for the REST the argument must plainly be the other way round. The levels have no *a priori* standing: a deep structure is merely a structure which is assigned by base rules, and a surface structure merely a structure which is derived by transformations, subject to various conditions, filters (Chomsky & Lasnik 1977), and so on. So, we have to ask on what grounds two distinct sets of syntactic rules – a base set and a transformational set – are still felt to be needed.

Of the arguments given in *Syntactic structures*, and in other works which follow immediately in that tradition, relatively few are valid from the *Aspects*-model onwards. We were told, for instance, that there was no way for a phrase-structure rule to handle linear recursion. Therefore we had to have a transformational component, if a succession of coordinated phrases (*I saw John, Jill, . . . and Mary*) was to be assigned an appropriate structure. Postal, for one, made great play of this argument (1964), and it still appears as late as Ruwet's *Introduction à la grammaire générative* (1967). But in the notes to *Aspects*, coordination is already handled in the categorial component (Chomsky 1965: 224), and in later work a phrase-structure schema of precisely the sort which Postal ruled out (S → S$_1$ . . . S$_n$; also NP → NP$_1$ . . . NP$_n$) is accepted without question. Not only was the argument never valid, but if it had been valid it would hold against the *Aspects*-model, and the EST or REST, and not in their favour.

A more interesting casualty is the form of argument based on a relationship between sentences. It was assumed, for instance, that the passive was syntactically related to the active . This was supported by the distribution of selectional or collocational restrictions (**Sincerity admired John*, **John was admired by sincerity*). We were also assured, though never quite shown, that the relationship had psychological reality. We therefore needed a rule which would map an active into a passive phrase-marker; this also ensured that the collocational restrictions need be stated only once. By definition that would be a transformational rule. So, once more, we needed a transformational component, with that sort of rule in it, as well as a phrase-structure component.

This argument has died more gradually, so gradually that some of Chomsky's followers may still imagine that it is alive. But in *Aspects* the base phrase-markers are already distinct, the passive having a so-called manner adverb, *by* + PASSIVE, in its underlying structure (Chomsky, 1965: chapter 2). At that level no particular relatedness is shown: a base string *John* + *admire* + *sincerity* + *by* + PASSIVE is distinguished from its former syntactic correlate, *John* + *admire* + *sincerity*, in exactly the same way that the deep structure of *John drinks heavily*, with a genuine manner adverb, is opposed to that of the adverb-less *John drinks*, or that of *John is shopping in London*, with a locative in the predicate phrase, from that of *John is shopping* (cf. Matthews 1967). Nor is there any relation between the surface structures; nor is there any form of syntactic description apart from the deep and surface structures and their intermediate stages. If the original relationship was genuine then, once more, an argument for *Syntactic structures* becomes an argument against the *Aspects*-model and its successors.

There remained, or seemed to remain, a problem of selectional restrictions. The choice of verb was limited by the nouns; so, there had to be selectional rules (Chomsky 1965: 95), or some equivalent mechanism, by which verbs reflect features such as 'abstract' (for *sincerity*), 'animate' (for *John*), and so on, in the surrounding base string. Such rules would have to be stated twice, once for the active and once for the passive, unless the latter had an underlying structure with the active word order. But that argument was in turn killed off by Chomsky's 'Remarks on nominalization' (1970). According to this article, a noun phrase with a subjective genitive (*the arrival of the children*) would bear no syntactic resemblance to its erstwhile kernel sentence (*The children arrived*). So, just as the verb *arrive* had features matching those of a subject which preceded it, the noun *arrival* would take its own features from one which followed. But the same technique could naturally be applied to the active and passive, or to predicative and attributive adjectives, or to any other case of that sort. Nor is there any need to duplicate rules in the individual lexical entries. A single function could be defined for two or more alternative structures – 'agent', let us say, for both the subject in the active and the passive *by*-phrase. The selectional rules could then refer to the function in general, not to particular positions.

Though such a treatment had become possible by the beginning of the 1970s, we might still have been told that it was wrong. For the active and passive form a regular semantic correlation, with shared interpretations of a sort which, in the EST as in the *Aspects*-model, could be handled only on the basis of a shared configuration (subject + verb + object) at the deep level. But even this is killed off by the introduction of the REST. The semantic interpretation of the passive must now be determined from the passive configuration at the surface level, by rules which are presumably distinct from those applying to the active. Likewise a phrase with an attributive adjective (*tall trees*) must be interpreted by a semantic rule referring to the surface order adjective + noun, and a clause with a predicative adjective ([*trees*] *which are tall, The trees are tall*) by a separate rule for surface subject + copula + adjective. If meanings are determined from the surface, it is at that level that a set of generalized syntactic or semantic functions (subject or agent, and so on) can best, or perhaps must, be defined. On the same basis we could also envisage surface lexical insertions (see Chomsky & Lasnik 1977: 18n). The vestiges of underlying structure would then be left with no substantive role.

Of the remaining arguments, the most significant were based on differences in constructional meaning and, in particular, on the ambiguities that arise between them. In *Flying planes can be dangerous*, the initial phrase could be interpreted in two ways: like the gerundial or exocentric *Flying planes* [*is dangerous*], or the endocentric *Flying planes* [*are dangerous*], with *flying* participial. This could be explained by positing two different transformational derivations or, in the *Aspects*-model, by establishing two different underlying structures for a single surface structure. There is also a difference in the interpretation of pairs such as *He is easy to please* and *he is eager to please*. This too was explained by differences in their syntactic descriptions (Chomsky 1964), both descriptions being assignable to an ambiguous sentence such as, for example, *It is ready to explode* (compare *It is ready to light* and *It is ready to go off*). To distinguish these descriptions a transformationalist again required two levels of syntactic representation: a transformation-marker in addition to the terminal phrase-marker, or a deep structure in addition to a surface structure.

In presenting such arguments, Chomsky and his followers had to make two crucial assumptions. First, they had to assume that a syntactic explanation was needed. For *flying planes* this seemed self-evident: the phrases are distinguished by their patterns of agreement (*is dangerous, are dangerous*), and agreement is, in part at least, a matter of syntactic rule. But for *He is easy* and *He is eager to please*, or the equally notorious *the shooting of the hunters* (Chomsky 1957: 88f), the assumption was naturally challenged. The argument here was bound up with the argument about relatedness between constructions (as in *tall trees* and *The trees are tall*). For the ambiguity of *It is ready to explode* would be explained by its relatedness, on the one hand, to the intransitive *It exploded* and, on the other hand, to the predicate *exploded it*. To a transformationalist, both the ambiguity and the relatedness belonged to syntax. To many of his critics both were purely semantic, just as, to them, there was a purely semantic connexion between an active and a passive, and so on.

The second assumption is one that Professor Haas, in particular, has often forcefully exposed. One of Chomsky's major achievements was the formalization of phrase-structure grammar, based in part on late

Bloomfieldian procedures of analysis (Harris 1946, 1951; Wells 1947; Hockett 1954) and in part on the mathematical theory of rewrite operations. But having formalized it he seemed very reluctant to abandon it. Phrase-markers could not distinguish two descriptions of *flying planes*; so, at least, we were told. But at some level, he assumed, it had to be represented by a phrase-marker. Therefore we had to postulate another level – that is, another syntactic level – at which the constructions could be differentiated. At the time, the majority of objections were directed to the first step in this argument; surely there was some way of labelling *flying planes* in two distinct ways. (Indeed there had to be, if agreement was to be handled by a normal transformation, instead of a global rule referring back to deep or kernel structures.) But the general assumption was also rather strange. A car cannot fly; if we want to fly we must therefore seek some other form of vehicle. But we do not assume that such a vehicle must have a car as one of its main components. Likewise, if a phrase-structure grammar cannot do the job required of it, we must simply give up phrase-structure grammars. There is no reason why a better syntactic structure should consist of a phrase-marker with something else added to it, let alone two phrase-markers in place of one.

Before we return to the first assumption, we can usefully remind ourselves of three particular ways in which phrase-structure representations, or so-called surface structures, are deficient. The first deficiency is that related substrings have to be contiguous. In *They brought up their daughter strictly* we may establish a constituent *brought up*, which in turn can form a constituent with *their daughter*. But the rules allow for no such unit when the verb and adverb are separate (*They brought their daughter up strictly*, *They brought her up strictly*). So, to overcome this failing, we were asked to posit a movement transformation, partly obligatory and partly optional, deriving the second pattern from the first. Some apologists made much of this and similar arguments, especially Postal (1964).

A second deficiency was that the only relationship is that of constituency. We can say that *flying planes* is a unit; we can classify it as a whole (noun phrase), and likewise classify its parts. But in *Flying planes is dangerous* we have no way of saying that the gerund governs *planes*, or has *planes* as its object, just as in *Flying planes are dangerous* we are unable to show that *planes* is modified by the participle, or has it as an attribute. It is only because the surface structure was restricted to a phrase-marker, and phrase-markers do not distinguish relations such as governance or modification, that a transformational treatment seemed to be illuminating.

A third deficiency is that the relations have to form a hierarchical structure. Let us imagine that we can link together discontinuous elements: so, in *John is eager to please* we could, among other things, establish a relationship between *John* and the infinitive. Let us also imagine that we can distinguish different types of relationship: so, the link here could be specifically that of (*to*) *please* and a subject, whereas in *John is easy to please* there could be a similar link with *John* as an object. Yet still the descriptions might seem problematic. For if *John* is related to the predicate *is* + adjective + *to please*, and the predicate is in turn split up with *to please* as the complement of the adjective, there is no way in which the infinitive can also be related to *John*, if a single tree structure is to be formed. Under this third limitation, we are still compelled to posit an additional level of tree structure, or an additional representation of some kind, in order that this subjective or objective link can be shown. In any case of this kind there would also be discontinuity; for that reason, perhaps, the argument was never stated as such. But it would be the final sticking point, if other and less fundamental deficiencies were eliminated.

The source of these restrictions was almost wholly Bloomfieldian. A Bloomfieldian 'discovery procedure' segmented utterances into phones, which it proceeded to classify under phonemes; it segmented strings of phonemes into morphs, which it proceeded to classify under morphemes; it segmented strings of morphemes into successively larger or successively smaller constituents, which it proceeded to classify under constructions. By the operation of segmentation, the basic relation is that of belonging to the same segment, as opposed to different segments. By the operation of classification, the basic property of a segment is that of belonging to a certain class (noun phrase, for example) and of having parts which themselves belong to the same or different classes (for example, noun or article). The construction as a whole could naturally be represented by a phrase-structure rule (noun phrase → article + noun). Naturally no substring could belong to overlapping constructions ($_x$[a $_y$[b]$_x$ a]$_y$), just as no phoneme, for example, could belong to merely overlapping morphs. Naturally, a discontinuous segment needed special treatment.

A second source was in the mathematical theory which Chomsky so brilliantly assimilated. But since a formal theory is not necessarily suited to empirical applications, and Chomsky himself abandoned the procedures of analysis which the Bloomfieldians had developed, his critics have found it hard to understand why syntactic structure should still be limited in such ways.

Let us now return to problems of constructional meaning and ambiguity. In its strongest form, this argument too has been destroyed by the introduction of the REST. *He is easy to please* and *He is eager to please* were said to be identical on the surface; therefore we needed different deep structures, to determine differences in their meanings. But now the meanings are to be determined from the surface structure; therefore their surface representations cannot be identical. So, there is in principle no need for any other representation which will show the difference.

But in Chomsky's newest model, the differences in surface structure would reside entirely in the 'traces' (Chomsky 1976; Chomsky & Lasnik 1977) which the underlying structures, or the subsequent movement transformations, leave behind them. For *He is easy to please* the surface representation would presumably be as follows:

He is easy [to please *t*]

where the trace (*t*) reflects the movement of *he* from its position as an underlying object. (Compare the structure *John is likely* [*t to win*], in Chomsky & Lasnik 1977: 445.) The semantic rules would then refer to the *t* in assigning an objective interpretation. For *He is eager to please* there would be no *t*:

He is eager [to please]

since the underlying subject of *please* is deleted rather than moved (Chomsky & Lasnik 1977: 93n). This simpler representation would then be interpreted subjectively. Likewise *the shooting of the hunters* might have representations with or without a *t* in front of *shooting*, the endocentric *flying planes* could presumably have a *t* in the original position of the participle (*flying planes t*), and so on. In this way the ghost of Chomsky's earlier arguments lives on, for we still need underlying structures − so he might tell us − in order that their traces can be derived.

All this is on the assumption which we made explicit earlier, that the differences must be registered in the syntax. If not, it is now a very short step to the alternative. In Chomsky's model, there are general transformational rules by which the underlying structure of *He is easy to please* will yield the surface structure which we have given; there is also a specific syntactic feature, assigned to *easy*, *hard* and similar adjectives, by which the operation of these transformations is constrained; finally, there is a general rule of semantic interpretation, constrained only by the presence or absence of the *t*, by which *please* and *he* are understood in a certain relationship. But if lexical features can constrain transformations there is no reason why they should not constrain semantic rules instead. Let us assign to *easy* a semantic feature by which its subject can be taken only objectively (i.e. as one of various semantic types of object) with respect to the infinitive. To *eager* we can assign a feature by which their relation must be taken as subjective, and to *ready*, in *It is ready to explode*, we naturally assign both. The traces are then redundant. Once more neither the transformations, nor the underlying structure, would have any effective role.

In such a treatment the semantic rules would also act as filters. According to the REST, a base string in which *easy* had an incompatible complement (thus *He is easy* [*he vanish*]) would be filtered out by the transformational component, since *easy* lacks the syntactic feature which would allow a transformation to apply. In this alternative, a surface structure in which *easy* was followed by an incompatible infinitive (*He is easy* [*to vanish*]) would find no semantic reading, since *easy* and *vanish* impose opposite relationships on *he*. Likewise, *It is ready* [*to light*] could only have a reading in which *it* is objective, since the subjective reading, though allowed by the semantic features of *ready*, is excluded by those of *light*. Chomsky's model has two sets of general rules (semantic rules and transformations) which between them distribute the traces, exclude incompatibilities, and assign meanings. The alternative model has a single set of rules (the rules of semantics), which either assign or fail to assign meanings, on the basis of structures in which traces are no longer needed. In this respect the alternative is plainly simpler.

But simplicity is not the decisive factor. By our earlier assumption, any general explanation had to be syntactic. If *It is ready to explode* is ambiguous, or *He is easy to vanish* cannot be interpreted, a connexion between these facts could be established only by resemblances and differences in syntactic description, not by the isolated collocations of particular verbs and adjectives. Now for *Syntactic structures* this was literally so: the syntactic rules were the only rules available, and the lexicon was no more than a series of word lists (adjective$_1 \rightarrow$ *easy*, *ready*, . . .; adjective $_2 \rightarrow$ *eager, ready*, . . ., and so on). Once more we must stress the fundamentally Bloomfieldian character of Chomsky's earliest work. The assumption was then incorporated into the 'integrated' model which emerged when a semantic component was added (Katz & Postal 1964), apparently without thought. But from then on each of Chomsky's theories offers us two general types of rule, between which we must choose in handling any particular pattern of regularities. For *He is easy to please* and *He is eager to please*, as for *the shooting of the hunters*, or the active and passive, and so on, the real question is not which mechanism is the neater, but whether a semantic or a syntactic explanation is correct.

I am not sure how Chomsky himself would see this issue. In his view of language, syntax and semantics are both part of a determinate grammar, both being reducible to rules. The choice is therefore just as we have presented it, between syntactic rules which are constrained by syntactic features of the adjectives, and semantic rules constrained by sets of semantic features which are equally clear cut. But for his critics the essential point is how far there are indeed 'constraints'. Could one say, for instance, *He was infelicitous to arrive yesterday*? It is not clear why we should try to write rules by which it is either grammatical or ungrammatical. One could say *He was unlucky to arrive yesterday*; but precisely which structure should it have? Should we take it like the sentence with *eager* ('He was unlucky for arriving yesterday'), or like one with *likely* ('His arriving yesterday was unlucky'), or is there yet a third pattern? It was for such examples that Bolinger first drew attention to the problem of 'syntactic blends' (Bolinger 1961). But are they truly syntactic? Blending is diagnostic not of rules, but of the less determinate type of regularity that Professor Haas has rightly characterized as a 'tendency' (Haas 1973a). Tendencies are at least more typical of semantics.

But let us grant the transformationalist his first assumption, at least for the distinctions of subjective and objective. So, in the *Aspects*-model and the original version of the EST, the semantic rules referred to syntactic functions such as 'subject of' and 'object of' (Chomsky (1965: 68ff) defined over the embedded sentences in underlying structure. Likewise, in the REST they must refer – to what? The functions could again be established in the base; but then the semantic component could not refer to them, unless we envisage precisely the sort of global rule (cf. Lakoff 1970a) which Chomsky's mechanism of traces is designed to avoid. Once more the natural alternative is to introduce them at the surface level; so, in *He is easy to please* we would establish a direct relationship by which *he* is, among other things, an 'object of' (*to*) *please*. It will be seen that this is just the sort of relation which, by Chomsky's original Bloomfieldian assumptions, surface structures could not have. If these relations are syntactic, and are referred to in the semantics, it now seems that they cannot but have them.

In what way might they be introduced? Chomsky himself would still define them on the basis of completed phrase-markers; so, we would need traces (as in *He is easy* [*to please t*]) to ensure that they were correct. Therefore we would still require the mechanism of deep structure and transformations – for by now it is scarcely more than a mechanism – to ensure that the traces, in turn, are in the right positions. But, once more, it is natural to envisage surface lexical insertion (cf. Chomsky & Lasnik 1977: 18n). So, let us start from a structure without lexical items: thus of the terminal string *he* + *is* + adjective + *to* + verb. For that configuration the rules would state that various functional relationships are possible; for example, there may be either a subjective or an objective link between the pronoun and the verb. This link is then a part of the syntactic description and, as such, will naturally limit the range of adjectives (*easy*, *eager*, *ready*, and so on) that can be selected. Once more, there is nothing that the traces, or any other relics of a transformational component, could add.

Here, as earlier, we have simply followed through the logic of Chomsky's latest general model. At the time of writing, he seems to be nearing a stage which I myself reached in the year of his *Aspects of the theory of syntax* (1965) in which I envisaged posttransformational lexical insertion and posttransformational rules for functions; doubtless I would also have had posttransformational semantics, if I had thought about that issue. Yet still I had the apparatus of base structures and transformations (Matthews 1965). Clearly, the next step is to sweep this apparatus away. It will be interesting to see how far Chomsky's own thoughts have advanced by the time this essay is published.

The English appearance of Aspect

T. F. MITCHELL

Brief general survey

If there is one thing that emerges from perusal of a large and heterogeneous literature on Aspect in many languages – which it is not my purpose to review, even if I were able, in this short, necessarily selective essay – it is that no two linguists agree on the subject. For some, not exclusively Slavists, it is a set of grammaticalized verbal forms of characteristic morphological shape and syntactic employment; for others, it is a multi-exponential property of verb phrases; for others again, it is a sentential category in whose terms aspectual devices are predicates of whole 'propositions'. The last position is adopted, for example, by Newmeyer (1975), who regards the apparently miscellaneous *begin*, *happen*, and *likely* as 'aspectual verbs' on the ground of their shared extrapolability from, say, *Bill begins/happens/is likely to annoy John* and equal applicability to a basic 'proposition' *Bill annoys John*. Apart from the somewhat hackneyed question of the derivability or not of adjectives from verbs, this view is a minority one in that it does not seemingly consider concepts of time and/or space as of any necessary relevance to Aspect, although most of Newmeyer's book is in fact devoted to a generally agreed aspectual class of verbs, labelled the *begin*-class, to which we shall return. For most scholars, however, Aspect is used in close contrast with Tense, so that, for instance, according to Palmer, 'In many languages there is what is called "aspect" as well as, or instead of, tense, tense supposedly referring to time and aspect to completion, duration, and similar concepts' (1971: 93). Presumably, however, these aspectual concepts ALSO refer to time, and the view adopted in this essay is of Aspect concerned with extension or spread, in time certainly but also often enough in space, while Tense and associated deictic categories relate rather to location in these dimensions. This was Sapir's view (1939: 114), when he spoke of Aspect as indicating 'the lapse of action, its nature from the standpoint of continuity', though one might wish nowadays to enquire more closely as to the intended scope of 'action'. Jespersen (1924) was also concerned with much of the conceptualization involved, yet, although he was writing over fifty years ago, agreement on the topic remains remarkably elusive, and concepts and terms are anything but consistently used. For instance, Palmer, on the subject of the morphology of the English verb phrase, points out that 'a distinction in terms of aspect, progressive and non-progressive, may be made, progressive forms being those that contain both a form of BE and an -ing form . . . The terms "continuous" and "non-continuous" are sometimes used. So too are "habitual" and "non-habitual" (habitual = non-progressive) but these are to be rejected as quite misleading' (1974: 34). The same author, following Joos (1964) and in contradistinction to, say, Quirk et al. (1972), treats 'perfect : non-perfect' under a category labelled 'phase', not generally employed elsewhere in this sense. Lyons (1977: 710–11) specifically rejects Palmer's use of 'phase' and follows Comrie (1976) in applying the term to the initiating, in-being, and terminating phases of a process. Focus on these phases is provided by the so-called 'imperfective' aspect of the verb in, say, Russian, in contrast with the indivisibility of the corresponding 'perfective' aspect. Comrie, for his part, seems somewhat caught up between the quite different conceptual areas of 'perfective' and 'perfect', which the earlier Lyons had apparently identified (1968: 313), and it is not absolutely clear whether Comrie wishes to recognize 'perfect' aspect relating to past events having current relevance in addition to the 'perfective' aspect of 'a situation as a single whole, without distinction of the various separate phases that make up the situation' (1976: 16). There is no doubt that the terminological similarity between 'perfective' and 'perfect' is decidedly inconvenient. There is equally no doubt that 'perfect' aspect should be distinguished in the analysis of some languages. A particularly clear case is in the many forms of spoken Arabic that develop contrastive relationships between the participle and two tenses of that language (cf. Mitchell 1952, 1978). When the terminology of Aspect is itself so evidently fluid, perhaps attention should also be drawn in passing to Comrie's and Lyons's use of the logical term 'situation' (= 'possible world') in quite a different way from other British linguists who use 'situation' as a shortened form of the well-known 'context of situation'. Comrie, for example, speaks of 'situations like that described by *make a chair*' (1976: 44). In present circumstances, it is clearly a matter of some importance for anyone approaching the analysis of aspectual distinctions among others in a given language to define his terms carefully.

The whole conceptual area of Aspect is further bedevilled by the notion and term of Aktionsart. Bolinger (1971b: 98) would replace Aspect by Aktionsart in most cases of English with the exception of the 'progressive' and 'perfect' aspects of the verb phrase; Lyons (1977: 705–6), on the other hand, would eliminate Aktionsart and introduces a new term, namely the 'aspectual character' or simply 'character' of a verb, which is 'that part of its meaning whereby it (normally) denotes one kind of situation rather than another'. The examples provided are *know* (state) versus *recognize* (event). Yet there are languages for which Aktionsart or some less cumbrous term would be suitably employed. In the cases of Arabic and Berber, for instance, by ringing a number of completely regular morphological changes on the so-called 'simple' form of the verb, the 'derived' forms are obtained, which, subject like the simple form to the same twofold distinction of tense (unsatisfactorily labelled 'perfect(ive)' and 'imperfect(ive)'), have somewhat haphazardly to do with such 'kinds of action' or 'meanings' as 'intensive', 'causative', 'reciprocal', 'conative', etc. and not therefore with spatio-temporal Aspect in any discernible way.

The confused picture that is being drawn is made no clearer by the long-standing insistence of some that the recognition of Aspect must depend on clear morphological distinctions in the verb. This, of course, derives from the facts of the Slavonic languages, which have bequeathed Aspect to the general study of language, but, as far as can be seen, there is no valid reason why differences of verbal morphology should be regarded in this way as prerequisite. It may, for example, be more difficult to recognize a class 'verb' in languages of east Asia than it is to observe distinctions for which aspectual semantic categories are appropriately employed. Nearer home, however, Kuryłowicz (1973: 117) unaccountably states with reference to the Semitic languages and Arabic in particular that he is 'far from attributing aspect to Semitic, especially to Arabic'. Similar reasons doubtless prompted Zandvoort (1962: 1–20) to believe the category was inappropriate to the analysis of English. French Arabists and others have spent long on the question of whether the Arabic tenses (in fact more closely associable *per se* with distinctions of person than those of time) are not 'really' aspects, more or less in a Slavonic sense, and have tended to ignore the rich resources of other kinds that, like English, spoken Arabic uses for picturing the phasing or otherwise of events and processes as well as for the indication of states (cf. El-Hassan 1978; Mitchell 1978). The confining morphologizing view of Aspect is illustrated by a Slavist's statement with reference to Russian and Polish that

What remains constant is only the opposition between the two sets of verbal forms. Two sets, and this must be emphasised at the very beginning, because there are unfortunately still (though very few) scholars who posit three aspects by including a frequentative one. This denotes, however, only a mode of action on the same lines as, say, inchoative, terminative, semelfactive, etc. verbs such as can be grouped together in all languages and which may also have certain formal characteristics in the Slavic languages . . . but this category is very far indeed from pervading the whole conjugation as the aspect does. (Galton 1964: 133–4)

There is obvious justification for according special status to the perfective and imperfective aspects in the Slavonic languages but the 'modes of action' referred to in the quotation are also unmistakably aspectual and will be unrepentantly regarded as such later on in this essay.

The basic reason for the recognition of aspectual categories seems to be the contrast diversely made in so many languages between what is seen as punctual or undivided versus what is extensive or durational, whether in time or space. Distinctions are perhaps most easily grasped from the usual temporal viewpoint, in accordance with which a threefold set of stages or phases of uninterrupted extensions may be singled out and labelled 'inceptive', 'progressive' (= in progress) and 'terminative', while interrupted extensions are, in varying degrees of periodicity, 'iterative'. 'States', whether perceptual (e.g. *He knows his French*), timeless (e.g. *The earth travels round the sun*), or perfect (e.g. *He is wearing his new suit*, i.e. having put on his new suit, he is still in the state of having done so), are also enduring but are seen from varying standpoints of changelessness. No further mention will be made of 'stativity' in this essay, nor has it seemed necessary to refer to 'habitualness' as a category separate from iterativity. There may be some terminological advantage to be gained from applying positive labels exclusively to extensions and their parts, so that the Russian perfective, for example, which has to be seen in systematic contrast with the imperfective and perhaps also other aspects yet which responds to the view of events and processes as indivisible and without extent, might be labelled 'zero'-aspect, thereby freeing the term 'perfect' for appropriate use elsewhere.

Another area in which a marked difference in the weight of attention paid to relevant categories has contributed to the general nebulousness of the subject, is that of auxiliaries and particles of Aspect, which loom large in English and which, taken mostly together with the -*ing* form of the main verb of the verbal periphrasis, will subsequently make up the greater part of the rest of this essay. It has already been said that Newmeyer devotes much of his book to English auxiliaries of aspect; there is, however, no separate chapter on the subject in Palmer's work on the English verb (1965, 1974). As to particles of aspect, Bolinger in his stimulating book on the English phrasal verb (1971b) dedicates a chapter to them under the heading 'Aspect', but Comrie and Lyons make little or no mention of them. Yet there can be no doubt that both of these categories, severally and conjointly, are closely involved with aspectual semantics in English and numerous other languages. For example, a prenominal particle /fi/ (lit. 'in') and a variously preverbal and prenominal /bi/ are among the means employed in many varieties of spoken Arabic to indicate progressive and iterative aspects, while the languages of north India and Pakistan make great use of aspectual auxiliaries. In Sindhi, for instance, a distinction by such means is regularly made between the temporary cessation of a process and its definitive termination. Thus, the compounded association or not of / d̲iiaṇ/ (lit. 'to give') with / chad̲aṇ/ ('to stop; finish') betokens either temporarily cessative aspect (Eng. *stop*) or completely terminative (Eng. *finish*), as in:

> /vaṇan ('The trees') pana ('(their) leaves') chaaṇaṇ ('to shed') chad̲ee (<chad̲aṇ) d̲inaa (<iiaṇ) /'The trees have stopped shedding their leaves' (i.e. some leaves remain)

versus

> /vaṇan pana chaaṇee) (<chaaṇaṇ chad̲iyaa (<chad̲aṇ)/'the trees have finished shedding their leaves' (i.e. have completely shed their leaves)

Some auxiliaries in these languages have no independent status as in the case of Urdu inceptive /lagnaa/, cf. /voh jaanee lagaa/ 'He's just going'. Aspects are indicated in some cases by a form of two-verb compound, e.g. /khaanaa/ 'to eat' +/jaanaa/ 'to go' >/khaa-jaanaa/ 'to eat up'. English, for its part, has only two tenses but considerable aspectual resources beyond the well-known progressive (*be -ing*) and perfect (*have -ed*) of the verb phrase. Typically involved are auxiliaries in replacement of progressive *be* (e.g. *begin*, *keep*, *stop*, *finish*), particles (especially *on*, *off*, *up*, *out*), and the *-ing* form of an accompanying main verb, to all of which we shall return.

There is one final factor conductive to present uncertainty over Aspect that should be mentioned. It is that a number of linguists plausibly see spatial position and locomotion as more basic than temporal counterparts, not least perhaps because at an early stage in his acquisition of language and experience the child is evidently much concerned with self-orientation in relation to phenomena and objects in the real world. J. M. Anderson, for instance, proposes 'a localist theory of aspect, in that various aspectual distinctions are interpreted as involving crucially the notions of location and direction' (1973a: 5). Bolinger in more than one place partly endorses this view (1971a: 246–50; 1971b: 110) and speaks of 'a deep-seated relationship between notions of action, state, progression, inception, completion, and the like, on the one hand, and notions of direction and position on the other – a kind of geometry of semantics'. A spatio-temporal view of Aspect has much to commend it on the evidence supplied by quite unrelated languages. It is striking, for example, that a link appears to occur between progressive aspect and position in a great many languages. In spoken Arabic, for instance, there is not only a noticeable use of /fi/ 'in' as a progressive indicator but also that of /gaaʕid/ 'sitting (at)', cf. Libyan (Cyrenaican Bedouin) /hu gaaʕid yiktib fi juwɑɑb/ 'He is (sitting a-) writing a letter'. Such structures closely resemble others, not only in contiguous Berber dialects but also in such remote languages as those of the Celtic family. Again, it is well known that seemingly locative constructions are used in innumerable languages to indicate the state of possession, and once again spoken Arabic is no exception, cf. Egyptian /ʔikkitaab ʕandak/? 'Have you got the book?' (lit. 'The book (is) with you?'). To the extent that, say, isolated /fi/ 'in' is punctual, it is aspectually zero, in contrast with the spread of aspectually continuative *on* in English (compare *He came on*). At all events, the equation between continuity in space and its correlate in time does not seem difficult to demonstrate.

Categories relevant to aspect in English sentences

Before we turn specifically to particles and auxiliaries of aspect in

English, it is well to consider the distribution of aspectual relevance among the parts of English sentences. There is probably something to be said for ascribing aspectual distinctions first and foremost to verbs, at least for the purpose of writing grammatical rules to the extent that these are formulable, but it seems unlikely that these distinctions are either produced or understood in such a way. True, verbs are classifiable on the basis of different behaviour in respect of aspectual features. Thus, although, as we shall see, the English sentence *John began to arrive* is perfectly acceptable if properly contextualized, it is nevertheless unacceptable if reference is to a particular arrival at a particular terminus; a similar contextual requirement, however, does not preclude *John began to eat*. Division between Newmeyer's 'continuous activity' verbs (*eat*) and Comrie's 'telic' verbs with 'built-in terminal points' (*arrive*) might seem justified. Yet it is also the case that *John began to pop in* is in fact immediately intelligible as iterative, thus contrasting with *John began to arrive*, which requires modifications and extensions that are dealt with below in order to permit iterative interpretation. Considering, then, examples of an SV 'intransitive' sentence pattern, we apparently find a preliminary threefold distinction between classes as follows:

(1) John began to eat (NON–TELIC, NON–ITERATIVE)
(2) John began to pop in (ITERATIVE)

and

(3) *John began to arrive (TELIC)

Now the aspectual classification of a verb may depend crucially upon features occurring at any point in the sentence. It is not any putatively inherent feature of 'punctuality' in *arrive* that decrees the unacceptability of (3); it is rather the singularity of the subject *John*, together with the sentence-finality of *arrive* that does not permit an iterative reading for the sentence. If a plural subject is substituted, the sentence is at once acceptable and iterative, cf.

(4) The guests began to arrive

Similar 'intransitive' behaviour is observable in the case of a class of verbs including *collect, mass, assemble, disband, separate, group, disperse, scatter*, etc. Cf.

(5) *John began to collect

and

(6) A crowd began to collect

Again, an adverbial or adjectival extension to (3) permits iterative interpretation, as in

(7) John began to arrive on time

and

(8) John began to arrive unshaven

Now the verb-class exemplified by *collect* at (5) and (6) also occurs with an object noun, in respect of which difference of number is as relevant as to the subject nouns in (3) and (4). Thus, cf.

(9) *John began to collect a stamp

and

(10) John began to collect stamps

In contrast with, say,

(11) *John began to burst a balloon

the following example

(12) The river began to burst a bank

may perhaps be less obviously acceptable than

(13) The river began to burst its banks

Yet it is none the less so, illustrating, I believe, SPATIAL iterativity, i.e. with the bank breached in more than one place, and is therefore not exceptional.

The foregoing facts could be formulated *prima facie* in terms of rules having something like the form

$$Vb_{telic/coll} \rightarrow *V/ \left[\frac{Subj}{+ sing} \right] \left[\frac{Aux}{+ inceptive} \right] \left[\underline{\quad\quad} ※ \right]$$

$$Vb_{coll} \rightarrow *V/ \left[\frac{Subj}{+ animate} \right] \left[\frac{Aux}{+ inceptive} \right] \left[\underline{\quad\quad} \right] \left[\frac{Obj}{+ sing} \right]$$

but these are no more than summations of the facts presented so far and are of doubtful value beyond. Examples of singular subject do occur with *begin to arrive*, cf. *The baby began to arrive* and, more importantly, the sentence *John began to arrive* is perfectly acceptable on a metaphorical reading of *arrive* = 'to "have it made", achieve material success'. Are we therefore to add [+literal] to the final bracket in the first rule as it affects 'telic' verbs? Surely not, since how is such a 'feature' recognizable, and how generalizable could it be in response to the infinitely varied use made of metaphor in everyday language? Again, although it has been said that *John began to pop in* and *The guests began to arrive* are at once interpretable as iterative, by what possible rule could *The guests began to pop in* be excluded from a grammar, when presumably its unacceptability depends on prior knowledge that includes the fact that 'guests' do not 'pop in', together with millions of other such particular facts of language-cum-experience? Nor, as Haas has most cogently argued (1975c), could we or should we try to cater for such things by the 'enrichment' of logical syntactico-semantics with simultaneous impoverishment of both logic and language study.

To continue with this review of sentence elements that may be relevant to aspectual interpretation, it is not of course a simple matter of grammatical number and similar categories (e.g. mass:count) as they affect the sentential functions of subject and object. The inceptive aspectual auxiliary *begin* was also necessary to the interpretation of *John began to arrive* as unacceptable in contrast with e.g. *John arrived*. So, too, was adverbial *on time* necessary for the iterative understanding of *John began to arrive on time*. Elsewhere the difference between *in* and *for* suffices to resolve the ambiguity of *read* (past) in *I read the book in five hours* (terminative) versus *I read the book for five hours* (cessative) without need of such expansions as *I finished reading the book in five hours* versus *I read the book for five hours, then stopped*. Adverbs, too, clearly play a most important role; compare the way in which they determine the different temporal readings to be attributed to the so-called 'progressive' form in *He is writing now, He is writing tomorrow, He is always writing, He is writing more clearly nowadays*. Again, if there is 'punctuality' or 'non-punctuality' anywhere, it is surely in the adverbs of, say, *He suddenly got better* versus *He gradually got better*. Finally by way of illustration, it can be the class of matrix verb in complex sentences that permits particular aspectual differences to be made in dependent clauses; compare the role of the perceptual matrix in, say, *I saw him climb the tree* (perfective *climb*) versus *I saw him climbing the tree* (progressive *climbing*). The fact is that, by whatever means we may seek to cut appropriate corners and sum things up in grammatical rules, any sentence element may play a part in the determination of aspect in English. The position of the verb in relation to Aspect seems rather like that of the noun as it concerns Concord in many languages (cf. Mitchell 1975: 137–45). There are few if any inherent features by which it 'controls' the aspectual interpretation of sentences but it must always be included in such interpretations and features may often be conveniently referred to it for the purpose of rule writing. Nevertheless in a sentence like *She went on chattering away to her heart's content all day long* every recognizable element, simple or complex, with the exceptions of *she* and *chat*, and including even phonaesthetic *-er*, contributes to the aspectual nature of the whole. Let us now turn specifically to consideration of English aspectual particles, the exemplar *on* having appeared in the last sentence cited.

English particles and auxiliaries of aspect

Indubitably locative particles, e.g. *by*, *at*, *near*, etc. are non-aspectual in accordance with the view taken here of Aspect as a matter of flow or spread rather than location. Other particles, however, notably *off*, *out*, *up*, and to a lesser extent *down*, are extremely productive in relation to terminal points of processes (i.e. beginnings and endings), while *on* is an important indicator of the middle or in-progress (otherwise, progressive–continuative) phase of a total process. There is thus, for example, a terminative spatial implication, a final covering of the distance between points X and Y, contained in the use of *up* in, say, *He came up (running)* or *he came (running) up*. It is not, of course, every use of a particle that is aspectual; the absence of *up* from *He tore the paper* and its presence in *He tore up the paper* is reminiscent of verb–case relationships in other languages but the particle here, totalitive versus the partitive case of its absence, seems to involve a semantic category of intensification belonging more to Aktionsart than Aspect. Word-meaning is a lexicographical fiction, attributable to shifts of register and the needs of memory, for words acquire most of their meaning from the company they keep and do not keep, actually or potentially, in discourse. Although it would be wrong to regard English aspectual particles as 'semantically empty', to search for their ESSENTIAL meanings is to succumb to the lure of the will-o'-the-wisp. Here are a few divisions which suggest themselves as appropriate to the uses, for example, of *out* — not incontrovertibly aspectual in all cases, it should be said, but clearly so in many:

TERMINATIVE:	sell out, pass out, peg out, peter out, give out (intransitive), carry out (= effect), last out
INCEPTIVE:	set out, break out (in a rash), burst out (laughing), strike out (for the shore), (bells) ring out
EXTENSIVE:	stretch out, spread out, string out, roll out (carpet), let out (trousers), line out (at rugby football), eke out, drag out
DISTRIBUTIVE:	mete out, deal out, hand out, give out
ABESSIVE:	cast out, ferret out, pop out, pour out
DISCRIMINATIVE:	stand out, make out, point out, find out, stick out (like a sore thumb)

But there is no 'out'-ness discernible for *out* in, e.g., idiomatic *hang out*, or in *deck out, do out* (a room), etc., and it would be impossible in many of the preceding examples to ascribe the designated meaning to either the verb or the particle considered severally. Although it is true that whatever *burns out* also *burns* beforehand, it is not the case that whoever *carries out* a plan carries anything. Again, one *carries on running* or *gives up running* and does not *carry running or *give running, so that it is not open to us to regard the particles as 'semantically empty' or a matter of so-called 'surface structure' or to label them indiscriminately 'prepositions', as transformationalists are apt to do. To complicate matters further, one must take into account collocational dependencies within comparable syntactic frames; thus, to take only aspectually terminative examples, it is *tracks*, *paths*, and perhaps *streams* that *peter out*, *candles* that *burn out*, *batteries* and *engines* that *give out*, *money* that both *gives out* and *runs out*, *fires* and *fireworks* that *go out*, and so on. It is, I believe, also noticeable that, of the four particles we are mainly considering (*up*, *out*, *off*, *on*), it is rare to find more than one ASPECTUALLY associated with a given verb; for instance, *He went up dancing is for practical purposes unacceptable, *He went out dancing* an example of adverbial *out*, *He went off dancing* triply interpretable, though in no case aspectually, between (i) he was dancing as he went off (adverbial *off*); (ii) he went off to a dance (adverbial *off*); (iii) he no longer liked dancing, so that, finally, *He went on dancing* and *He went dancing on* are alone aspectual. Moreover, Lyons's 'sense relations' seem hardly applicable when, for instance in the earlier examples, *out* is both inceptive and terminative, when at least in my own usage apparently antonymous particles *up* and *down* are semantically indistinguishable in, e.g., *He slowed up/down to let the car behind overtake*, when optional choices of particle are open to us, as between *up* and *off* in the case of *the chain reaction* that one *sets* either *up* or *off* or between *off* and *out* with reference to the *walking* on which one *sets* either *off* or *out*, or when once again the choice of particle is a matter of collocational or syntactic (and mnemonic) constraint, as when one *starts up an engine* but *sets off an alarm* and *starts (someone) off (laughing)*. What is yet more, I feel sure that not everyone will agree with my own judgments in these matters, for idiolectal and dialectal variation is another important source of complexity. For example, it often seems difficult for British speakers to believe what Americans say they do linguistically, and vice versa. Not only, then, do I find it hard personally to come to terms theoretically with Newmeyer's statement that *on* in *keep on* is 'inserted by a very late rule of the grammar' but it is also hard to accept that two of the three sentences quoted in this context as ungrammatical are in fact so, namely *Mary's condition kept on steadily worsening* and *Jack kept on not working* (1975: 54–5). It seems to me, then, that all the evidence (not only of this essay) supports a theoretical view of language, the object of the linguist's study, as simultaneously embodying continuity and change, stability and flux, and that it must indeed be so if it is to meet the demands we make of it in response to our own nature. It has its rules but it has at the same time the flexibility that permits planned and impromptu innovation; it is not the homogeneous, tightly organized affair in which many wish to believe but rather a 'chunky', regularistic, 'more-or-less' structure of the kind that Haas and Bolinger have described so perceptiently (Haas 1973a, 1975; Bolinger 1976).

In face of the evident semantic heterogeneity of *out* (and *up* and *off* are no less heterogeneous; cf. Mitchell 1975: 108–14), the more or less constant continuative aspectual meaning of *on* is remarkable. Perhaps, however, before relevant examples are supplied, it would be well to identify the category still to concern us, namely the verbal auxiliaries of aspect, since these and the particles so often work in unison. In some cases the particle provides aspectual meaning to phrasal verbs (e.g. *go on*, *carry on*, *give up*), elsewhere the verb is itself aspectual, tolerating or rejecting a particle as in the cases of *keep* (± *on*) and *begin* respectively. I believe that a special relationship obtains between the verbal auxiliaries and the progressive (*be -ing*) of the verbal periphrasis to the extent that any member of the class should be substitutable for *be*. This is not to say that the auxiliaries do not participate in the periphrasis on their own account, so to speak, cf. *keep* (± *on*) in association or not with perfect *have* in, e.g., *He keeps asking, He has kept asking*, with progressive *be* in, e.g., *He keeps on trying, He is keeping on trying*, with passive *be/get* in, e.g., *He keeps being/getting caught*, and with combinations thereof in, e.g., *He has kept on being/getting caught*. It seems that the support of two kinds of research finding, statistical and distributional, would strictly be necessary to support the recognition of the open-ended list of aspectual auxiliaries given below. At present I can say no more than that they appear to be the most significant| members of an extensible class. I am aware that these and other verbs are used aspectually in environments other than [– -ing], also that other verbs with aspectual interpretability occur before -*ing*, but a ranking of criteria must prevail in the corner-cutting process of descriptive analysis and among these the substitutability for progressive *be* and a characteristic pattern of distribution within the verbal periphrasis should, I think, be paramount, together of course with unequivocal interpretation in aspectual terms. I should personally agree, too, with Newmeyer's 'self-embedding' hypothesis, by which the subject of the auxiliary and of the main verb should be coreferential and the auxiliary extrapolable in the way spoken of earlier with reference to the extrapolability of inceptive *begin* from, say, *John begins writing a letter every day at 9 o'clock* (= [S]$_{inc}$). Nevertheless, criteria must again be ranked, so that I should not wish, for example, to exclude *start*, which shares synonymously a good deal of the aspectual distribution of *begin* and is substitutable, for instance, in the preceding sentence. Here now is the promised list, with the auxiliaries presented within a framework of substitution for progressive *be*:

He	was	reading when I came in
INCEPTIVE {	began	
	started	NOTE

For stylistic reasons, *resume* (= start again) and *commence* are not included. *Continue* also differs from *go on*, *carry on* as to stylistic employment and frequency of occurrence, though it may still belong to standard

PROGRESSIVE– CONTINUATIVE (including ITERATIVE) { kept (on) carried on went on

TERMINATIVE (including CESSATIVE, COMPLETIVE and NON- COMPLETIVE)	{ stopped left off gave up finished	spoken English, it seems to me, in a way that *resume* and *commence* do not. *Cease* has been excluded for similar reasons. Once again, not everyone is likely to agree

The infinitival forms of the auxiliaries are, of course, *begin, start, keep (on), carry on, go on, stop, leave off, give up, finish*. Let us look now at some of the facts concerning individual auxiliaries with and without the ubiquitous particles.

The overlapping – here of the synonymous kind, elsewhere cross-classificatory – which is a pervasive indication of the essential flexibility of language, characterizes the relationship between *begin* and *start* but, though the substitution of one for the other is often permissible, there are also noticeable differences of use between them. *Start* (cf. the phonaesthetically related *startle*) is, unlike *begin*, associated as a non-auxiliary verb with a component of 'instantaneousness' in, e.g.

He started up with alarm

which to my mind is also present in

He started the car/the race

but not in

He began the book/the interrogation

More generally, however, a verbal *-ing* form (specifically *reading* and *conducting* in the examples given) may plausibly be considered, as Newmeyer suggests, to have been deleted from the latter sentences containing *begin*, but not, it would seem, from the preceding sentences containing *start*. The latter in, say,

He started the car

seems to refer to two events, the operation of the appropriate control and the starting of the engine, and may reasonably be seen as causative and to embody the sentence *The car started*, from which *began*, of course, is excluded (**The car began*). Causative interpretation of *start* seems even more clearly justified in, e.g.

He started her (off) laughing

where the change of subject between *started* and *laughing* is overt and the reading 'He did something as a result of which she started laughing' apparently clear. But the inclusion of the sentence

> She started laughing

is crucial to the inclusion of *start* in the foregoing list of auxiliaries of aspect, and the frequent substitutability of *start* for *begin* is further justification. This is not, of course, to say that we should not regard *start* as the same verb among the diversity of

> He started up with alarm
> He started the car
> The car started

and

> She started laughing

There is no regular causative relation between other verbs of the list, it may be noted in passing; typically, *make* is required in causative forms, e.g.

> He made him keep on trying

though *stop* is both causative and non-causative, cf.

> He stopped (her) laughing

Other types of relationship involve constraints between auxiliaries indicative of different phases in a process, especially when these are consecutive; thus, for instance, the inceptive auxiliaries concerning us permit a following terminative, cf.

> He began to stop, leave off, give up going

but preclude a progressive–continuative auxiliary, cf.

> *He began to keep on, carry on, go on going

Such constraints deserve closer examination than it is possible to accord them here.

The particles are often interestingly used in association with the auxiliaries to mark contrasts between phases of an extended or including process (or processes), e.g.

> He started off grumbling but finished up laughing

Again, by their inclusion or exclusion, or by contrasts between them, the particles may serve to identify types of process involved and accompanying grammatical categories. Thus, gerundial *painting the kitchen* is an object noun phrase in

> He finished off painting the kitchen (i.e. having started (painting) and left off (painting))

but the homophonous form is participial in

> He finished up painting the kitchen (i.e. instead for instance of going to the football match)

In the latter case, *painting the kitchen* indicates the terminative phase of some including process, as in

> He started off wanting to see the football match but finished up painting the kitchen

The difference between the two is relatable to that between

> What did he finish (off)?

and

> How did he finish up?

Three particles may be used to mark the three principal phases of such including processes; thus, when for example talking of someone's progress from A to B, we may say

> (INCEPTIVE) He set off (OR out) running, (PROGRESSIVE–CONTINUATIVE) carried on running (for a few miles), but (TERMINATIVE) finished up walking

Here *finish* belongs to a total process (*set off–carry on–finish*) but in the earlier example to the single process of *paint the kitchen*. It is only in the including case that the pattern exemplified by

> He finished up walking

is paraphrasable as

> He was walking when he finished

It is *finish*$_1$ of

> He finished (off) painting the kitchen

that is essential for the inclusion of *finish* in the list of auxiliaries, not least since other verbs, e.g. *end (up)*, *wind up*, may be substituted for *finish*₂, i.e.

He ended up/wound up walking

At the same time the role played by the particles *off* and *up* in resolving any potential ambiguities is noteworthy.

Turning now to progressive–continuative auxiliaries and to *keep* ±*on* in particular, I see no justification for identifying the *keep* of

They keep rabbits

with

They keep grumbling

or for thinking that all occurrences of *keep* are aspectual and to be equated with the auxiliary in some way. At the same time, as we have seen in the case of *begin* and *start*, the flexibility and built-in mechanisms for change that abound in language show themselves in the language as a whole between *keep* and *stay*. Once again, there seems to obtain a good deal of synonymous overlapping, especially where reference is to location as in

Keep/Stay off the grass

or

The rain kept/stayed away

But it is *stay*, not *keep*, that is 'inherently' locative, with a possible gloss 'remain *in situ*' applicable also to e.g.

He stayed with us overnight

where *keep* may not be substituted. *Keep* often stands in 'causative' or 'transitive' relation to *stay*, cf. *to keep someone away* versus *to keep/stay away*. To return to the auxiliaries of our main concern, however, the association of *stay* with *-ing* is restricted and of a different order from that applicable to *keep*, whence the exclusion of *stay* from the earlier list of auxiliaries. The relationship between *stay* and *-ing* is in a sense a reverse one from that between *keep* and *-ing*, so that in sentences like

You stay there reading, I'll go and do the shopping

or

He stayed reading when he should have gone out

participial -*ing* 'modifies' *stay* and is omissible in a way that does not apply to *keep* in

You keep reading, I'll go and do the shopping

and

He kept on reading when he should have gone out

Any uncertainty that one feels over the acceptability of the *keep*-sentences here doubtless springs from the iterativity so frequently associated with the auxiliary and which is discussed below. In the meantime, it may perhaps be said again that one cannot plausibly regard all occurrences of the verb *keep* as classifiable semantically with the auxiliary. For example, I believe that it is a case of locative *keep* in

The rain kept off

but of continuative auxiliary *keep* in

The rain kept on

The latter is synonymous with and regularly relatable syntactically to

It kept on raining

to which the support of other examples like

The snow kept on/It kept on snowing

might be added. The view of things taken here is also supported by the looseness of association between *kept* and *off* in *The rain kept off*, indicated for instance by the substitutability of *away* for *off* and *held* for *kept*.

Keep ±*on* is progressive–continuative ±interrupted, i.e. iterative or not. If the main verb is 'inherently' limited as to duration, e.g. *interrupt*, *yawn*, then interpretation is uniquely iterative, cf.

He kept interrupting/yawning

but, in the absence of further contextual indices, the majority of cases are 'ambiguous' between iterative and non-iterative, cf.

He kept coming

Nor does the inclusion of *on*, in my own speech at any rate, serve to eliminate the 'ambiguity'. It may be included 'otiosely' in the iterative

He kept on interrupting

but equally in a non-iterative reading of

He kept on coming

As we have seen, *on* is essentially continuative and provides pertinent exemplification of the associability under Aspect of time and space. In, say, the direction-giving sentence

Keep on to the traffic lights, then turn left

it is presumably plausible not only to regard, e.g., *walking* or *driving* as deleted following *keep* but also *on* as simultaneously spatial and temporal. There is, however, an interesting difference of positional occurrence between temporal and spatial *on* in the company of main verbal *-ing*. Thus, although

They kept on coming

is ambiguous between (i) continuative versus iterative, with a possible preference for the latter interpretation, and (ii) temporal and spatial readings, nevertheless the order

They kept coming on (in spite of heavy losses)

is unmistakably spatial as far as *on* is concerned. Although *carry on* and *go on* are, in contrast with *keep ±on*, predominantly non-iterative, and *on* forms a unitary auxiliary with the preceding verb, the particle retains throughout its continuative meaning. *Carry on*, frequently temporal, is clearly interpretable spatio-temporally in, say, the report of the footballer's progress

They hacked at him but somehow he carried on and scored

where it is presumably again legitimate to consider that an *-ing* form, e.g. *dribbling*, has been deleted. In this case, the reverse order

*He carried dribbling on

versus

He carried on dribbling

is inadmissible, in contrast with the duality of possible order permitted by *go on*, cf.

He went dribbling on

and

> He went on dribbling

This difference of order in the case of *go on* permits differences of focus as between the highlighting of *dribbling* in

> He went on dribbling (when he should have passed)

and of continuative *on* in

> He went dribbling on (and nobody could stop him)

A continuing, apparently interminable process imposes the order cited in

> He went droning on

but not in, say,

> He went on talking

It was said that *carry on* and *go on* are predominantly non-iterative; this is not to say that they do not occur in iterative sentences, cf.

> He does carry on (grumbling) (so)

or

> He will go on (talking) (interminably)

but the iterative interpretation depends, as in the examples shown, on other items in the text or on 'prosodic' features of pronunciation. There are other differences between these auxiliaries and between each of them and *keep ±on*, notwithstanding a large measure of 'synonymous overlapping' between the three. For instance, where, in an extended process of the kind recognized earlier in relation to *finish*, the type of constituent process changes, as in

> He started off walking, then carried on trotting, and finished up running

kept on is not substitutable for *carried on*, but when reference is to the continuation of the same initial process, as in

> He started off running and carried on running all the way home

kept on may be freely substituted.

The cohesion between particle and verb is, as we have seen, of several degrees, so that *on* is omissible from association with the non-auxiliary *ramble* in

He rambled on

without prejudice to the sentential status or semantic identity of the remainder; but it is one of a set of inomissible 'directional' complements in

He shambled on

and is likewise inomissible from its unitary association with *carry* in

He carried on (talking)

Yet, despite the range and intricacy of its distributional employment, *on* is remarkably stable as to its interpretability in comparison with *off*, *out*, and *up*, which, together with *on*, form as far as particles are concerned the backbone of this interesting (Auxiliary ± Particle) area of English aspect.

We have now seen something of the inceptive and progressive–continuative of the generally agreed three main phases of a process. It is appropriate, therefore, to draw the process of writing this essay to a close on a cessative and terminative note. Rather, however, than ask Vendler's questions (1967) *Has it stopped?* versus *Has it finished?* (quoted in Lyons 1977: 711), I shall first look briefly at the uses, for instance, of the auxiliaries *stop* and *finish*. Sufficient examples of *finish* have already been provided. *Stop*, for its part, in contexts of contrast with *finish*, is cessative, i.e. it betokens a presumed or potential resumption of the process where the substitution of *finish* would be finalitive or terminative. Thus, cf.

He stopped painting the kitchen

and

He finished painting the kitchen

Just as at the other (inceptive) end of the process scale we saw that *begin* was acceptable with verbs like *eat*, cf.

John began eating, to eat

but not with those like *arrive*, cf.

*John began arriving, to arrive

unless the latter was extended to permit iterative reference to a plurality of events, cf.

John began arriving, to arrive late

so, at the terminative end, there are comparable constraints in the case of *stop*. It is not so much, *pace* Lyons (1977: 712), that verbs like *arrive* or *leave* 'cannot normally be used in a durative aspect (e.g. in the English progressive)', cf.

He was arriving/leaving as I left/arrived

nor is it just that such 'achievement-denoting verbs' refer to events rather than processes. What seems to matter most about any event is that it should be a single one, since although we do not say

*John stopped arriving

we have no difficulty in saying

John stopped arriving late

which implies a plurality of arrivals. There seems to be some tendency for the main verb following *finish* to require an object noun but there is more than a tendency for reference to be to a single event or process. For example, if I wish to report John's renunciation of the smoking habit, I should not say

*John finished smoking

which needs completion as in

John finished smoking his cigar

I would say rather

John stopped smoking

or

John gave up smoking

to refer to John's earlier iterative activity. On the evidence so far, the following pattern would suggest itself, as far as contrast between *stop* and *finish* is concerned:

(a) *John stopped arriving   *John finished arriving
(b)   John stopped eating   John finished eating
(c)   John stopped smoking   *John finished smoking

But any measure of exclusion between *stop* and *finish* at (c) may involve not only a necessary singularity of event or process for *finish* but also differences involving the multivalent *-ing* form of the main verb. Is it this latter factor or is it the pervasive variation already commented upon that allows me to use *finish* as well as *stop*, perhaps even to prefer *finish*, in

John finished/stopped playing (football) (years ago)?

In fact, I suspect that I should most often replace them both in such a context by the unequivocally terminative *give up*. Indeed, the availability of a number of auxiliaries in this general 'terminative' area responds to the recognition in non–iterative contexts of more than two degrees of termination; cf., for instance,

John stopped writing the letter   (CESSATIVE)
John finished writing the letter   (COMPLETIVE)
John gave up writing the letter   (NON–COMPLETIVE)

The abovementioned multivalence of *-ing* cannot be ignored. The sentence

John gave up running

variously refers to a single race or to John's iterated activity as a runner. The former reading does not permit the transposability allowed in the case of the latter, i.e.

John gave running up

A comparable 'minimal' contrast, involving in this case the presence or absence of the particle *off*, occurs between

John left off lecturing

where reference is to a particular lecture and transposition again inadmissible, and

John left lecturing

where reference is to John's former career as a lecturer. Nor is the particle associated only with non–iterative processes, cf.

John left off going there

which does not correspond to any form

*John left going there

The absence of the particle seems to specify the 'career' use of *-ing*, cf.

> John left off swimming (EITHER after a few strokes OR on doctor's
> advice)

versus

> John left swimming (altogether)

A point of departure within Logic is usually not very helpful, however irritated one may feel over the untidiness of language. Vendler's 'accomplishments', for example, are said to be processes moving towards natural conclusions, so that the culmination of the process *decide*, for instance, is taking a decision. *To run a race*, but not just *to run*, is similarly an accomplishment. Of such accomplishments it is held that one can ask: 'How long did it take John to decide/run the race?' But the verb *decide* seems to behave *grosso modo* in the manner of *arrive*, cf.

> *John stopped deciding

but

> John stopped deciding matters years ago

and the question 'How long did John take to run the race?' seems quite irrelevant to the culmination of John's participation in the race, as a result of injury or from whatever cause, which is referred to in the form

> John stopped running

and not

> *John finished running

The possibility of John's resuming running is, to my mind, not in question. Not only do we need to take into account differences of number and transitivity as well as the multivalence of *-ing* but I also believe that behaviour in, say, the perfect may not be in parallel with that described here predominantly in terms of the past tense of report, nor again, for instance, as between the tenses and the imperative. All should be accounted for in a comprehensive treatment from linguistic beginnings, not to mention the pervasive manifestations of variability in language.

I can do no better than conclude with reference to the writings of the scholar to whom we gladly do honour in this volume, for I believe this paper is fully in accord with his teaching on questions touching the very foundations of Linguistics. William Haas recognizes the existence of obligatory grammatical rules but attaches greater importance to those infinitely more numerous grammatico-semantic regularities that cannot be said to be rules in any 'watertight' sense. Drawing attention to the transformationalists' 'animate subject' rule by which, for instance,

> The chimpanzee is eating the banana

is more normal than

> The banana is eating the chimpanzee

but

> The chimpanzee is eating up the car

less normal than

> Rust is eating up the car

Haas has conclusively demonstrated that 'rules' of this kind require further specification to such a degree of accumulated detail that would amount to a description of the universe and be quite irreducible to any system of rules. Yet Haas would not reject this or similar 'rules' but say rather that there is SOME truth to them and that what we have to deal with as linguists is for the most part types of regularity not binding any individual sentence but characterizing sets of sentences. 'We are concerned with something akin to probability statements; though, since we have to rely on judgments of acceptability and of comparative normality rather than on statistical measures, we might refer to *habits* and *tendencies*, rather than probabilities' (1973a: 146). As Haas says, within the fixed form of the rule requiring the verb *permit* to be preceded by subject and followed by object in a declarative sentence, we can observe the TENDENCY (repeated with other verbs) for both nouns to be 'animate', although we are always free to ignore such tendencies and to say, for instance,

> The ceiling did not permit the grandfather clock to stand upright

Moreover, a balance must always be struck by individual linguists making their cognitive judgments and cutting their corners in the process of analysis; any kind of utopian or totalitarian approach is inappropriate to the nature of the subject matter. Haas returns to his thesis of meanings presented within the framework of syntactic rules in a powerfully argued paper (1975c) in which he also shows that, although logical syntax is derived from ordinary language, it is fallacious to believe that the reverse is ever possible. The more 'enriched' the language of logical idealization, the greater the necessary 'intrusion' for instance of 'pragmatics' or 'modality' and, correspondingly, the more remote the possibility of providing 'non-arbitrary', non-linguistic base structures for the description of syntax. At the same time, the scope for the study of sentences within a limited propositional framework of truth value is drastically reduced. Such 'enrichment' is in accord with Haas's view of the structure and nature of ordinary language but is highly inimical to the kind of 'deep structure engineering' that for two decades now has quite failed to characterize our object of study. Rules there must be in life and language, as imperative as continuity; tendencies, too, are as inevitable as flux. Come to think of it, continuity and change are at the heart of the matter of Aspect.

Non-assertion and modality

F. R. PALMER

There is a *prima facie* plausibility in the attempt to analyse modality within a language such as English in terms similar to those suggested by logicians for quantification. In particular there seems to be a close parallelism, especially in relation to negation, between 'possible' and 'necessary' on the one hand and 'some' and 'all' on the other. Some support for this view may be seen in the table suggested by von Wright (1951: 1–2), in which the existential mode with its terms 'universal', 'existing' and 'empty' parallels the alethic mode with 'necessary', 'possible' and 'impossible' and the deontic mode with 'obligatory', 'permitted' and 'forbidden'. (I shall not, however, use von Wright's terms or classifications and shall, in fact, use 'necessary', 'possible' and 'impossible' more generally when referring to any kind of modality.) It is also relevant, perhaps, to note that the modal verb CAN may be used not only in a modal sense, but also in a quantificational or existential sense in, for instance, *Lions can be dangerous* which may mean 'Some lions are dangerous' (though it can also mean 'Lions are sometimes dangerous' and is usually indeterminate between all three).

We must, of course, be very careful in adapting logical notions to the description of natural languages, but it is nevertheless true that some aspects of the English modals can be accounted for in terms of such notions as 'necessary' and 'possible' together with negation, and certain logical or semi-logical relations between them. It is these that I wish to investigate.

1. Non-assertion

So far I have spoken only of negation, but mentioned non-assertion in the title. This term is used by Quirk *et al.* (1972: 54) to include both negation and interrogation. It is clear that in many respects, negation and interrogation function similarly in English (and probably in many other languages).

Within the modal system we may note the following pattern for epistemic possibility:

> John may be there
> John can't be there
> Can John be there?

MAY, we can see, is used for assertion and CAN for non-assertion, both negation and interrogation. There is a similar pattern with the quantifiers SOME and ANY (though there are also complexities that must not concern us here):

> John has some money
> John hasn't any money
> Has John any money?

When talking of 'negation', however, we must not simply be concerned with forms with final *-n't* or with *not*, but also with negative words such as *never, no-one, nothing* and even the semi-negatives (Palmer 1974: 28) such as *hardly* and *scarcely*. For instance, in suggesting that auxiliary NEED (not followed by TO) will occur in non-assertion, we must include all of these:

> John needn't come
> Need John come?
> John need never come
> No-one need come
> John need hardly come

There are also some environments of a negative kind, that are included under Klima's (1964: 313) heading of 'affective'. In general some rules apply to these, but there is no place for a detailed discussion here.

2. *Modality and event*

When it is said that a modal verb is formally negated, it is important to ask whether the negation belongs semantically with the 'modality' or the 'event'. I use the term 'modality' to refer to the meaning of the modal and 'event' in the sense of the meaning of the following main verb, recognizing, with Joos that it may specify 'relations [RESEMBLE, etc.] and states [WORRY, BE COLD] as well as deeds [SHOW]' (1958: 243).

It is also important to distinguish between the formal negation of the modal (as discussed in the last paragraph) and the semantic negation of the modality and event. (There would have been some advantage in using two different terms instead of the one, but there are no obvious candidates – but see below on interrogation.)

In general, if it is possible for either the modality or the event to be negated, this is achieved by using different modal verbs. Thus for the epistemic modals *may not* negates the event ('it is possible that . . . not . . .'), while *can't* negates the modality ('it is not possible that . . .'); similarly non-epistemic *mustn't* negates the event ('it is necessary for . . . not . . .') and *needn't* negates the modality ('it is not necessary for . . .'). Some of the details will be the concern of later sections.

With interrogation it is only the modality that can be questioned (here we can distinguish formal 'interrogation' and semantic 'question'). What is important, of course, is that in general the form used for negating the modality will be the one that is used for questioning it as we saw for epistemic MAY and CAN in §1.

3. *Epistemic modality*

There is no doubt that English uses the verbs CAN, MAY and MUST (at least) to express epistemic modality, though of a 'subjective' kind (Lyons 1977: 792), to express judgments by the speaker. MAY and MUST express assertive possibility and necessity respectively:

John may be in his office
John must be in his office

('Necessity' may seem a misleading term because *necessary* is not used in an epistemic sense in English, but that is, perhaps, merely a fact about the English word; we need a term to express the strongest epistemic modality, that of a firm conclusion, and 'necessity' is the obvious choice.)

There are regularly only two negatives:

John can't be in his office
John may not be in his office

These can be interpreted respectively as the modality-negative ('not possible that . . .') and event-negative ('possible that . . . not . . .')

forms of epistemic possibility. Yet it could be argued that *can't* is the event-negative of epistemic necessity ('necessary that . . . not . . .'), and so related not to MAY, but to MUST. By a continuation of the argument, but less plausibly, *may not* can be seen as the modality-negative ('not necessary that . . .') of necessity.

The fact that these alternative interpretations are possible can, perhaps, be explained by the equivalence of 'not possible ≡ necessary not' and 'not necessary ≡ possible not'. For if these equivalences hold, as they seem to in epistemic modality, there is no need for four different forms ('not-possible', 'possible-not', 'not-necessary', 'necessary-not'), but only two.

Halliday (1970: 333) concludes from the fact that there are regularly only two forms for negation in epistemic modality that there is 'no negative modality', i.e. that the modality is never negated, but only the event. He interprets the two, that is to say, as 'possible-not' (*may not*) and 'necessary-not' (*can't*). But this is not what is suggested by the language. If there are only two possibilities they are 'possible-not' and 'not-possible', since MAY and CAN are clearly both possibility modals.

Epistemic possibility thus seems to be the more basic (cf. Lyons 1977: 801), and the negative forms for necessity are not really required because there are equivalent possibility forms.

Nevertheless it is not true that there are no negative necessity forms in English. Both of the following are possible in an epistemic sense:

> John needn't be in his office
> John mustn't be in his office

These are, however, unusual and would be likely only if there was some reason to stress necessity rather then possibility. For instance, either might be used after the positive sentence *John must be in his office*, the first simply to deny the necessity, the second to affirm, by contrast, that the opposite conclusion should be drawn. Rather more likely contexts are:

> He may be there, but he needn't be
> He mustn't be there, after all

In the first there is a contrast between asserting possibility and negating necessity. In the second the emphasis is on what, after all, must not be, rather than what cannot be.

It is worth noting that there is, or may be, a similar occurrence of only one form where there are two logically equivalent possibilities elsewhere – in the quantification system. For there is no single correct logical analysis of:

I didn't see anybody

It can be argued that this is to be analysed in terms of 'not-some' ($\sim \exists$). This is, in effect, the solution that Bolinger (1960: 387) would suggest. Yet it can equally be seen as 'all-not' ($\forall \sim$). The order of the quantifiers in the English sentence, *not* and *any*, seems to suggest the former solution. If so, 'some' is basic, just as epistemic possibility is. But we then must ask about:

I saw nobody

Is this the 'all–not' form? There is nothing in the language to show that it is. It is better seen as an alternative with a fusion of the two logical words. By contrast, there is no problem about distinguishing the logically equivalent 'not-all' and 'some-not':

Not everyone came/Everyone didn't come
Some people didn't come

In spite of such problems, it seems fairly clear that epistemic modality, in fact, follows a fairly logical pattern in relation to negation, that there are equivalences, and that these equivalences can account for the occurrence or non-occurrence (rare occurrence) of forms.

4. *Non-epistemic modality*

There are certainly several kinds of non-epistemic modality. I shall concentrate here on what I call 'deontic' and '(neutral) dynamic'. The former is essentially performative and has its most typical expression in the giving of permission with MAY or CAN. The latter merely expresses the notions of 'possible for' and 'necessary for' with no involvement of the speaker. But while it is usually easy enough to distinguish deontic and dynamic possibility, it is much less easy to distinguish deontic and dynamic necessity. When MUST is used, it is seldom clear whether the speaker is personally laying an obligation or merely stating what is necessary (though, in contrast HAVE TO and HAVE GOT TO clearly deny the speaker's involvement).

Taking deontic possibility first, it is clear that we can negate the modality, i.e. refuse permission to act:

You can/may go now   (possible)
You can't/may not go now   (not-possible)

There is, however, no obvious form to negate the event, to give permission not to act. This may, perhaps, be achieved by accenting the negative *nót*:

You can/may nót go now

Yet this is ambiguous. It might equally be taken as a very firm refusal of permission. Accenting *nót* merely indicates that there is something unusual; it might be, but it is not necessarily the case, that *not* belongs with the main verb, and so negates the event. This will certainly be the case in, e.g.:

You can always nót go
You can go or nót go

With deontic necessity *mustn't* negates the event, while *needn't* seems to negate the modality:

You mustn't go   (necessary-not)
You needn't go   (not-necessary)

It is abundantly clear that the equivalence 'not-possible ≡ necessary not' does not work for deontic modality, for *You can/may not go* does not have the same meaning as *You mustn't go* (though Seuren (1969: 160) argues that *mustn't* is the negative of 'universal permission'), even though they have the same perlocutionary effect. The reason is, presumably, that giving permission normally presumes that the speaker is in a position where the action will not take place without his permission, whereas laying an obligation does not imply that he has the authority needed, though he may well take upon himself authority to prevent it. With permission, then, positive action by the speaker is needed to permit the event, while with obligation positive action is needed to prevent it, and, thus, not giving permission ('not-possible') is not the same as laying an obligation not to ('necessary-not').

But there is still the worrying point that there is no simple way of giving permission not to act. Is it, then, necessarily the case that *needn't* is the 'not-necessary' form, or could it equally be seen as 'possible-not', the means of giving permission not to act? There is no clear answer to this question. In general the meaning of NEED suggests that it is a necessity, not a possibility, modal. It may be, then, that here we must say that the necessity is basic, but that the 'not-necessary' form is used where 'possible-not' is required. If so, in contrast with the distinction between *can't/may not* and *mustn't*, the 'not-necessary ≡ possible-not' equivalence seems to be valid, since one form may be used for either.

With dynamic modality ('possible/necessary for' with no involvement of the speaker) there are some differences. First, *can't* is used to negate the modality, but there is in effect no way of using a modal to negate the event with possibility (and a paraphrase of some kind is needed):

He can get a job	(possible)
He can't get a job	(not-possible)
It is possible for him not to get a job	(possible-not)

With dynamic necessity, we again have the negative forms *mustn't* and *needn't*, but also *don't have to* (or *haven't got to*). *Don't have to* usually negates the modality and not the event; but it may be ambiguous as shown by:

I don't have to go to work today

This would normally be taken to mean that it is not necessary for me to go to work, but it could mean that I must not go (e.g. because I am not fit enough).

What of the equivalences? Clearly *can't* is not the same as *mustn't*, so that it is not the case that not-possible ≡ necessary-not. I am not so sure, however, whether *needn't* (again) and *don't have to* serve as equivalences to the 'missing' 'possible-not' as in:

He needn't/doesn't have to get a job

When we look at the past tense, the position is complicated by the fact that MUST has no past tense forms. This is important because *mustn't* in the present is the only form available for negating the event. There is, then, no problem with 'not-necessary'; this is expressed by *didn't have to*. But there is no obvious way of expressing 'necessary-not'. Thus:

I don't have to go to London	(not-necessary)
I mustn't go to London	(necessary-not)
I didn't have to go to London	(not-necessary)
? ? ?	(necessary-not)

How, then, can 'necessary-not' in the past be expressed? One solution is to use *didn't have to*, but that is, of course, ambiguous and likely to be taken in the other more usual (not-necessary) sense. A second possibility is to use the paraphrase *It was necessary for me not* . . . . Thirdly, however, it might seem that the required meaning can be indicated by *couldn't*, i.e. by using the potentially equivalent 'not-possible' form. Consider:

> Since I want to get well, I mustn't smoke
> Since I wanted to get well, I didn't have to smoke
> Since I wanted to get well, I couldn't smoke

If we are to ask which is the more reasonable past tense analogue of the first example, the answer must surely be the third. The second is ambiguous, although the context may force the 'necessary-not' meaning. But that forcing is a little unnatural.

All of this leaves us with a messy situation. It is clear that in both deontic and dynamic modality there are in general no equivalences in terms of negation. But in certain cases a modal that belongs formally either to possibility or necessity may seem to fill a gap in the other set. Where there are contrasting forms we have no doubt that the equivalences are not valid. Where there is no contrast we are not so sure.

5. *Interrogation*

Let us now look in a little detail at interrogation. Generally, the form used is the same as that used for negation (negation of the modality, since only the modality can be questioned). For epistemic possibility there is no problem. CAN is used (as it is in negation):

> Can John be in his office?

For necessity there is a problem, because there is no normal form for negating the modality. Instead of 'not-necessary' the 'possible-not' form, *may not* is used. But we saw that *needn't* is also used as 'not-necessary' and, therefore, we might expect to find:

> Need John be in his office?

In fact, this seems to me to be less likely than:

> Must John be in his office?

Yet this is surprising since *mustn't* negates not the modality, but the event. The explanation for its use is, presumably, that English has no completely obvious form and there is, with interrogation, no danger of ambiguity.

With deontic and dynamic modality there is no real problem. For the former, both MAY and CAN ask permission and NEED asks if there is any obligation. For the latter MAY is no longer used while HAVE TO and HAVE GOT TO are available for necessity:

> Can/may I leave now?
> Need I leave now?
> Can he get a job?
> Does he have to get a job?

Yet MUST may also be used:

> Must I leave now? Must he get a job?

There is, perhaps, some suggestion that the necessity is already implicitly or explicitly in the context – a MUST somewhere already understood by the participant is being questioned. In a similar way, *mustn't* may be used to negate the necessity if there is what Halliday calls 'verbal crossing out' (1970: 333) as in, e.g.:

> He must go now. – Oh, no he mustn't

6. *Negative interrogatives*

The situation with negative interrogatives is rather more complex. In general they seem to be questions that, in traditional terms, 'expect the answer "Yes",' like Latin *nonne*. Certainly they are not simply questions about the negative; *Aren't you coming?* does not ask 'Is it the case that you are not coming?', but is nearer to 'Isn't it the case that you are coming?' (and it is certainly more like *You're coming, aren't you?* than You're not coming, are you?).

It is not surprising, perhaps, that with epistemic modality MAY and MUST are used, i.e. the forms that are used for assertion; this is either because negative interrogatives are often rhetorical assertions, or because negation and interrogation 'cancel each other out'. An excellent example from the Survey of English Usage (University College London) is:

> I like to think about those days and how tough it was for the average Englishman what a hard life they must have had and mustn't there be endless stories about this mansion (*S*.12.6.75)

There is little to be said about deontic and dynamic possibility where MAY and CAN are used for the former, and CAN for the latter, e.g.:

> May I not go now?
> Can't I go now?
> Can't he get a job?

With necessity, however, the situation is far more complex. To begin with there is the normal type of negative interrogation (with HAVE TO for dynamic modality only):

> Mustn't John come?
> Doesn't John have to come?

These, on this interpretation, expect the answer 'Yes'. However, both of them may also question the proposition in which the event is negated, i.e. they may question *John mustn't come*. Alternatively, of course, *Doesn't John have to come?* may be seen as questioning *John doesn't have to come* with its alternative, rarer meaning with the event, not the modality, negated, though curiously I find this event-negation interpretation much more likely for the negative interrogative than for the simple negative.

It is tempting to distinguish these two interpretations simply in terms of the negation of modality and of the event. In the more usual sense the modality is negated, in the second sense it is the event that is negated. We have, then, in effect:

> (a) Question + neg-necessary + *come*
> (b) Question + necessary + neg-*come*

But this is not satisfactory for two reasons. First, if this is so, we should expect a regular use of HAVE TO for (a) and of MUST for (b) as is found with non-question forms. *Mustn't* ought not to question negative modality, but only positive modality with a negative event. Secondly, there is a third possibility with *needn't*:

> Needn't I come?

Now it is clearly this form (but not *mustn't* or *don't have to*) that questions the negative modality. It asks 'Is it true that I needn't come?' It is clearly not the case, then, that the normal negative interrogative can be interpreted as question together with negative modality.

The correct solution, I believe, is that negative interrogatives are best seen as negating the question and not either the modality or the event. We have, then, three possibilities which may be tabulated as:

Question	Modality	Event
(a) Negative	Positive	Positive
(b) Positive	Negative	Positive
(c) Positive	Positive	Negative

Mustn't and *don't have to* are used for (a) and, less commonly, for (c), while *needn't* is the form for (b). The paraphrases are:

(a) Isn't it the case that it is necessary . . .?
(b) Is it the case that it is not necessary . . .?
(c) Is it the case that it is necessary . . . not . . .?

One might then ask what are the forms for:

(d) Isn't it the case that it is not necessary . . .?
(e) Isn't it the case that it is necessary . . . not . . .?

But, perhaps, one should not ask, for languages do not have and cannot have simple regular forms for all theoretical possibilities (though one can always provide some kind of paraphrase).

Functional syntax in mediaeval Europe

R. H. ROBINS

The establishment of basic units and structures at different levels of analysis has been a preoccupation of linguists throughout the history of the subject. It will continue so to be, despite the changes through which linguistic theory has been passing in the past few decades. Indeed, new theories, embodying new models of language analysis, require new sets of basic elements, as one sees, for example, in the array of terminology currently being developed by the stratificational-ists, among others.

Mediaeval linguists in Europe, though their work is less widely known than, perhaps, it deserves to be, are no exception, and a brief notice of their contribution to syntactic theory and to the creation of a specifically syntactic terminology may be of some current interest. It is, additionally, a pleasure to offer such a paper for publication in a volume of studies honouring William Haas, who has himself given us some valuable writings on the identification and definition of basic units and elements in linguistic science (see especially 1954a, 1957a, 1960b, 1966).

It would be generally admitted that in Ancient Greek linguistics and in the Latin linguistics derived from it, syntactic theory and syntactic analysis were less developed than were morphological and phonological theory and analysis. Dionysius Thrax's grammar of Greek, basically orthographic phonology and morphology, was written three centuries before Apollonius wrote his standard books on syntax, which rested on Thrax's prior work and provided the model for Priscian's *Institutiones*.

Greek and Latin phonological and morphological statements are in several places in need of correction; their phonetics is inadequate, and they perpetrate some morphological misstatements, for example describing Latin future perfect forms (*amavero*, etc.) as future subjunctives (Priscian 8.55 *passim*). But these faults are corrigible within the descriptive system that they used. They had established their basic elements. The *grámma/littera* was the minimal phonological unit of articulate speech, and the word and the sentence were the minimal and maximal limits of grammatical description; antiquity was, in Hockett's famous term (1954) wholly WP in orientation. Eight word classes had been distinguished and defined by reference to morphological categories (case, tense, etc.), *Grundbedeutungen*, or syntactic functions (e.g. the conjunction). But there seems to be no evidence of a specific theory of syntax or a set of specifically syntactic categories in the main stream of ancient western linguistics: the scholars of Alexandria, Dionysius Thrax, Apollonius, and the later Latin grammarians.

Certainly the Stoics had a distinct theory of syntax, with syntactic categories and structures not directly tied to morphological features and classes, but arising from their propositional logic (Mates 1953). Chrysippus (third century BC) wrote at least three books specifically on syntax (Barwick 1957: 21). But Stoic linguistics was not very influential in the main tradition of Greek and Latin grammar, and though it formed the basis of Augustine's *De dialectica* it does not appear to have had any influence on the later mediaeval scholastic grammarians. Apollonius and Priscian refer to the Stoics in a few *obiter dicta*, and there is one term clearly of Stoic origin to be found in the twelfth-century didactic grammarian Alexander Villadei (l. 1501), carried over from Priscian. But Priscian clearly misunderstood what Stoic terminology he misused, and it played no role in his description of Latin grammar. As Steinthal said, 'Priscians Bericht ist erst verstümmelt und dann verwirrt worden' (1890: 1. 307). As far as modern scholarship is concerned, we are greatly hampered by the total lack of surviving primary texts dealing with Stoic linguistics.

In Apollonius and in the syntactic books of Priscian, what we seem to find are masses of detailed accounts of constructions into which different word classes enter. These are justified and explained by reference to each other; for example, the use of the genitive case with verbs like βασιλεύειν 'to rule', is referred to the possessive meaning of the genitive, and its use with verbs of perception is explained by the fact that we are affected by the objects concerned and therefore the case appropriate to the agent in (Greek) passive constructions is the right one; the construction of ὁρᾶν 'to see', with the accusative is explained (away) by the statement that in seeing we take a more active part in perception (Bekker 1817: 290–3). What we do not find is any general theory of sentence structure embodying its own basic components. This is precisely what the scholastic grammarians, though their work largely derives from Priscian, set themselves to provide.

The writings of the scholastic grammarians were generally known under the heading *De modis significandi*. *Modus significandi* was a technical term designating the specific grammatical categories, both essential and accidental, of each part of speech or word class. Their work amounted to a reinterpretation of Priscian's Latin grammar in scholastic terms and in conformity with scholastic logical and metaphysical theory. From their use of *modus (significandi)* as the basic term in their grammars they were often called the *modistae* and the adjective *modistic* is used to refer to their approach to grammatical theory.

Syntax occupied the central place in later mediaeval grammar: 'Studium grammaticorum praecipue circa constructionem versatur' (thirteenth-century text cited by Thurot 1869: 213). The scholastic grammarians laid great stress on the syntactic component of grammar and on syntactic theory, devising a set of basic syntactic elements and relations which were not directly tied to morphology. Their whole grammatical exposition was, of course, executed within the bounds of Aristotelian philosophy as interpreted by the scholastics (notably St Thomas Aquinas), and their main concern in syntax was with declarative sentences.

There were, naturally, some differences of theory between different writers on grammar (Pinborg 1972: 120–6), but there was general agreement overall, and we may take the relatively late grammar of Thomas of Erfurt (Bursill-Hall 1972) as representative of scholastic doctrine.

Two basic structures were recognized: NP VP, and NP VP NP. The order of these elements was taken as normal, and positional categories were employed in description. The first NP was designated *suppositum* and the VP *appositum*.

This is the standard scholastic use of *appositum* as a technical term (Bursill-Hall 1971: 61). It is explicitly so defined by Thomas of Erfurt: in *Socrates currit*, *Socrates* is *suppositum* and *currit* is *appositum* (§95) 'solum verbum est suppositum' (§116); in copulative constructions like *(ego) sum albus* and *(ego) vocor Adrianus*, *albus* and *Adrianus* are described as *appositi determinatio* (§102). This use of the term is also

constructio intransitiva
compositio

NP
modus entis
suppositum

VP
modus esse
appositum

dependentia

Socrates ——— currit

determinabile determinans

sum ← albus

vocor ← Adrianus

(ego) → sum albus

(ego) → vocor Adrianus

currit ← bene

(ego) → currit bene

determinabile determinans

Socrates → albus

Socrates → currit

si Socrates → currit

constructio intransitiva
compositio

NP
modus entis
suppositum

VP
modus esse
appositum
dependentia

Socrates ——— percutit

Socrates currens
modus esse
indistantis

laedit
modus esse
distantis → pedem

(ego) → video

(Socrates) → laedit

constructio transitiva
significatio

NP
modus entis

Platonem

similis Socrati
filius Socratis

pedem

legentem librum

pedem

found in Petrus Helias (twelfth century): 'nomen per se supponitur, et verbum per se apponitur', and in a thirteenth-century manuscript: 'verba fuerunt inventa ad significandum appositum' (Thurot 1869: 217).

There are, however, at least two other recognized designations of *appositum*. As Pfister remarks, 'Der terminus "appositum" bleibt während der gesamten Dauer seines Gebrauches unpräzis' (1976: 109). This may well be due to the conflicting claims of syntactic relations in the sentence on the one hand and the logical association of *appositum* with a propositional predicate on the other. Petrus Helias, for example, wrote: 'sicut nomen repertum est ad significandum de quo dicitur, ita et verbum ad significandum quid de aliquo dicitur' (Thurot 1869: 217). This treatment of the verb, of course, goes back to Aristotle *de Interpretatione* 3: 'ῥῆμα . . . ἔστιν ἀεὶ τῶν καθ᾽ ἑτέρου λεγομένων σημεῖον.

On some interpretations of the term, *appositum* includes adverbs in construction with the verb: in 'Sor bene legit' (thirteenth-century manuscript, Thurot 1869: 218) *Sor* (= Socrates) is the *suppositum* and *bene legit* the *appositum*, a use not really incompatible with Thomas's *appositi determinatio*. John of Genoa (end of thirteenth century) makes the *appositum* include the postverbal NP: 'verbum principale cum toto illo quod sequitur est appositum'; notice that in the same paragraph he writes 'appositum est illud quod de altero dicitur, et appellatur in dialectica praedicatum' (Percival 1975: 213–14).

A third usage confines the term *appositum* to the postverbal NP. This is made explicit in some humanist grammars, such as Guarino Veronese (c. 1400) and Giovanni da San Ginesio (fourteenth or fifteenth century): 'quid est appositum? Est quicquid ponitur post verbum principale vel intelligitur poni' (Percival 1976a: 248–9; 1976b: 240–1). As this use of the term is mainly found in Italian grammars of the fourteenth century and after, where it became the standard use, (Percival 1975: 234) it may be suggested that it was a humanistic trend, part of the rise of humanistic grammar in southern Europe, where modistic theory never secured a strong foothold. *Appositum* as the VP alone was the standard modistic use of the term, but we find the start of a move away from this in the Paris manuscript of the thirteenth century cited above (Thurot 1869: 218), which otherwise belongs within the modistic tradition: in sentences like *Sor est albus*, *Sor* is taken as the *suppositum*, *albus* as the *appositum*, and *est* is 'mera copula', in direct contradiction to Thomas's treatment of such sentences.

In Thomas's syntax the *suppositum* and the *appositum* were basic to every sentence, though the personal pronouns could be understood from the inflections of first and second person verbs (Bursill-Hall 1972: §119). We notice that the *modistae* did not use the logical terms *subiectum* and *praedicatum* as technical terms in grammar.

NP VP formed a *constructio intransitiva*: *Socrates currit*, also *Socratis interest* etc.

NP VP NP involved a *constructio intransitiva* and a *constructio transitiva*, with the verb entering into both: *Socrates percutit Platonem*.

The criterion is whether two grammatical persons, or non-coreferential NPs, are involved (reflexives are a special case of transitives: *Socrates diligit se*). In the most usual form of the *constructio intransitiva* the termination of the verb refers to the *suppositum*, expressed or understood.

The same distinction is used in the analysis of subordinate constructions in more complex sentences: *Socrates albus currit bene*. *Socrates albus* and *currit bene* are each *constructiones intransitivae*, only one person being involved. Nominal phrases like *similis Socrati* and *filius Socratis* are *transitivae*, because there is *transitio personarum* and two non-coreferential NPs are involved. Complex NPs like those just exemplified are *constructiones personarum* (intransitive and transitive), which are non-sentence-forming, as distinguished from *constructiones actuum*, which include a verb and are sentence-forming (Pinborg 1972: 123).

The relation between the *suppositum* and the *appositum* (NP and VP) is *compositio*. Mediaeval grammar was modelled on mediaeval understanding of reality. The sorts of categories, *Modi significandi*, found in grammar had their counterparts in the external world (*modi essendi*). Nouns were designed to express the stability of things, persons, etc.; verbs were designed to express the phenomena of temporal change and process, as both of these conditions are in the world of reality. 'Nomen est pars orationis significans per modum entis' (Bursill-Hall 1972: §16); 'verbum est pars orationis significans per modum esse distantis a substantia' (§48); 'participium est pars orationis significans per modum esse indistantis a substantia' (§65). The distinction between the verbal *modus esse distantis a substantia* and the participial *indistantis a substantia* reflects the difference between a judgment already made and incorporated in an NP and the judgment actually expressed by the sentence as a whole or by its main clause. In a participial construction the process has already been associated with the head noun, i.e. the *modus esse* has already been united with the substance designated by that noun, as in *Socrates currens* (*laedit pedem*). A complete sentence expresses a judgment or proposition which *ab initio* links a person or thing with a process etc., and the act of forming such a judgment is *compositio*. *Compositio* thus bridges the gap that otherwise keeps apart the *modus entis* of nouns and the *modus esse* of verbs until they are brought into a sentence comprising *suppositum* and *appositum* (in participial constructions this has already been done in the sentence that is embedded in the newly formed matrix sentence).[1]

Significatio (Thomas of Erfurt §58) is the counterpart of *compositio*, and expresses the relation between the VP and a following oblique case NP in *constructiones transitivae*, active or passive (§59). '(Petrus Helias) per significationem vult intelligere modum transeuntis' (§58). *Significatio* is, of course, here used in a highly restricted technical sense, and presumably must be zero with intransitive verbs and transitive verbs used without expressed or recoverable object (Bursill-Hall 1971: 225).

Compositio and *significatio* are specifically syntactic categories derived from Priscian's morphological categories of *modus* (mood) and *genus* (voice). Thomas uses these categories to subclassify types of *compositio*, relations between *suppositum* and verb (indicative, imperative, etc.), and *significatio*, relations between verb and following NP, if any (active, passive, neutral, etc.); 'sicut se habet modus verbi ad compositionem, sic se habet genus ad significationem' (§59; notice that *modus* (mood) is here a separate, though homonymous, term distinct from *modus* (*significandi*, etc.)).

Compositio and *significatio* are both relations of dependence, another basic relationship in mediaeval syntax. Every verb requires or depends on a (usually) prior *suppositum*, and transitive verbs with expressed

---

[1] Thomas of Erfurt is very clear and explicit on the relation between *modus essendi* in the world and *modus significandi* in language. His §36 on the pronoun is worth quoting *in extenso*:

Modus significandi essentialis generalissimus pronominis est modus significandi per modum entis et indeterminatae apprehensionis . . . Modus vero indeterminatae apprehensionis oritur a proprietate, seu modo essendi, materiae primae. Materia enim prima in se extra indeterminata est respectu cuiuslibet formae naturalis quae inest de se, ita quod nec includit nec excludit formam nec determinationem formae. Ab ista ergo proprietate materiae primae, quae est proprietas de se indeterminata, determinabilis tamen per formam, sumitur modus significandi per modum indeterminatae (apprehensionis), qui est modus significandi essentialis generalissimus pronominis; non quod pronomen materiam primam significet tantum, sed ex modo essendi reperto in materia prima intellectus movetur ad considerandum aliquam essentiam sic indeterminatam et ad imponendum sibi vocem sub modo significandi per modum indeterminati. Et hunc modum generalissimum essentialem pronominis grammatici (e.g. Priscian 13.29) expresserunt dicentes pronomen significare substantiam meram vel substantiam sine qualitate; dantes intelligi per *substantiam* modum entis, qui in substantia principaliter reperitur, ut dictum est; per *meram vel sine qualitate* modum indeterminatae apprehensionis (Bursill-Hall 1972: 196).

objects depend on a (usually) following NP. The mediaeval and Romance SVO order was taken as standard (*ordo naturalis*); it could be varied for stylistic reasons or for emphasis (*ordo artificialis*), but this was always referable to a basic *ordo naturalis* (Thurot 1869: 344).

Syntactic structures (*constructiones*) are all binary (§89) and comprise a constituent that is dependent and a constituent that satisfies or terminates that dependency; verbs depend on their *supposita* and in *constructiones transitivae* on their following NP as well (first and second person verb forms can supply their own *supposita*). This relation of dependency appears in the analysis of other constructions: adjectives depend on nouns and adverbs on verbs; in these cases a determinant depends on a determinable. Nouns and adjectives in *constructiones transitivae* consisting of a complex NP depend on their associated noun: *similis* depends on *Socrati*, and *filius* depends on *Socratis*. Subordinate clauses depend on their main or matrix clause: *si Socrates currit* (*laedit pedem*). The possibility of nesting or recursive dependencies was allowed for: in *video legentem librum, legentem* both satisfies the dependency of *video* and itself depends on *librum*. Complex sentences are analysable into sets of embedded dependencies (Bursill-Hall 1972: §92, §107–8, §118).

Scholastic syntax did not involve a thorough-going immediate constituent or tree-type analysis, but made the main verb the centre of the sentence, rather as Tesnière (1959) did and as some of the case-grammarians do (Anderson 1973b). These modern authors write of verbs in this sort of relation as governing (*régissant*) or dominating their NPs, but the terms *dependere* and *regere* were, despite their opposed literal meanings, very similar in mediaeval technical linguistic terminology; Petrus Crocus (thirteenth-century commentator on Alexander Villadei) wrote: 'Oportet quod regens significet per modum dependentis' (Pinborg 1967: 74).

Several of these scholastic syntactic concepts and relations had been in part suggested or outlined by the didactic grammarians and even by Apollonius and Priscian; Alexander Villadei used *regimen* of the relationship between various word classes and nouns in specific case forms (1,074–1,368), and with it the notion of the ungoverned 'ablative absolutes' (*rectore soluti*, 1,339, 1,411), the syntactic functions *supponere* and *apponere*, and the distinction between transitivity and intransitivity (1,372–3). Apollonius used the phrase διάβασις τοῦ προσώπου (Bekker 1817: 202), translated by Priscian (13.23, 14.14) as *transitio personarum*, and both were feeling towards a technical term for the relationship between words that were linked with nouns in a specific oblique case (ἀπαιτεῖ πλαγίους, ἐπὶ γενικὴν φέρεσθαι, Bekker 1817: 116, 241–2), in Priscian's Latin *exigere* and *adiungi* (18.10, 18.127). The term *compositio* can be traced back via Boethius's translation to Aristotle's σύνδεσις (*de Interpretatione* 16b 25), where it is part of the specific semantic function of the verb εἶναι: προσσημαίνει δὲ σύνδεσίν τινα (cf. Reichl 1976: 179).

While, therefore, the syntactic terminology of the scholastic grammarians was not wholly original and some embryonic syntactic concepts had appeared in earlier work on grammar, it is nonetheless true that the elaboration and exposition of a system of functional syntactic analysis not based on particular morphological classifications and covering in principle the syntax of all possible Latin sentences was their achievement, and it was they who set this system within a comprehensive theory of language.

Four 'principles' (*principia constructionis*) underlay any syntactic structure and made it possible (Thomas of Erfurt §89). These were clearly modelled on the four Aristotelian causes:

MATERIAL: *constructibilia*, words in their grammatical status as *partes orationis*.

FORMAL: *unio constructibilium*, effected by their *modi significandi*, the combination of words in constructions.

EFFICIENT: (a) INTERNAL: the syntactically relevant grammatical categories (*modi accidentales respectivi*): case, tense, gender, number, etc.[2]

(b) EXTERNAL: the human intellect which constructs sentences.

FINAL: the expression of a judgment (*expressio mentis conceptus compositi*).

George Lakoff has sought to place his system of generative semantics within a general system of 'natural logic' (1970b). The speculative grammarians of the latter Middle Ages for their part aimed at the creation of a coherent system of syntax, which they set firmly within what they sincerely believed was a 'natural' metaphysical system, scholastic philosophy as expounded by such thinkers as St Thomas Aquinas.

---

[2] The speculative grammarians were the first to distinguish the syntactically relevant categories (inflectional categories) from the syntactically irrelevant categories (derivational categories): diminutive, inceptive, etc.

Speculative grammar was self-righteously rejected by men of the Renaissance. But several of its basic concepts and formulations were kept and have remained in use up to the present day, e.g. subject and predicate (logical terms taking over from the distinctively syntactic terms of the speculative grammarians), the relationship of government or rection (cf. Wackernagel 1926: 23), and the statement of prepositional syntax (cf. Bursill-Hall 1972: §80: 'modus significandi per modum adiacentis alteri casuali ipsum cotrahens, et ad actum retorquens'), clearly the correct analysis of the main function of prepositions in languages like Latin, which the classical grammarians, from Dionysius Thrax to Priscian, never succeeded in achieving.

In the European linguistic tradition, the conception of syntax as a theory of sentence structure embodying its own specific elements and relations can be regarded as part of the legacy of the Middle Ages.

Some remarks on the stylistics of written language

JOSEF VACHEK

One of the outstanding achievements of Professor William Haas is undoubtedly his confrontation of spoken and written language phenomena (see especially Haas 1970b). That such a confrontation can lead to interesting results was foreseen by quite a number of linguists: on the phonemic–graphemic level such confrontation had been already attempted by Pulgram (1951). Problems of orthographic reform were to lead, later on, to confrontations on 'higher' language levels, mainly on the morphological and lexical (cf. Vachek 1959); confrontation of intonational phenomena with facts of punctuation touched, at least in an elementary way, upon the relations of spoken and written utterances reflecting the syntactic level. It appears, however, that so far hardly any attempt has been made at a confrontation of the two spheres, spoken and written, on the stylistic level. In view of the vast complexity of the implied problems we can hardly do more in this essay than present a first attempt at such a confrontation by offering a handful of remarks on some of its aspects.

Before this very limited task is undertaken, three important provisos must be stated. First, it should be pointed out that we want to discuss only the purely material means serving stylistic purposes and their organization in concrete written utterances. In other words, we will leave aside, e.g., lexical and phraseological signals of stylistic differentiation because they do not reflect material means of written language but only register by graphical means what are, in fact, specific features of spoken language, mainly on its higher levels, lexical and syntactic.

The second proviso follows logically from the first: we will confine our attention mainly (though not exclusively) to printed utterances, as opposed to hand-written ones, for the simple reason that it was the printed, rather than the hand-written, subvariety of written utterances that developed, for purely technical reasons, a richer inventory of the marked, graphical devices. See, e.g., various sizes and ducts of letters as well as specific letter types (italic, bold, etc.). Admittedly, some devices for serving the purpose of stylistic differentiation will also be found in hand-written utterances, e.g. capital letters (though not small capitals) as well as most punctuation marks, etc. Some are even found to be specific to hand-written utterances, e.g. various kinds of under-lining of either individual words or whole word-groups. In such instances one can speak about 'infrasegmental features' (while their suprasegmental counterparts, so important in the spoken utterances, are virtually absent in written communication).

Finally, as the third proviso, it should be added that, as a rule, we will confine our remarks to those languages whose written utterances are based on an alphabetical principle (on the Latin alphabet espe-cially). In other words, those writing systems whose units correspond to syllables or even words of spoken utterances (as is the case, e.g., in Japanese or Chinese writing, respectively) will not be analysed here.

In the study of the material means available to the written language for the purpose of signalling stylistic aspects of written utterances, and in confronting these means with those available for analogous pur-poses in spoken utterances, much depends on a safe starting point of such study. This would appear to consist in singling out, on the one hand, what may be regarded as the unmarked basic style of language and, on the other, what set of graphical means is at the disposal of the written utterances implementing the written variety of this stylistic category.

As we have shown in another paper (Vachek 1975), the status of the unmarked, basic stylistic variety of language seems most probably to belong to simple, quiet, unemotional narratives or descriptions (the so-called simple communicative style); in other words, anything that deviates from the qualities indicated above introduces some feature of marked, superimposed quality into the examined stylistic specimen – i.e. formulational complexity, emphasis or emotion, a deeper or more sophisticated approach to the content of the examined specimen. In the graphical domain, the set of small roman characters ('upright, light-faced, and with serifs', as Webster (1947) defines it) would appear to be the analogous unmarked basic set, while all other graphical sets may be regarded as having a marked, superimposed material status.

At the very outset it should be pointed out that written languages of different communities may differ in the evaluation of materially identical items found in their respective inventories of graphical symbols. Thus, e.g., in written German the item conventionally called 'exclamation mark' signals not only genuine exclamatory utterances but also quiet, unemotional commands (e.g. *Komm her! Passen Sie auf!*), so that it is functionally ambivalent in that language, inasmuch as it ranks there both with the unmarked and with the marked sets of graphical means. On the other hand, in written English the same graphical item can only occur in genuine exclamatory sentences, not in unemotional commands (see the English equivalents of the German sentences adduced above, namely *Come here, Pay attention*), and thus its function is clearly limited to being a member of the marked set only. (Needless to say, written norms of language may differ in this point at various stages of their developments: written Czech in its earlier variety followed the German pattern, while its modern variety agrees with the English practice.)

Conversely, the device of spacing out the graphemes of a printed word is quite frequently used in Czech and German printed texts as a signal of emphasis, while this is rarely found in English printed texts. In English newspaper columns, such spacing serves, rather, as a technical device enabling the compositor to fill a part of the line which otherwise would have to be left empty – in other words, it does not constitute an item of any linguistic significance but is employed for purely technical purposes.

The use of some other marked sets of graphical symbols, however, is parallel in most languages written on an alphabetic basis. The use of the italic symbols, signalling the emphatic and/or emotional quality of the words or word-groups (which may extend to whole sentences) printed in these symbols, undoubtedly belongs here. The marked value of such symbols is obvious not only from their semantic function but also from their graphical shapes (described by Webster (1947) very aptly as 'starting upward to the right'), and it stands out especially when an utterance is printed in roman type except for small or more extensive 'islands' printed in italic type.

In signalling emphasis and/or emotion, the italic set of symbols, naturally, does not stand alone. Another very interesting means of achieving the same purpose is the use of quotation marks (except when they denote a newly coined or suggested terminological item), if they include, not a whole sentence (signalling direct speech), but only one word or a small word-group placed inside a sentence. In such situations, of course, the signalled emotion often has a special colouring: it is accompanied by an ironical (or even sarcastic) approach on the part of the author of the given sentence.

A further usage of italic symbols also deserves a mention. In some languages (e.g. English), the italic set may also signal the foreign status of the word or phrase printed in it – here again the marked, superimposed status of such 'islands' is readily recognized inasmuch as they constitute items of a different language system, items of almost quotational character. Such items are inserted into the native context with some obvious stylistic intention (it may either signal a highbrow approach to the discussed content by the author, or his intention to put the content in a more euphemistic manner than could be mediated by a synonymous native expression).

Incidentally, it will be of interest to note that in written languages based not on Latin but on the Cyrillic alphabet (e.g., Russian) the italic shapes of graphemes are only used to signal emphasis or emotion, while the signalling of 'foreignisms' does not require the italicization of their graphemes. Such italicization is obviously not necessary in Russian since the contrast of the roman, non–italic graphemes used to print such foreignisms and the Cyrillic symbols of the native context is in itself sufficiently distinctive. It achieves the same stylistic effect on the recipient of the message as is evoked in the recipient of the English text by the contrast of the roman and italic sets of what is essentially one and the same graphical system.

There is another interesting structural feature which deserves to be noted here in connexion with the use of the italic set of symbols. Sometimes (especially in German or Czech) one may find a whole article printed in italics. This may be, e.g., a foreword or an epilogue which an editor thought it necessary to annex to a novel by some other author, or a short essay in a newspaper. Such an essay usually deals with some lighter, often non–political theme. The use of the italic types in such instances signals a literary genre different from, and usually more ambitious than, the other materials included in the given publication (an essay commenting on a novel or a short story, or opposed to the purely informative sections of the same newspaper issue).

The interesting point is that if the author of such an essay wants to emphasize a word or a phrase, he has to indicate this by printing it in a different type. In such a case, as a rule, Czech printers signal such emphasis by using the common roman set of types. Clearly, they are convinced that the optical contrast in which the roman types stand to the italics will guarantee the functional interpretation of the former as transmitting a signal of emphasis. This conviction is obviously based on the exceptional occurrence of the roman 'islands' in what is otherwise an exclusively italic context. But the practical experience of Czech readers (and most probably also of the German ones) does not confirm this aprioristic assumption. It appears that the unmarked, basic stylistic quality of the roman type has been so firmly fixed in the scale of values of the material means of written Czech (or German, for that matter) that it cannot be evaluated as possessing the marked, superimposed stylistic quality within the italic context (which again would have to be evaluated, in that case, as basic, unmarked). In other words, if in an italic context some words or phrases really have to be signalled as emphatic or strongly emotional, this can only be done efficiently by printing such words or phrases in bold italics, or if, as often happens, typographers disapprove of this on aesthetic grounds, by some other set of letters, e.g. small capitals (in Czech also spaced italics might be used for that purpose).

Two remarks should be annexed to the preceding paragraph. First, what has just been said on the inability of italics to figure as the unmarked member of the opposition 'italic type – roman type' appears to be of more general linguistic significance. It appears, that is to say, that the values of the two members in the opposition 'marked – unmarked' are not interchangeable in the system of graphical language means. In other words, the above opposition must obviously be formulated as 'non-slanted – slanted', not as 'upright – non-upright'. This seems to furnish an interesting parallel to the Prague conception of phonological correlative oppositions where again the marked and the unmarked members are evaluated as non-interchangeable (so that, e.g., the opposition of Russian consonant phonemes /t/ – /t̡/ must be evaluated as 'non-soft – soft', not as 'hard – non-hard'). As is well-known, the conception of markedness worked out by Chomsky & Halle (1968: 404, 4n) differs from the Prague conception exactly on this point. In the light of what has just been said here, the Prague conception appears to obtain further support.

Second, it should be noted that hand-written contexts, in which emphasis is not signalled by a different set of symbols but simply by underlining, one can find nothing that would correspond to a whole article printed in italics – as a matter of fact, if such a thing were possible, it would necessitate underlining the whole of a hand-written article. An important conclusion can be drawn from this fact: in hand-written utterances underlining can be used exclusively for signalling emphasis, not for the purpose of characterizing some specific literary genre (as, e.g., a short essay). As a consequence of this, hand-written utterances do not face the problem of how to indicate emphasis within the context of such a genre – if any situation of the kind could exceptionally emerge, one would perhaps have to resort to double underlining.

In the preceding paragraphs a reference was also made to two other specific sets of graphemes which undoubtedly also have the status of marked sets, i.e. bold type and small capitals. These two sets may serve the same purpose as the italic set, i.e. the signalling of emphatic or emotional words or phrases, but interestingly, they do so rather rarely – mostly they are used for other purposes.

As already noted, bold type is not frequently used for signalling emphasis since this is often considered unaesthetic inasmuch as it is apt to destroy the 'balanced' outlook of the printed page. For this reason, bold type is mostly used for other stylistic purposes, especially for captions briefly summarizing what is contained in the following chapter or chapters or even in smaller sections of the printed utterance concerned (in this function bold type is particularly frequent in Journalese contexts).

What has just been said about bold type may also be applied to the other set mentioned above, small capitals. Although the latter can also be used for headings introducing following chapters or sections and (briefly) summarizing their contents, they appear to be much more frequently used to make printed utterances easier to survey and so more quickly understood. Thus, e.g., in the texts of theatrical plays small capitals commonly identify the person(s) speaking the sentences following. In printed interviews the questions are sometimes printed in small capitals whilst the answers are printed in ordinary roman (or, of course, vice versa). Again, in theoretical treatises the names of the scholars referred to by the author are sometimes also presented in small capitals (e.g. JESPERSEN – note, however, that the first grapheme of the name in such cases continues to be printed in a large capital, not a small one).

Thus, the uses of both graphemic sets, bold type and small capitals, again clearly belong to the sphere of stylistic material means: they give evidence of the conscious effort of the author to facilitate the work of the recipient of the message, ensuring that he is able to survey it as quickly as possible and grasp its content more easily than would be the case if no such marked sets were employed.

Large roman capitals also deserve some comment. They, too, constitute a marked set of graphemes (in opposition to the unmarked 'small' roman) and their function is again, in principle, to increase the legibility of the whole context. The functional motivation is obvious in the sequences of large capitals in sign-posts informing of shops and offices, in street name signs, in various traffic signs, in chapter titles and titles of books, articles and periodicals, etc. – in all such cases the aesthetic motivation also plays its part. However, in more extensive contexts consisting mostly of small roman type, the use of large capitals is functionally motivated only at the beginning of proper names, and perhaps in titles of institutions (e.g. Government, Labour Party, Post Office, etc.). Incidentally, if small roman type is used in titles of books, posters, etc., this is only due to intentional instances of 'forwarding' (in French, *actualisation*), motivated by a specific aesthetic purpose intended by the author or editor; an analogous use of small roman type is seen in the practice of some poetic schools (e.g. the Futurists).

However, the use of capitals to open the sentence is, in fact, redundant, because the beginning of the new sentence is sufficiently signalled by the presence of the full stop at the end of the preceding sentence (or by the absence or any preceding context). Still, one can hardly object to the use of capitals in sentence beginnings; it is commonly admitted that some degree of redundancy helps the recipient of the message to decipher it more easily than could be done otherwise. (Analogous arguments might be adduced in defence of the use of capitals for nouns in Modern German written utterances, although German authorities themselves of late appear to be willing to abolish this redundant feature; cf. Nerius 1975.) The relatively small linguistic significance of large capitals is also evidenced by the fact that one can only very rarely find 'islands' of words and phrases consisting of them within a context printed in small roman type (among exceptions to this, let us mention technical terms like ALGOL, etc.) – such islands more often consist of small capitals. It should also not be overlooked that in hand-written contexts longer sequences of large capitals are quite unknown. The frequent practice of capitalizing autosemantic words in Modern English captions is again a linguistically redundant phenomenon; it too, in its own way, is motivated by an intention to facilitate the recipient reader's work.

Parenthetically, it should be added that even the full stop at the end of the sentence may become redundant if some other typographical feature reveals that the sentence has been completed. As is well known, this is clearly already the case in captions introducing articles or chapters of a book, of titles of books, of sign posts, of names and addresses on visiting cards, of signatures closing down letters, of all sorts of official documents, etc.

If a sentence is unfinished, this is usually signalled by the punctuation sign of dash (–) or by three points (. . .). The dash implies that what is unexpressed may be supplemented, roughly at least, from the general context, while the three dots rather signal some embarrassment on the part of the author or the presence of more alternatives. Inside the sentence the dash signals some surprise called forth by what follows after it. (Incidentally, in Russian the dash inside the sentence can, in some specific situations, perform the function of the copula which, as is well known, does not exist in Russian sentences using the indicative present tense. In other written languages, especially those employing roman characters, this grammatical function of the dash is obviously unknown.) Three points inside the sentence signal, at least very frequently, some hesitation and/or uncertainty on the part of the author of the utterance.

Contrary to all the punctuation marks enumerated above, the comma appears to have only grammatical, not stylistic function, in most written languages. An exception to this general rule may be found in English, where one notes the presence of the so–called 'rhetorical comma' (see Fowler & Fowler 1930). It is sometimes explained as due to a 'slight pause', but even if such a pause is present, its motivation is to be looked for in some (at least slight) emotion on the part of the author, and thus it again belongs to the stylistic domain.

To go back again to the marked sets of graphemes, we have already noted that the use of bold type and of small capitals is, for the main part, also stylistically motivated, inasmuch as it is aimed at making the written utterance easier to survey and its content thus more intelligible to grasp. A similar stylistic function is also performed by another marked set of graphemes, small print. Admittedly, it differs from roman type only by its smaller size, not by any special shapes of the graphemic materials. But the very difference in size of the two sets shows, in this particular case, an important iconic significance: while the bigger type (roman) presents the main information, the smaller type supplies facts of only marginal or auxiliary character, so that the recipient of the message easily perceives the hierarchy of the content communicated to him by the material aspect of the printed utterance.

It should be added that the opposition 'roman – small print' is an asset to the stylistics of written utterances which cannot be matched by the stylistics of spoken utterances, at least not by primary means. The corresponding hierarchization in spoken utterances can only be induced by secondary means (e.g., by phrases like 'By way of a footnote it might be added that . . .', or 'In connexion with what has just been said, a few details may be of interest . . .', etc.). This confrontation of written and spoken utterances again has some more general linguistic significance: it supplies new evidence for the assertion that written utterances do not merely constitute inadequate quasitranscriptions of their spoken counterparts but can claim some communicative (in this case, stylistic) primary material means to which no analogous primary means can be found in the corresponding spoken utterances. In other words, there are at least some communicational situations in which the written utterances are found to be ranking higher than their spoken counterparts.

Another point remains to be briefly touched upon here. In discussing the stylistic material means of written utterances, we have not yet tackled the question of how differentiated are these material means with regard to what is usually called the functional styles of language (see *Cercle linguistique* 1958: 51).

In general it may be said that there is little differentiation of the material means of written utterances when examined from this viewpoint. Seen from the purely material angle, an essay does not differ by any essential features from a short story or from a scientific treatise. Of course, texts of some functional styles can be quite easily identified by their formal features: see what has been said above of theatrical dialogues. Also Journalese contexts will also be recognized by their bold type captions, often extending over two or more printed columns. Another special case is, obviously, poetical contexts, in which one can readily identify verses by the unequal length of the lines which, as a rule, do not reach the end of the page or column. (It should be noted that this is true not only of rhymed verses but also of cases of vers libre.) These, however, are exceptions that only prove the rule.

Finally, let us note that, as a rule, functional styles are not differentiated, for the purpose of quick identification, by the use of specific sets of symbols. One interesting exception to this rule is constituted by the headings of some German or English daily papers, by sign boards of some old–established shops, etc. In such instances one can sometimes find the Gothic script as an instrument which is deliberately employed to call forth venerable archaic atmosphere, appropriate to a paper or place of time-honoured tradition.

Our analysis has been able to mention only very briefly some of the most striking material features of written utterances which are utilized for the purpose of stylistic differentiation. Undoubtedly, a more detailed analysis of written utterances would be necessary to find out and to present a more exhaustive survey of graphical means used in them for stylistic aims. Even so, we hope to have convincingly demonstrated that in this domain, too, the written norm of language is able to vindicate its remarkable linguistic autonomy within the language system taken as a whole.

List of references

(excluding the work of W. Haas)

Ajdukiewicz, K. (1934) 'W sprawie universaliów' ('On universals'), *Przeglad Filozoficzny* 37, 219–34. Reprinted in K. Ajdukiewicz, *Jezyk i poznanie (Language and knowledge)* 1, 196–210, Warsaw 1960

—— (1935) 'Die syntaktische Konnexität', *Studia Philosophica* 1. Available in an English translation by H. Welser, 'Syntactic connexion', in *Polish Logic 1920–1939*, Storrs McCall, (ed.), 207–31, Oxford 1967

Allen, W. S. (1964) 'Transitivity and possession', *Language* 40, 337–53

Allerton, D. J. (1969) 'The sentence as a linguistic unit', *Lingua* 22, 27–46

—— (1970) 'Intuitions in grammatical theory'. In *Actes du Xᵉ Congrès International des Linguistes* Bucharest

—— (1978) 'Generating indirect objects in English', *Journal of Linguistics* 14, 21–34

Allwood, J., Andersson, L-G. & Dahl, Ö. (1977) *Logic in linguistics* Cambridge

Anderson, J. M. (1971) *The grammar of case; towards a localistic theory* Cambridge

—— (1973a) *An essay concerning aspect* The Hague

—— (1973b) 'Maximi Planudis in memoriam'. In F. Kiefer & N. Ruwet (eds.), *Generative grammar in Europe*, 20–47, Dordrecht

d'Ardenne, S.T.R.O. (1936) *þe Liflade ant te Passiun of Seinte Iuliene* Liège

Austin, J. L. (1950) 'Truth', *Proceedings of the Aristotelian Society, Supplementary Volume 24*, 111–28. (Reprinted in Austin 1970)

—— (1962) *How to do things with words* Oxford

—— (1970) *Philosophical papers* (2nd edition), Oxford. (First edition, 1961)

Bach, E. (1974) *Syntactic theory* New York

Barwick, K. (1957) 'Probleme der stoischen Sprachlehre und Rhetorik', *Abhandlungen der Sächsischen Akademie der Wissenschaften zu Leipzig, phil.-hist. Klasse* 49.3

Bekker, I. (ed.) (1817) *Apollonii Alexandrini De constructione* Berlin

Benveniste, E. (1960) ' "Être" et "avoir" dans leur fonctions linguistiques'. Reprinted in *Problèmes de linguistique générale* Paris, 1966

Bolinger, D. L. (1960) 'Linguistic science and linguistic engineering', *Word* 16, 374–89

—— (1961) 'Syntactic blends and other matters', *Language* 37, 366–81
—— (1969) 'Judgements of grammaticality', *Lingua* 21, 34–40
—— (1971a) 'The nominal in the progressive', *Linguistic Inquiry* 2, 246–50
—— (1971b) *The phrasal verb in English* Cambridge, Mass.
—— (1976) 'Meaning and memory', *Forum Linguisticum* 1/1, 1–14
Brentano, F. (1976) *Philosophische Untersuchungen zu Raum, Zeit und Kontinuum* Hamburg
Bursill-Hall, G. L. (1971) *Speculative grammars of the Middle Ages* The Hague
—— (1972) *Thomas of Erfurt: grammatica speculativa* London
Campbell, A. (1959) *Old English grammar* Oxford
Cercle linguistique (1958) Collective theses presented by B. Havránek, K. Horálek, V. Skalička and P. Trost. In *Réponses aux questions linguistiques au IVe Congrès International des Slavistes*, 50–3, Moscow
Chomsky, N. (1957) *Syntactic structures* The Hague
—— (1964) *Current issues in linguistic theory* The Hague
—— (1965) *Aspects of the theory of syntax* Cambridge, Mass.
—— (1966) 'Topics in the theory of generative grammar'. In T. A. Sebeok (ed.) *Current trends in linguistic theory*, 1–60, The Hague
—— (1970) 'Remarks on nominalization'. In R. Jacobs & P. S. Rosenbaum (eds.) *Readings in English Transformational Grammar*, 184–221, Waltham, Mass.
—— (1972) *Studies on semantics in generative grammar* The Hague
—— (1976) *Reflections on language* London
—— & Halle, M. (1968) *The sound pattern of English* New York
—— & Lasnik, H. (1977) 'Filters and control', *Linguistic Inquiry* 8, 425–504
Comrie, B. (1976) *Aspect* Cambridge
Cruse, D. A. (1973) 'Some thoughts on agentivity', *Journal of Linguistics* 9, 11–24
Davidson, D. (1967) 'The logical form of action sentences'. In N. Rescher (ed.) *The logic of decision and action*, 81–95, Pittsburgh
—— (1969) 'On saying that', *Synthese* 19, 130–46
Detienne, M. (1967) *Les maîtres de vérité dans la Grèce archaïque* Paris
Dummett, M. A. E. (1975) 'What is a theory of meaning?' In S. Guttenplan (ed.) *Mind and language*, 97–138, Oxford
El-Hassan, S. A. (1978) 'Variation in the educated spoken Arabic of Jordan, with special reference to aspect in the verb phrase'. Unpublished PhD thesis, University of Leeds.
Firth, J. R. (1957) *Papers in linguistics 1934–1951* London
Fowler, H. W. (1954, 1965) *A dictionary of Modern English usage* New York and Oxford
—— & Fowler, F. G. (1930) *The King's English* (3rd edition), London
Fries, C. C. (1952) *The structure of English* New York
Galton, H. (1964) 'A new theory of the Slavic verbal aspect', *Archivum Linguisticum* (old series 16), 133–44
Halliday, M. A. K. (1970) 'Functional diversity in language as seen from a consideration of modality and mood in English', *Foundations of Language* 6, 322–61

—— (1977) 'Text as semantic choice in social contexts'. In T. A. Dijk & J. Petöfi (eds.) *Grammars and descriptions* (research in text theory 1), 176–225, Berlin and New York

—— & Hasan, R. (1976) *Cohesion in English* London

Harris, Z. S. (1946) 'From morpheme to utterance', *Language* 22, 161–83

—— (1951) *Methods in structural linguistics* Chicago

—— (1952) 'Discourse analysis', *Language* 28, 1–30

Hill, A. A. (1958) *Introduction to linguistic structures: from sound to sentence in English* New York

Hockett, C. F. (1954) 'Two models of grammatical description', *Word* 10, 210–34

—— (1958) *Course in modern linguistics* New York

—— (1968) *The state of the art* The Hague

Huddleston, R. D. (1965) 'Rank and depth', *Language* 41, 574–86

Hudson, R. A. (1967) 'Constituency in a systemic description of the English clause', *Lingua* 18, 225–50

—— (1972) 'Evidence for irregularity', *Linguistic Inquiry* 2, 227–8

Jackendoff, R. S. (1972) *Semantic interpretation in generative grammar* Cambridge, Mass.

Jakobson, R., Fant, C. G. M. & Halle, M. (1952) *Preliminaries to speech analysis: the distinctive features and their correlates* Cambridge, Mass.

Jespersen, O. (1924) *The philosophy of grammar* London

Jones, L. G. (1968) 'English phonotactic structure and first language acquisition', *Lingua* 19, 1–59

Joos, M. (ed.) (1958) *Readings in linguistics* 1 New York

—— (1964) *The English verb: form and meanings* Madison

Kahn, C. H. (1966) 'The Greek verb "to be" and the concept of being', *Foundations of Language* 2, 245–65

—— (1973) *The verb 'be' in Ancient Greek* (Part 6 of J. W. M. Verhaar *The verb 'be' and its synonyms, Foundations of Language Supplementary Series* 16), Dordrecht

Kamp, J. A. W. (1975) 'Two theories about adjectives'. In E. L. Keenan (ed.) *Formal semantics of natural language*, 123–55, Cambridge.

Katz, J. J. & Postal, P. M. (1964) *An integrated theory of linguistic descriptions* Cambridge, Mass.

Kempson, R. M. (1977) *Semantic theory* Cambridge

Klima, E. S. (1964) 'Negation In English', In J. A. Fodor & J. J. Katz (eds.) *The structure of language: readings in the philosophy of language*, 246–323, Englewood Cliffs, N. J.

Kneale, W. & Kneale, M. (1962) *The development of logic* Oxford

Körner, S. (1970) *Categorial frameworks* Oxford

—— (1973) 'Material necessity', *Kant-Studien* 64, 423–30

—— (1975) 'On the identification of agents', *Philosophia* 5, 151–68

Kripke, S. (1971) 'Naming and necessity'. In D. Davidson and G. Harman (eds.) *Semantics of natural language*, 253–355, Dordrecht

Kuryłowicz, J. (1973) 'Verbal aspect in Semitic', *Orientalia* 42, 114–120

Lakoff, G. (1970a) 'Global rules', *Language* 46, 627–39

—— (1970b) *Linguistics and natural logic* Ann Arbor

Lees, R. B. (1960) *The grammar of English nominalizations* The Hague

—— (1965) 'Turkish nominalizations and a problem of ellipsis', *Foundations of Language* 1, 112–21

Lejewski, C. (1958) 'On Leśniewski's Ontology', *Ratio* 1, 150–76

—— (1967) 'A theory of non-reflexive identity and its ontological ramifications'. In Paul Weingartner (ed.) *Grundfragen der Wissenschaften und ihre Wurzeln in der Metaphysik*, 65–102, Salzburg-Munich

—— (1974) 'A system of logic for bicategorial Ontology', *Journal of Philosophical Logic* 3, 265–83

—— (1975) 'Syntax and semantics of ordinary language I', *Proceedings of the Aristotelian Society, Supplementary Volume 49*, 127–46

Leśniewski, S. (1930) 'Über die Grundlagen der Ontologie', *Comptes rendus des séances de la Societé des Sciences et des Lettres de Varsovie*, Classe 3, 23 Année, Warsaw

Lewis, D. (1972) 'General semantics'. In D. Davidson & G. Harman (eds.) *Semantics of natural language*, 169–218, Dordrecht

—— (1975) 'Adverbs of quantification'. In E. L. Keenan (ed.) *Formal semantics of natural language*, 3–15, Cambridge

Linsky, L. (1971) 'Reference, essentialism, and modality'. In L. Linsky (ed.) *Reference and modality*, 88–100, Oxford

Lyons, J. (1964) *Structural semantics (Publications of the Philological Society, 20)*, Oxford

—— *(1967) 'A note on possessive, existential and locative sentences', Foundations of Language* 3, 390–96

—— (1968) *Introduction to theoretical linguistics* Cambridge

—— (1975) 'Deixis as the source of reference'. In E. L. Keenan (ed.) *Formal semantics of natural language*, 61–83, Cambridge

—— (1977) *Semantics* (two vols.) Cambridge

Maclay, H. & Osgood, C. E. (1959) 'Hesitation phenomena in spontaneous English speech', *Word* 15, 19–44

Martinet, A. (1975) *Studies in functional syntax* Munich

—— (1977) 'Les fonctions grammaticales', *La Linguistique* 13/2, 3–14

Mates, B. (1953) *Stoic logic*. University of California publications in philosophy, 26

Mathesius, V. (1911) 'On the potentiality of the phenomena of language'. In J. Vachek (ed.) *A Prague School Reader in Linguistics*, 1–32, Bloomington, Ind.

Matthews, P. H. (1965) 'Problems of selection in transformational grammar', *Journal of Linguistics* 1, 35–47

—— (1967) Review of Chomsky (1965), *Journal of Linguistics* 3, 119–52

Miller, G. A. & Johnson-Laird, P. N. (1976) *Language and Perception* Cambridge

Milsark, G. (1972) 'Re: doubl-ing', *Linguistic Inquiry* 3, 542–49

Miner, K. L. (1974) 'English inflectional endings and unordered rules', *Foundations of Language* 12, 339–65

Mitchell, T. F. (1952) 'The active participle in an Arabic dialect of Cyrenaica', *Bulletin of the School of Oriental and African Studies* 14, 11–33

—— (1958) 'Syntagmatic relations in linguistic analysis', *Transactions of the Philological Society*, 101–18

—— (1975) *Principles of Firthian linguistics* London

—— (1978) 'Educated spoken Arabic in Egypt and the Levant, with special reference to participle and tense', *Journal of Linguistics* 14, 227–58

Nerius, D. (1975) 'Untersuchungen zu einer Reform der deutschen Orthographie', *Linguistiche Studien* A 35, Berlin

Newmeyer, F. J. (1975) *English aspectual verbs* The Hague

Osthoff, H. (1906) 'Gab es einen Instr. Sing. auf *-mi* im Germanischen?', *Indogermanische Forschungen* 20, 163–218

Palmer, F. R. (1965) *A linguistic study of the English verb* London

—— (1971) *Grammar* Harmondsworth

—— (1974) *The English verb* London

Percival, W. K. (1975) 'The grammatical tradition and the rise of the vernaculars'. In T. A. Sebeok (ed.) *Current trends in linguistics* vol. 1, 231–75, The Hague

—— (1976a) 'Deep and surface structure concepts in renaissance and mediaeval syntactic theory'. In H. Parret (ed.) *History of linguistic thought and contemporary linguistics* Berlin

—— (1976b) 'On the historical source of immediate constituent analysis', *Syntax and semantics* 7, 229–42

Pfister, R. (1976) 'Zur Geschichte der Begriffe von Subjekt und Prädikat', *Münchener Studien zur Sprachwissenschaft* 35, 105–119

Pike, Kenneth L. (1959) 'Language as particle, wave and field', *The Texas Quarterly* 2, 37–54

Pinborg, J. (1967) *Die Entwicklung der Sprachtheorie im Mittelalter* Münster

—— (1972) *Logik und Semantik im Mittelalter* Stuttgart

Popper, K. (1972) *Objective knowledge* Oxford

Postal, P. M. (1964) *Constituent structure* Bloomington, Ind.

Priscian (c. 500) 'Institutiones grammaticae'. In H. Keil (ed.) *Grammatici Latini*, vols. 2–3, Leipzig 1855–8

Pulgram, E. (1951) 'Phoneme and grapheme: a parallel', *Word* 7, 15–23

Pullum, G. K. (1974) 'Restating doubl-ing', *Glossa* 8, 109–20

—— (1975) 'PEOPLE-DELETION in English', *Ohio State University Working Papers in Linguistics* 18, 173–80

Putnam, H. (1975) *Mind, language and reality* Cambridge

Quine, W. V. O. (1948) 'On what there is', *Review of Metaphysics* 2, 21–38. Reprinted in *From a logical point of view*, 2nd edition 1961, New York

—— (1960) *Word and object* Cambridge, Mass.

Quirk, R., Greenbaum, S., Leech, G. & Svartvik, J. (1972) *A Grammar of contemporary English* London

Reichl, K. (1976) *Tractatus de grammatica*, eine fälschlich Robert Grosseteste zugeschriebene spekulative Grammatik. Edition und Kommentar. Munich

Ross, J. R. (1972) 'Doubl-ing', *Linguistic Inquiry* 3, 61–86

Russell, B. (1940) *An inquiry into meaning and truth* London

Ruwet, N. (1967) *Introduction à la grammaire générative* Paris

Sampson, G. (1975) *The form of language* London

Sapir, E. (1939) *Language* New York

Seebold, Elmar (1974) 'Gothisches *gasinþa "Reisegefährte"* und *gasinþi "Reisegesellschaft"* ', *Beiträge zur Geschichte der deutschen Sprache und Literatur* 96, 1–11

Seuren, P. A. M. (1969) *Operators and nucleus* Cambridge

Shoemaker, N. (1952) 'The nature of the gerund and participle', *American Speech* 27, 108–12

Silva, C. M. (1975) 'Adverbial -ing', *Linguistic Inquiry* 6, 346–50

Smiley, T. J. (1959) 'Sense without denotation', *Analysis* 20, 123–35

Steinthal, H. (1890) *Geschichte der Sprachwissenschaft bei den Griechen und Römern* 2nd edition, Berlin

Strawson, P. F. (1974) *Subject and predicate in logic and grammar* London

Sweet, H. (1913) *Collected papers* Oxford

Tarski, A. (1944) 'The semantic conception of truth', *Philosophy and Phenomenological Research* 4, 341–75

Taylor, A. (1976) ' "Ergative-based" or "transitive-based"?' *Foundations of Language* 14, 1–17

Tesnière, L. (1959) *Eléments de syntaxe structurale* Paris

Thurot, C. (1869) *Extraits de divers manuscrits latins pour servir à l'histoire des doctrines grammaticales au Moyen Âge* Paris

Trubetzkoy, N. S. (1939/58) *Grundzüge der Phonologie* Prague (reprinted Göttingen)

Vachek J. (1959) 'Two chapters on written English', *Brno Studies in English* 1, 7–36

—— (1975) 'Some remarks on functional dialects of standard languages'. In H. Ringbom (ed.) *Style and text*, 101–7, Stockholm

Vendler, Z. (1967) *Linguistics in philosophy* Ithaca, N.Y.

—— (1968) *Adjectives and nominalizations* The Hague

Villadei, Alexander (twelfth century) *Doctrinale*, D. Reichling (ed.), Berlin, 1893

von Wright, G. H. (1951) *An essay in modal logic* Amsterdam

Wackernagel, J. (1926) *Vorlesungen über Syntax*, vol. 1, Basel

Webster, N. (1947) *Webster's new international dictionary*, 2nd edition, Springfield, Mass.

Wells, R. S. (1947) 'Immediate constituents', *Language* 23, 81–117

Wimsatt, W. K. (1950) 'Verbal style: logical and counterlogical', *Publications of the Modern Language Association of America* 65, 5–20

Wittgenstein, L. (1953) *Philosophical Investigations*, trans. G. E. M. Anscombe, Oxford

Zandvoort, R. W. (1962) 'Is "aspect" an English verbal category?', *Gothenburg Contributions to English Syntax and Philology* 14, 1–20

Index

abessive, 169
ablative, 143, 147, 203
abstract, 151
abstraction, 7
accent, nuclear (tonic), 46, 68–9, 142
acceptability, see deviancy, rectification
accusative, 197
acquisition: of language, 164; of literacy, 25
active, 127, 150–1
active mode of meaning, 59
actor, 64–5, 73
addressee, 130
adequacy, 111, 120, 138
adjective, 10, 151, 156, 159, 166, 203;
    attributive, 9, 151; evaluative, 9; of
    degree, 9; predicative, 151
adverb, 9, 10, 129, 146, 150, 153, 166–7,
    169, 200
affective environments, 186
affirmation, 117
agent, 151, 197
agreement, 152
Ajdukiewicz, K, 99, 100
Aktionsart, 161–2
Alexandria, 197
allative, 146
Allen, W. S., 112
Allerton, D. J., 15, 17, 19
alliteration, 41–2
allomorph, 14, 23–4
Allwood, J., 128, 138
alphabet, 207ff
ambiguity, 152, 155–6, 167, 175–6, 193
analogy, 37–8
Anderson, J. M., 112, 126–7, 164, 203
animate, 151, 183
anomaly, categorial, 4, 10
anthropology, 71
antonym, 170
Apollonius, 196–7, 203

apposition, 76
Aquinas, St Thomas, 198, 204
Arabic, 160–4
archaism, 30
d'Ardenne, S.T.R.O., 35
Aristotelian Society, 4, 80
Aristotle, 80–1, 94, 121–2, 198, 204;
    Metaphysics, 122
artificial language, 95–7, 117–18
Asia, 161
Aspect, 159–84
assent, 118, 122
assertion, 121, 130, 134–5, 185–95
asterisk, 42
attitudes, 120, 142
Augustine, 197
Austin, J. L., 113, 117–18, 121
auxiliary, 46, 48, 50, 163–4, 167, 170–9, 186;
    quasi–, 50
aversion, 41

Bach, E., 140
Barwick, K., 197
Bedouin, 164
Bekker, I., 198, 203
belief, 91–2, 132, 136
Benveniste, E., 112
Berber, 161, 164
bicategorial languages, 99ff
binary, 203
biuniqueness, 58
blends, 157
Bloch, B., 23
Bloomfield, L., 23, 148, 153–5, 157–8
Boethius, 204
Bolinger, D. L., 18, 157, 161, 163–4, 170,
    189
boundaries, 23–4, 69, 72
bracketing, 20–1, 65, 139
Brentano, F., 80, 81n, 85, 89, 90

burden, semantic, 19
Bursill-Hall, G. L., 198, 201–3, 205

Campbell, A., 30
Carnap, R., 123n
case grammar, 143
categories, semantic, 95–7; syntactic, 9, 12, 19
causative, 129, 131, 133–4, 161, 172–5
Celtic, 164
cessative, 167, 172–3
change: linguistic, 11–12, 30, 37–8, 143, 170; semantic, 14, 40; syntactic, 40
characters, 58
Chesterton, G. K., 111
Chinese, 63–4, 207
Chisholm, R. M., 80n
Chomsky, N., 8, 17, 20, 23, 25, 111, 113, 125n, 138–9, 148–58, 160, 210
Chrysippus, 94, 197
classification, 142, 144, 154
clause, 68–9, 77–8
co-application, 88–90
code, 57
co-designation, 88–90
cohesion, syntactic, 20, 179
co-implication, 88–90
colligation, 48
collocation, 115–16, 118, 133, 139, 141, 150, 156, 170
completion, 159
completive, 172
complex, 76
compound monadic predicates, 85ff
Comrie, B., 160, 163, 165
conative, 161
concord, 168
condition, 76
conjugation, 162
conjunction, 76
conjunctives, 70
connotation, 67
consciousness, 59, 63
consistency, 91
consonants, 22
constant, 16
constituents, 65, 67, 71, 78, 153–4
constraints, 157, 173
constructions, 154
content, 7, 57, 124, 144
context, 5, 8, 9, 10, 12, 18–19, 22, 39, 42, 54, 60, 81, 122, 143, 165, 171; of situation, 62
contiguity, 153
contingency, 89, 90
continuative, 164–5, 168, 171, 176–9
contrast, 15, 41, 68, 160, 162, 167, 181, 192
conversation, 134

cooccurrence, 20
coordination, 76, 147, 150
copula, 127, 151
co-reference, 88–90
correspondence, 116ff, 122
corrigibility, 42, 129, 132
counting, 75
count-noun, 19, 33–7, 167
creation, 134
Crocus, Petrus, 203
Cruse, D. A., 4, 19
culminative, *see* structure
culture, 136
Curme, G. O., 35
cycle, 57
Cyrillic, 209
Czech, 208–10

dative, 30–5, 38, 146–7
Davidson, D., 10
declarative sentence, 95, 183
deep structure, *see* structure
definitions, 58, 103
deictic expressions, 139, 160
deletion, 17; people-deletion, 33–4
dependency, 20–1, 202–3
derived forms, 161
determinant power, 16, 21, 24
determination, 145
determiners, 17, 144–5
Detienne, M., 122n
deviancy, 10–11, 14, 18, 32, 42, 46, 91, 126, 130, 157, 165, 167, 170, 176, 183
diacritical power, 16, 21
dialect, 143, 170
discontinuity, 154
discourse, 60, 66, 68–70, 119
discovery procedures, 17–18, 154
discriminative, 169
disjunction, 25
distribution, 23, 141, 170, 179
distributive, 169
diversification, 58
double *-ing*, 41–56
Dummett, M. A. E., 10
duration, 159, 176
durative, 180
dyslalia, 24

Egyptian, 164
El-Hassan, S. A., 162
embedding, 54, 74, 137, 171, 203
emphasis, 208
empirical validation, 17
emptiness, 168–9
endocentric, 20, 152, 155
English, 118–20, 122, 124, 127, 131, 137, 140f, 146, 161–2, 165, 168, 185–95, 208–9,

212–14; American, 170; Early, 33–5;
   Middle, 34–5; Old, 30–1, 35, 37
epistemic modality, 112–37
epistemology, 111, 118, 132, 135–6
equivalence, 88, 90, 115
EST, *see* standard theory, extended
euphemism, 209
evaluation, 17, 138
exceptions, 11
exclamation mark, 208
existence, 6, 120–2
existential expressions, 125
exocentric, 152
exophoric reference, 62
expansion, 17, 167
expeditionary, 50
experience, 59
experiential mode of meaning, 59, 63–6, 72
extension, 162, 169
extent, 64–5, 73

familiarity, 48–9, 56
features: distinctive, 8, 22, 24; graphemic,
   25; prosodic, 8; relative, 22–3
field, 62, 73
filters, 156
Firth, J. R., 15–17, 21, 23, 71
focal distribution, 14
focus, 41, 68–9, 178
form, 147
Fowler, H. W., 42, 213
Frege, G., 94, 96
French, 39, 114–15, 146
frequency of occurrence, 48, 50, 115
frequentative, 162
Fries, C. C., 16
function, 8, 12–13, 15–16, 20–1, 23, 64–5,
   88, 135
functionalism, 142
functional load, 24
functional relations, 16, 22, 158

Galton, H., 162
gender, 37–8
generalization, 73
generic noun, 33–7
genitive, 197
genre, 70
German, 23, 32, 114, 147, 207–14; Old
   High, 30, 32
Germanic, 30, 32
gerund, 41–56, 152–3, 174
Given, 68–70
Givón, T., 41
goal, 64–5, 73
Goldbach's conjecture, 132–3
Gothic, 30–1, 38
Gothic script, 215

governance, 154, 205
gradience, 55
grammar, 41, 78, 111, 119, 124, 137ff, 140,
   196–205; categorial, 9–10; generative
   (transformational), 17–18, 38, 71, 119,
   138ff, 148ff; phrase-structure, 152–3;
   speculative, 196–205; traditional, 139
grammaticality, degrees of, 11
grapheme, 24–5, 206ff
graphical devices, 206–15
Greek, 31, 112, 115–16, 122, 196–7
Gröber, 63n

Haas, W., 1–29, 111, 113, 115, 119, 139,
   152, 157, 167, 170, 183, 196, 206
Halle, M., 25, 210
Halliday, M. A. K., 16, 18, 20, 62, 188, 193
Harris, Z. S., 42, 153
Hasan, R., 20
having, 112
hearer, 68
Helias, Petrus, 200–2
hierarchy, 8, 19, 142, 154, 214
Hill, A. A., 8
Hjelmslev, L., 7
Hockett, C. F., 13, 18, 153, 197
hocus-pocus, 22, 23
Hogg, R. M., 36
homonymy, 14, 41, 147
homophony, 33, 38
Huddleston, R. D., 76
Hudson, R. A., 38, 65
Hungarian, 22
Hymes, D., 60

idea, 5
idealization of ordinary language, 94ff
ideational mode of meaning, 59
identity, 142; relational, 7
ideogram, 58
ideographic, 26
idiolect, 170
idiom, 14, 169
illocutionary acts, 120, 124, 134, 137
immediate constituent analysis, 203
imperative, 39, 182
imperfective, 160–2
inceptive, 49–50, 162–3, 167, 169, 171, 173
inchoative, 162
India, 163
Indo-European, 38, 127, 147
inference, 101
infinitive, 154
ing-form, *see* gerund, participle
insertion, 17, 170; lexical, 152, 158
instantaneousness, 172
instrumental, 30–2, 38
intensification, 168

intensionality, 84–5, 123, 128–9, 134
intensive, 161
interdependence, 61
interpersonal mode of meaning, 59, 66–7, 72
interrogation, 186–7, 192–5
interrupted, 176
intonation, 66, 68, 71, 72, 142
intransitive, 165
intuitions, 8–9, 17, 113, 138
inventory, 145
Isaiah, 87
isomorphism, 5, 8, 117
iterative, 162, 165–7, 171, 176, 178, 180–1

Jakendoff, R. S., 149
Jakobson, R., 23
Japanese, 207
Jespersen, O., 19, 160, 211
jingles, 41–2
John of Genoa, 200
Johnson-Laird, P. N., 129, 130, 133
Joos, M., 160
juncture, 45–6

Kahn, C. H., 112, 122n, 123n
Kamp, J. A. W., 10
Kant, I., 86–7
Katz, J. J., 157
Kempson, R. M., 116
Klima, E. S., 186
Kneale, W. & M., 89
knowledge, 112–16; performative (know₁), 113, 133; by acquaintance (know₂), 113, 131–2; propositional (know₃), 113, 120, 129, 131, 133, 136
Körner, S., 81n, 87n, 90n
Kripke, S., 87n
Kuryłowicz, J., 161

labelling, 20–1, 153
Lakoff, G., 157, 204
Lamb, S. M., 58
language: formal, 4, 8–9; natural, 4, 8–9, 73, 119, 124, 136, 138; written, 206–15
langue, 7
Lasnik, H., 148–9, 152, 158
Latin, 39, 115, 127, 143, 147, 196–7
Lees, R. B., 140
Lejewski, C., 9, 99, 104
Leibnitz, G., 80, 87
Leśniewski, S., 96, 104, 110
levels, 8, 16, 21, 41, 57ff, 149, 153
Lewis, D., 10
lexeme, 112, 115
lexicon, 137, 140, 156
Libyan, 164
linearity, 64, 75
Linsky, L., 92n

lip-reading, 24
literature, 73
Lithuanian, 32
localism, 112, 127, 164
locative expressions, 112, 125–6, 137, 139, 164, 175
locomotive, 50, 164
logic, 182–3, 185; history of, 94; mathematical, 80
logical mode of meaning, 59, 73–7
Luther, 32
Lyons, J., 14, 17–18, 20, 112, 114, 116, 125, 128–30, 134, 137, 139, 160–1, 163, 169, 179, 180, 187–8

Maclay, H., 42
magic, 122n
manner, 64–5, 73
markers, 13, 16–17, 21, 42, 68, 146, 208ff
markedness, 37–8, 208ff
Mates, B., 197
mathematics, 153–4
Mathesius, V., 63
Matthews, P. H., 18, 20, 150, 158
meaning(s), 4–8, 10, 12, 14–16, 18, 23, 41, 57ff, 91–2, 146, 156, 161, 168–9, 186; cognitive, 14; constructional, 152, 155; difference of, 16; orders of, 58; theories of, 10
metalinguistics, 17, 121, 124, 132–3
metanalysis, 30–3, 38–9
metaphor, 14, 73, 167
metaphysics, 92, 111, 113, 198, 204
methodology, 8, 119
metre, 48, 70, 73
middle, 127
Mill, J. S., 123n
Miller, G. A., 129, 130, 133
Milsark, G., 41, 43–5
Miner, K. L., 33
Mitchell, T. F., 18, 66, 160, 162, 168, 170
modals, 137, 185–95
modality, 61, 66, 77, 81, 86–9, 112, 116, 137, 183, 185–95
mode: alethic, 185; deontic, 185, 189; existential, 185; of discourse, 62; of meaning, 58ff
models, 18, 65, 71–3, 139, 148–58, 196
modification, 154
modistae, 198ff
modus significandi, 198
monadic predicates, 82–93
moneme (*see also* morpheme), 142, 144ff
mood, 61, 77
morph, 14, 33, 154; empty, 38
morpheme, 13–14, 20–1, 142, 154
morphology, 32, 143, 159–61, 196ff
morphophonemics, 23

names, 9, 10, 73, 81–4, 87–9, 94ff, 124, 132; general, 96, 100ff; non-referential, 96; referential, 96; singular, 96, 100
naturalness, 23, 38
nature (and function), 143–4
necessity, 86–9, 185ff; deontic, 189ff; dynamic, 189ff
negation, 117, 185–95
Nerius, D., 212
neutralization, 14
New, 68–70, 77
Newmeyer, F. J., 159, 165, 170–2
nominalization, 123–4, 137, 140
nominalist, 123
non-assertion, 185–95
normality, 115
Norse, Old, 30, 38
noun, 144, 146, 151, 154, 198ff
noun phrase, 198ff
number, 147, 167

object, 19, 145–6, 151, 154ff, 166–7
oblique, occurrence, 81–3, 89ff
Occam's razor, 123
omission, *see* deletion
ontology, 5, 80, 91, 100, 111, 114ff, 123, 135, 139, 141
opacity, referential, 10
open-ended list, 170
opposition, 23, 162, 210
order, 75
orthography, 206
Osgood, C. E., 42
ostension, 6–7
Osthoff, H., 31–2
orthography, 24, 196
overkill, 41
overlap, 172, 175; phonemic, 22
overspill, 34–5, 38

Pakistan, 163
Palmer, F. R., 159, 160, 163, 186
paradigmatic reducibility, 20
paradigmatic relations, 15–16, 78
paraphrase, 191–2, 195
paratactic, *see* structure
participial adjectives, 43
participial prepositions, 43
participle, 41–56, 152–3, 174, 201
particle, 73, 163–4, 168–70, 172–3, 182
partitive, 168
passive, 127, 150–1
past, 167, 191–2
perception, 22, 197
perceptual, 162
Percival, W. K., 200
perfect, 160, 162–4, 171
perfective, 160–2

performative, 113, 189
periodicity, 69, 70, 73
permutation, 17, 20
person, 127, 162
Pfister, R., 200
phase, 160, 162, 173–4
Philological Society, 21
philosophy, 4, 12, 71, 112–13, 120, 132
phone, 154
phoneme, 8, 21, 142, 154, 206; pitch, 71
phonetics, 142, 148, 196
phonoaesthetic, 168
phonology, 7, 16, 21–4, 41–2, 46, 143, 196; generative, 23
phrase-marker, 150, 152–3, 158
phrase-structure component, 150
physiology, 143
pictographic, 26
Pierce, C. S., 94
Pinborg, J., 198, 203
Plato, 81
plural, 33ff, 165, 180; count, 33–8; generic, 33–4
pluralia tantum, 31
plurifunctionality, 145
poetry, 41, 70, 214
Polish, 114, 116, 162
polysemy, 14
Popper, K., 129, 132, 135ff
possession, 164
possessive, 112, 125, 197
possibility, 89, 185ff; deontic, 189; dynamic, 189, 194; epistemic, 186, 188, 192
Postal, P. M., 150, 153, 157
pragmatics, 183
Prague, School, 4, 21, 23, 210, 214
predicate, 39, 40, 80–4, 91, 117, 154, 205
predicate calculus, 80, 86–7, 92
prepositions, 169
prerequisites, grammatical, 23–4, 41
presuppositions, 13, 126
primitive notions, 10
Priscian, 196–8, 203, 205
probability, 183
probability adjectives, 38–40
process, 63–5, 162
progressive, 19, 43–6, 160, 162, 164, 167–8, 171–3, 176, 179
prominence, 46, 69; thematic, 67; tonic, 68, 72, 142
pronoun, 158
propositions, 82ff, 94ff, 118, 120ff, 128, 131ff, 134ff, 159, 183
prose, 41
prosodic analysis, 21, 73
prosodic features, 178
prosody, 42, 45, 47–8, 56, 66–7, 126, 137
psychology, 71, 136, 139

Pulgram, E., 206
Pullum, G. K., 33, 55–6
punctuality, 162, 165, 167
Putnam, H., 117

qualifiers, 185–6
quantification, 86, 94, 123, 185
question, 126
Quine, W. V. O., 119, 123
Quirk, R., 160, 186
quotation, 76, 124, 208

rank, 77, 171
rank shift, 74
reading, 24
reality, 73, 77, 81, 93, 117, 120–2, 164
realization, 57, 60–3, 66–7
reciprocal, 161
rectification, 82–3, 91–3
rection, 205
recursion, 74–7, 150
reducibility, 21
reduction, 17; vowel, 25
reductionism, 71
reference, 5–7, 24, 81, 96, 139; exophoric
    (situational), 62; internal, 62; isolated, 6
reflexive, 127
Reichl, K., 204
reinterpretation, *see* metanalysis
reiteration, *see* repetition
relations, logical, 59, 73, 80ff; sense, 169
relative, 74–6
relevance, 16, 60, 142–3, 165
religion, 122n
reordering, *see* permutation
repetition, 7, 41–4, 47, 76
reporting, 76, 182
representation, 59
REST, *see* standard theory, revised extended
rheme, 69, 70
rhyme, 41, 214
rhythm, 47, 68, 78, 88
role, 73
Ross, J. R., 41, 44–45
rules, 70, 74, 149, 157, 165–8, 170, 183;
    base, 149; contextual, 25; global, 153, 157;
    grammatical, 10–12, 18–20, 37; natural,
    38; phrase-structure, 149, 154; rewrite,
    153; selectional, 151; semantic, 155–7;
    syntactic, 152, 156–7, 184;
    transformational, 25, 149, 155
Russell, B., 6, 80, 96, 114, 123n
Russian, 113, 127, 160, 162, 209–10, 213
Ruwet, N., 150

salience, 42
da San Ginesio, Giovanni, 200
Sampson, G., 140

Sapir, E., 23, 160
de Saussure, F., 7, 146
scale, 22
science, 132, 136
scripts, 25
Seebold, E., 30–2
segmentation, 17, 21, 154
selectional restrictions, 151
semantic category, 95–7, 161, 168;
    component, 148; correlation, 151;
    deviancy, 32; value, 15
semantics, 8, 11, 13–15, 18–19, 42, 116, 119,
    138, 144, 152ff, 167
semelfactive, 162
semiotic, 57–8, 62
Semitic, 161
sentence, 8–11, 15, 19, 77, 80–7, 95, 116,
    123–4, 128, 134, 138, 150, 167, 178, 183,
    197, 201–2, 208; accent, *see* accent,
    nuclear
separation, 44–6
sequence, 64, 75
Serbian, 37
Seuren, P. A. M., 190
Shoemaker, N., 43
sign, 4–7, 13, 20–1, 24, 57, 146
simplex, 76
Sindhi, 163
singular, 5, 9, 165–6, 181
situation, 160–1
Slavonic, 37–8, 161–2
Smiley, T. J., 9
sociology, 71
space, 159, 161–2, 164, 166, 177
Spanish, 146
speaker, 68, 77, 138, 144
speech: direct, 130; indirect, 130
speech act, 121, 137
speech therapy, 24
spelling, 24–5; reform, 24–5, 206
standard theory, 148; extended (EST), 148ff;
    revised extended (REST), 148ff
statistics, 170, 183
stativity, 162
Steinthal, H., 197
Stoics, 94, 197
strata, 57–8
stress, 68, 142
structuralism, 23, 38, 71
structure, 64, 78; constituent, 65ff, 80;
    culminative, 69, 70; deep, 19, 20, 40, 119,
    120, 126, 139, 140, 148ff; generic, 73;
    hypotactic, 75–7; paratactic, 75–7; phrase-,
    150; surface, 20, 40, 119, 120, 125, 139,
    140, 169; syntactic, 132; tree, 154
style, 41–2, 206ff
subject, 19, 127, 145–6, 151, 154ff, 205;
    raising, 38–40

substitution, contrastive, 8, 17, 21, 23, 88, 139
Survey of English Usage, 193
swearwords, 66
Sweet, H., 19
syllabary, 58
syllable, 33–5, 42, 142, 207
syllogism, 94
syncretism, 34
synonymy, 40, 47, 171, 176, 178
syntagmatic dependence, 20
syntagmatic relations, 15–16, 78, 143
syntax, 10, 11, 19, 20, 143, 145, 148–58, 183, 196–205
system of signs, 7, 57; semantic, 57–9; social, 76; stratified, 57

Tarski, A., 121, 124n
Taylor, A., 20
telic, 165, 167
temporal relationship, 51
tendencies, 11–12, 18–20, 25, 70, 74, 157, 183
tenor of social relationships, 62
tense, 76–7, 159, 161
terminal string, 158
terminative, 162, 167–9, 172, 181
Tesnière, L., 203
text, 81
textual mode of meaning, 59, 67ff, 72
Theme, 68–70
Theophrastus, 89, 90
Thomas, of Erfurt, 198, 200–4
Thrax, Dionysius, 196–7, 205
Thurot, C., 198, 200, 203
time, 159, 161–2, 164, 167, 177
tone group, 68–9
tones, 142
totalitive, 168
traces, 155
Trager, G. L., 23
transformation, 44, 123, 125, 129, 153ff, 169
transformational derivation, 152
transitive relations, 75
transitivity, 77
translation, 5, 24–5, 122
trees, 65, 203

tree-structure, 154
Trubetzkoy, N. S., 16, 23
truth, 112, 116–18, 120–4, 129, 132
truth functors, 95
truth values, 9, 14, 82, 86, 92, 95, 117–18, 128, 130, 134–6
Turkish, 140

underlying form, 33
ungrammatical, *see* deviancy
unicategorial languages, 99
unifunctionality, 145
universal base, 140
universals, 70, 122
Urdu, 163
use, 8, 81

Vachek, J., 206–7
value, 16–17, 20–1, 94, 143, 146; nominal, 94; propositional, 94
variables, 16, 83, 94, 97, 102
Vendler, Z., 140, 179
verb, 147, 151, 153, 158–9, 161ff, 168, 187, 200, 203–4; aspectual, 159, 161; phrasal, 163, 170; -phrase, 159, 160, 198ff
verificationism, 17
Veronese, Guarino, 200
Villadei, Alexander, 197, 203
von Wright, G. H., 185

Wackernagel, J., 205
wave, 73
Webster, N., 207–8
Wells, R. S., 153
Whitehead, A. N., 81
Wimsatt, W. K., 42
Wittgenstein, L., 6
word, 8, 143, 168, 197, 208; class, 197–8; order, 203
worlds, possible, 128, 134–5
WP (word and paradigm), 197
writing, 24
writing systems, 25, 58

Zandwoort, R. W., 161
zero: -aspect, 163–4; class-index, 14; morphological, 13–14